What educators are saying . . .

"I will definitely nominate Secr... ... Bonnet Award. As a public librarian, ... young adults, knowing that it will ho... ... ...rest in additional reading. I can also ... ...vanced readers and not have to worry about the content being offensive."

April Dillon, Library Director, Hemphil County Library, Canadian, TX

"For teachers and librarians this book can be an invaluable tool to teach character education with the added bonus of developing interest in Civil War history. The book is enthralling. I found it hard to put down. The characters are down to earth and realistic. This is truly a book that will appeal to young and old."

Dee Gutshall, elementary school teacher, Hamilton, MO.

"This many-faceted book is certainly a teacher's dream! . . . The experiences of the teens as they explore the cave, make a historically signficant discovery, and deal with the surprising aftermath, will grip the attention of youngsters and adults. Of equal importance, they will trigger dialogue about teamwork and relationships, dealing with emotions and prejudices, and often-forgotten aspects of our country's history."

Jean Bell, retired teacher, Chillicothe, MO

By having both boys and girls of different ages playing important roles, pre-teens and teens will find a hero or heroine with whom to identify. I can't wait to share it with our students. I can recommend this to parents as, not only a good story, but also, one that will whet their child's appetite and interest in reading and history as well as promote strong values. . . . To me this book is reminiscent of the days when money was in short supply, but manners, family togetherness and respect were not. Parents will appreciate Secrets of Rebel Cave for giving their children appropriate values to aspire to and examples to follow.

Sandra Denning, school librarian, McMinnville, TN

To Brianna —

Secrets of Rebel Cave

A Stoneworth Teen Adventure

By Philip Dale Smith and Lisa Kay Hauser

Lisa Kay Hauser

Philip Dale Smith

05-05-'02

Golden
Anchor
Press

Tacoma, Washington

Publisher's Cataloging-in-Publication
(Provided by Quality Books, Inc.)

Smith, Philip Dale, 1932-
    Secrets of Rebel Cave : a Stoneworth teens adventure/
Philip Dale Smith and Lisa Kay Hauser -- 1st ed.
    p. cm. -- (Stoneworth teens adventure series)
    Includes bibliographical references.
    SUMMARY: Two teens from Kentucky visit their cousins
in Tennessee and explore Rebel Cave in search of proof that
Confederate soldiers hid there. They make major
discoveries, including a hoard of Civil War artifacts.
They carefully research what they have found and learn
a lot on their visit--including things about prejudices
and conditions in the U.S. after World War II.
    Audience: Grades 5-12.
    LCCN 2001118028
    ISBN 1-886864-05-5
    ISBN 1-886864-06-3 (series)

    1. Caves--Juvenile fiction. 2. United States--
History--Civil War, 1861-1865--Juvenile fiction.
3. Prejudices--Juvenile fiction. 4. Tennessee--Juvenile
fiction. [1. Caves--Fiction. 2. United States--History
--Civil War, 1861-1865--Fiction. 3. Prejudices--
Fiction. 4. Tennessee--Fiction.] 1. Hauser, Lisa Kay.
II. Title.

PZ7.DI526Se 2001   [Fic]
                    QBI01-700791

Printed in the United States of America
02 03 04 05 06 07 08 - 9 8 7 6 5 4 3 2 1
Cover photos by courtesy of Dan Silvestri and Jack Engle

This book is dedicated ...

To Bill and Melinda Coleman for your constant demonstration of love for children and youth. You touch and enrich them. You inspire me.
                                                                    —Philip Dale Smith

To my generation of the *"Stoneworth Teens*: "Lequeta Bowman Sweeney, Jeff Rhoads, Jeanie Bowman Morris, Debby Rhoads Eason, Sandy Bowman Short, and Kent Smith. Your lives are an example to all who follow in your footsteps. Thanks for letting me, the youngest of the cousins, tag along.
                                                                    — Lisa Kay Hauser

Acknowledgements

Once again we're reminded that a book is the joint effort of many. We owe a debt of gratitude to those who contributed to the creation of this work. They include those whose knowledge of the Civil War we've tapped: The staff at Stones River Battlefield; the folks at "The Blockade Runner," near Wartrace, TN; the team at Magness Library in McMinnville, TN; Shirley Farris Jones, historian and Civil War site preservation activist; and researchers Jerry Jones and John Sibley. Fellow cave enthusiasts who impacted this work are: Roy Davis, S.R.(Tank) Gorin, Dr. Tom Barr, Barbara Munson, Louie Lamon Jr, and Bill and Christine Walter. Next are those who helped with the manuscript. Early readers whose feedback we highly value are: Bill Brown, Harold and Mary Winstead, Mary Jo Smith, Darlene Mindrup, Sandra Denning, and Jean Bell, who doubled as a proofreader. Special kudos to our chief editor, Dr. Henriette Anne Klauser. Cover designer George Foster deserves an enthusiastic nod of approval. And we are especially grateful for the great cave pictures used on the covers. Those unique shots are by Dan Silvestri and Jack Engle, whose skills are complimented by their own "Cave Impressions" team.

A person deserving a paragraph of her own, and much more, is Susan Vaughn. Susan, a "Stoneworth Cousin" herself, is the artist whose pencil sketches add a special touch to each chapter heading and at other key locations in the book. Susan, we're all indebted to you—especially those who have never seen a carbide light. Thanks!

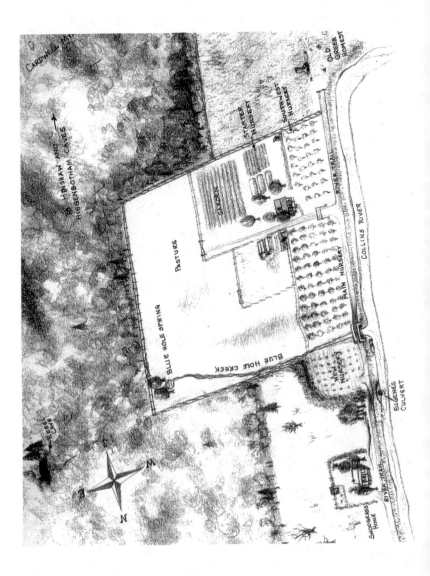

1

The Race

Deadly, thought Dulcie Delaney. *An absolutely deadly combination: Mr. Harman Kirby and geometry. Worse yet, Mr. Kirby and geometry in the last class period.* She tapped her pencil on the top of her wooden school desk and stifled a yawn. She half listened to Mr. Kirby, who stood at the blackboard, droning on and on in his high-pitched, monotonous nasal voice.

"And so it's obvious," he said, "when you add all the angles of a parallelogram, you end up with 360 degrees."

Dulcie bit her lower lip and tried to concentrate on the lecture. *If I'm going to go to college, I have to pass this class with a decent grade. I'll never get a scholarship without good marks. Why, oh why does geometry have to be my last class of the day?*

Dulcie brushed her dark, curly hair off her forehead and tried to focus on her lecture notes. She lethargically drew a circle around October 12, 1945 at the top of the page, adding little curls and flowers to dress up the day's date. *With the war just ending when Japan surrendered in August, a history class might be interesting enough for last period. But not geometry.* Her eyes wandered to the bright October sunlight streaming through the classroom window. Tiny motes of dust sparkled in the shaft of light. *Adventure—I need an adventure! Fat chance!*

Maggie Brown, her best friend, caught her eye. There was a piece of paper half hidden behind Maggie's geometry book. It had Dulcie's name written at the top. Maggie scribbled quickly, glancing up at the lecturing teacher as she wrote. The next time Mr. Kirby turned to write on the blackboard, Maggie slipped the note across the aisle.

> *Dulcie, guess what! Arnie's taking me to see Casablanca tonight and afterward we're going to "Chat and Chew on 62"—the new drive-in restaurant between Greenville and Depoy!*

Mr. Kirby turned to the class. "You can see from the diagram I've drawn on the board that while a square has four equal angles, the parallelogram's two narrow-angled corners combine with its two-broad angled corners to have the same number of degrees as the square." He turned back to the board.

Reading the note, Dulcie's brown eyes widened. Quickly she responded with a note of her own.

> *Rub it in! I haven't had my first date, and you've already been on three. Now you're going out with Arnie? If you were my true friend, you'd wait for me to catch up. Ha! Ha!*

Mr. Kirby's back was still turned as he lettered the lines that made up the diagram on the blackboard: a, b, c, d. Dulcie slipped her note to Maggie. With her lips slightly moving, Maggie read it. Dulcie caught her breath when she saw Mr. Kirby watching her friend. If he had seen them passing notes, they'd have to stay after school. Dulcie glanced quickly back and forth between Maggie and the teacher. *He couldn't have seen me. I was too careful. Please don't make me stay after school! I'm sick of sitting in this building on such a beautiful day!* Her heart jumped when Mr. Kirby called on her best friend.

"Maggie," said Mr. Kirby, "would you please stand and summarize for the class what we've learned today?"

Maggie rose. She quickly turned Dulcie's note over and wrote a large word on the back. Smiling at the teacher, then at the class, she held up the sheet and turned so each could see its single word: *"SAME!"*

"Mr. Kirby, we've learned that whether we're dealing with a square, rectangle, parallelogram, or even a circle, the total number of degrees will be the same. In the case of the parallelogram, narrow angles are offset by wide angles, so the total is 360 degrees. This sameness gives a constant we can depend on to make various calculations. That sameness makes consistent and reliable results possible for engineers, mathematicians and others."

"On target! Maggie, on target!" responded the teacher. He turned back to the board to tap each diagram with his chalk and reiterate the accuracy of Maggie's analysis.

Maggie grinned at Dulcie. Dulcie rolled her eyes and good-naturedly stuck her tongue out at Maggie. *Disgusting!* thought Dulcie. *You weren't paying any more attention than I was. You get caught with the note, and instantly turn it into a demonstration of your brilliance. Well, Miss Valedictorian, at least you won't have to worry about college. You'll have scholarships galore. Disgusting!* Secretly, though, she was proud of her friend.

The bell rang just as the 3 o'clock whistle blew at Black Diamond Coal Mine. Drakesboro, a small coal-mining town in Muhlenberg County, lay within the Western Kentucky Coalfield. Muhlenberg County often topped the nation in coal production. Drakesboro was proud of its mines—and of its schools. The three-story grade school stood between the high school and one of the finest gymnasiums in the state. All three buildings were constructed of brick, while most structures in the town were of wood.

"How'd you do that?" Dulcie asked Maggie as the two and Jenny Martin, a new girl in their class, walked across the school grounds. "How did you come up with that answer when Mr. Kirby called on you?"

Maggie giggled, then pointing her nose in the air, she said, "I did the homework—and a little extra—last night. So I knew where

Mr. Kirby was going with the discussion before he got there. And, as you know, I never have any trouble talking."

Dulcie laughed. "You sure don't!"

"It woulda scared me spitless if he'd called on me!" said Jenny.

"Me, too! But you have an excuse, being new here," said Dulcie. They neared the road running past the school toward Mondray, the little community where Dulcie lived. The village lay in a valley just to the west of Drakesboro.

Walking toward town in a steady, limping gait was a slender, gray-haired man.

"Hi, Daddy!" called Dulcie, waving the hand that wasn't wrapped around her schoolbooks.

He waved a response. "Hi, Sweetheart! Hidy, girls!"

"Hello, sir," Maggie and Jenny replied together.

"Where you girls headin'? Wouldn't be skippin' out of school now, would you?"

"Daddy! School's out and you know it." Dulcie giggled.

"That's good. 'Specially if you're headin' home. Dulcie, you and Jackie have a thick letter from Tennessee waitin' for you. When I get back from Radburn's store, I wanna hear all about it." He winked and grinned a lopsided grin. "Anything that ain't a secret, anyway. I got a suspicion there's somethin' important in it."

"Wow! I'll hurry then—Oh, unless you need me to go with you and help carry stuff home." She had noticed his limp was getting more pronounced.

He shook his head and walked on. "Nope. Just gettin' a couple of things. See you in a bit."

Dulcie called to him, "Daddy, wait! Was the letter addressed to me, or to Jackie?"

"Both." He waved a goodbye and limped toward the store.

"Oh fiddle!" Dulcie exclaimed to her friends as they walked down the road. "If it's addressed to both of us, I won't be able to open it until that brother of mine gets home. No telling when that'll be!"

Jenny turned to watch the man walking toward town, then looked at Dulcie. "Was that really your daddy? I mean—he looks old enough to be your grandpa—and why's he so crippled up?" Suddenly Jenny stopped and blushed. Her hand flew to her mouth. "I reckon that wasn't very polite. I'm sorry, I didn't mean to—"

"That's okay, Jenny, he is over fifty, but—"

"Jenny!" interrupted Maggie, laying a hand on the other girl's arm. "Don't you know who Dulcie's daddy is? That was Smith Delaney!"

"*Smith Delaney?*" The girl's eyes opened wide. "Oh, my gracious! That explains the limp." Jenny turned back to Dulcie. "Was that *really* Smith Delaney?"

Smith Delaney was a legendary character throughout the region, especially in mining communities. The story continued to be told of how, a dozen years earlier, Delaney and two companions had squeezed themselves down a tiny airshaft into a mine to rescue a group of miners trapped by an explosion. Against tremendous odds, they succeeded. Seven men were rescued that day, including Dulcie's uncle, Eldon Stoneworth, and her cousin, Ben Stoneworth. Delaney, though, was crushed by a cave-in while they were making their way out of the mine. He was crippled for life.

As the girls walked, Dulcie explained. "Actually, my real father's name was Jack Crowe. He died after a mine accident when I was three. Mother needed help around the home place, so she hired Smith Delaney. They fell in love and got married. He's the only daddy Jackie and I have ever known. I don't guess we'd love him more if he *was* our natural dad."

"Gangway!" yelled a voice from behind them. "Clear the road for Jackie and Derrick, the dynamic-duo successors to Batman and Robin!" Dulcie's brother and his friend charged up.

"Hold up, Harmless Handful," said Dulcie. She held out an arm to stop the boys. "Guess what, Jackie! Daddy says we have a letter from Tennessee waiting at home."

Dulcie put a hand on Jackie's shoulder. "Let's agree right now

11

that I get to read it out loud first, since you read the last letter. It's my turn."

Jackie wiggled out of her grasp, and rubbed his chin as though considering a life-altering dilemma. "Hold yer horses, Sis! Last time *was* your turn. This one's mine. I arm-wrestled you for first dibs on the last one, remember? Can I help it that, me being a boy—an' you being a girl, I naturally won?"

Dulcie put one hand on her hip and glared at her younger brother. "My being a girl had nothing to do with it!" she exclaimed. "You had Derrick holler, 'A mouse! Look out—there's a mouse!'" Dulcie shuddered at the memory. "When I panicked, you slammed my hand down. You cheated, but I let you go ahead and take what should have been my turn. So I get to read this one."

Jenny, Maggie and Derrick grinned at the goings-on between the brother and sister.

"Tell you what I'll do for ya, little lady," Jackie chanted in a carnival barker sing-song. "Take a risk, take a chance. Step right up and agree to race me down the hill. For winning a mere foot race—be the first one to the front step, you read the letter to me. If I win, I read to you. Whatta ya think? Is it a deal? Or do you just wanna concede right now?"

"It's a deal, and I'll beat you, you little worm!" Dulcie tried to look stern, but could hardly suppress a smile as she looked at his freckled, upturned face.

"Ummmm! What you said! I oughta tell. You know what Mother says about 'derogatory name-calling' and 'insensitive put-downs.' But I won't tell—instead, I'll raise the ante. The winner not only gets to read the letter out loud, the loser will serve glasses of lemonade to the winner and our guests. Mother said she was making fresh lemonade today. The iceman was to come this morning, so it'll be good an' cold."

Jackie stuck his hand out to his sister. "Deal?"

"Deal!" said Dulcie, grabbing his hand to shake on the bargain.

"Me and Derrick will run ahead and draw a starting line across the road."

With that the two boys sprinted ahead.

"Your little brother is a stitch!" said Jenny. "But, what's the big deal about who gets to read to the other?"

Maggie spoke before Dulcie had a chance, "Her little rascal of a brother is the biggest tease in the world. To make it worse, he thinks so fast it makes you sick."

"We have a rule about reading to each other," said Dulcie. "No reading over the shoulder while the other reads out loud. So, when it's his turn to be the reader, he thinks up stuff as he goes along and sticks it in. He does it so naturally that it sounds like he's actually reading it. By the time he's finished he has me so excited, or upset, I'm just about beside myself. Then, when I finally realize I've been had, he cackles like a hen that laid a double-yolked egg! He's such a card!" She chuckled.

Jenny laughed. "I know all about brothers. I've got a herd of 'em myself. I wish I could see the race, but this is where I turn off. I got to get on home, or I'll be in big trouble."

"Shoot!" said Maggie. "I have to go too, Dulcie, but I'll walk with you to the top of the hill if you promise to tell us all about the race and the letter tomorrow."

"Of course," answered Dulcie.

The girls said their good-byes and Jenny walked away down a street to their left.

Dulcie called to her, "Jen, don't forget that you're going with me to church at Jackson Chapel Sunday."

"Okay," Jenny called back. "Meet you in front of Mrs. Collier's at 9:30."

Maggie linked her arm through Dulcie's. "You know, Jackie's really growing. I can't believe how he's shooting up. You agreed to race him—won't he beat you?"

"I don't think so, not if I can keep my feet under me running down the hill. He's getting faster, and I've let him beat me a couple of times so he'd think he's faster than he is—for just such an occasion as this. He'll go all out, but I think I can win."

When the girls passed the Sumners' house at the top of the

hill above Mondray, Jackie and Derrick were part of the way down the hill, waving for them to hurry.

"C'mon, slowpokes! We marked the start here at the hump. I told Derrick that you wouldn't race from the top because Mother is so antsy about us falling if we start up there."

"No wonder!" said Maggie. She looked down the dirt road just beyond the Sumners' place. There the road left the level area at the top of the hill and plunged toward Mondray valley. A third of the way down, the rutted road crossed over a sandstone brow and dropped even more sharply until it flattened at the foot of the hill. At that point, the main road made an abrupt turn to the left. Directly opposite the turn was the driveway up the slope to Dulcie and Jackie's home. Their white wood-frame house stood among a stand of ancient oak, elm, and maple trees.

"Toe the line, Dulcie," ordered Jackie. He lined up at the mark stretching across the road. "Derrick will give us the 'One, two, three, go!'"

Dulcie held up her hand. "Hold your 'tater, kiddo! The last time we raced, Derrick did a quick count between 'three' and 'go,' and you jumped off to a head start. Maggie will do the count—agreed?"

"Awww! Some people have no faith in their fellow man! What a sore loser." Jackie shook his head dramatically. "Give the signal, Maggie, and get ready to eat some dust, Sis!"

"Okay," said Maggie. "I'll do the count, then I'm heading home. Get ready. One—two—three—go!"

Sure enough, Jackie lunged into the lead. With reckless abandon, he dashed sure-footedly over the washboard-rutted dirt road. Dulcie's longer strides kept her close on his heels. By the time they hit the flat, he was a few feet ahead. He turned up the driveway with legs driving like pistons, but she gained on him with graceful long strides, then passed him. Dulcie slapped the side of the house beside the front steps.

"I win!" she gasped.

The red-faced siblings flopped onto the steps and sat there

panting until Derrick arrived. Just then the screen door opened and a smiling Hattie Delaney, their mother, stepped out on the top step.

"Hello, children," she said, with a sparkle in her dark eyes. "I was just stirring the lemonade when I heard a bang against the house. I figured it was the two of you—have you been racing again? Your tongues are hanging out."

"Yes, ma'am." The brother and sister grinned at their mother.

"Dulcie, a sixteen-year-old girl, …" Mother began.

"… shouldn't be racing around like the wild man from Borneo,'" Dulcie said, with a grin. "I know, but it was for a good cause."

Mother laughed. "You children come around to the side porch, and I'll bring each of you a glass of lemonade. Dulcie and Jackie, you have a letter from Tennessee. I've got it in my apron pocket."

"Thanks, Mother. We saw Daddy and he told us about the letter, but I believe Jackie, young gentleman that he is, wants to serve the lemonade."

Jackie arose from the step, swept an imaginary top hat from his head, bowed to the group, and said, "But of course, Your Highness. As my close personal friend Willie Shakespeare once remarked, 'I am the very pink of courtesy—A proper man as one shall see in a summer's day. A most lovely, gentleman-like man.' Gracious damsel, proceed to the aforementioned meeting place. 'Twill be my delight to serve you. Brave knight, follow me." With a flourish he made his way up the steps and into the house.

Derrick tagged along up the steps and Mother followed them.

Behind her brother's back Dulcie rolled her eyes. She stood up and walked around the side of the house to the porch. Hanging from the eaves was a wooden porch swing. She set her books on the fieldstone floor and sat down on the swing and began pushing it back and forth. *What a ham!* thought Dulcie. *I'm glad Jackie's such a good sport.* She bent over and rubbed her aching calves. *I really had to work to win the race. Next time he'll probably beat me!*

Mother pushed open the kitchen door and joined Dulcie on the swing. She laughed softly. "I think I created a monster when I brought home that book of Shakespeare's plays."

Dulcie smiled. "You may have. No one at school, not even the high school kids, has a vocabulary like Jackie's."

You reckon Jackie gave us an actual quote a moment ago?"

"I don't have the slightest notion." Dulcie shrugged. "One thing is certain, if Jackie ever read it, he'll remember it from now on."

Mother leaned back in the swing. "Oh, my! It feels good to just sit and rest a minute. How was your day?"

"Fine. I just wish I could get the hang of geometry."

"You'll get it, Honey. Maggie will help you if you ask her."

"She's great, isn't she, Mom?" Dulcie's eyes widened. "And she's got *another* date. This time she's going out with Arnie Bixby!"

Mother frowned. "Isn't he a bit wild? I've heard he is."

"I've heard that, too. But Maggie says he's been a perfect gentleman up to this point—though not quite to the level of young 'Sir Galahad,' who's coming out the door." She nodded at Jackie who was backing out through the screened door that opened onto the side porch from the kitchen. He carried a tray with four glasses of lemonade. Derrick followed him with a plate of sugar cookies.

When each had a glass of lemonade and a cookie, Jackie turned to Dulcie and said, "Your Highness, you may read to me."

The boys seated themselves on the steps.

Mother reached into her pocket and drew out a fat envelope and handed it to Dulcie.

"You don't mind if I listen, do you?" Mother asked. "Daddy and I got a letter, too, so we know about the special invitation inside."

"Invitation—did you say 'invitation'?" exclaimed Jackie. "Hurry, Dulcie."

"Would you wait just a minute, Jackie!" said Dulcie as she opened the letter. "Of course you can listen, Mother."

Dulcie pulled the folded pages from the envelope.

2

Adventure Ahead

"All right, Sis, get to reading!" said Jackie.

Dulcie held the letter in her hand but looked at the envelope. "It's postmarked 'McMinnville, Tennessee.' The return address says it's from 'The Tennessee Stoneworth Teens.' And below, in red ink it says, 'Adventure Ahead!'"

"Yea!" said Jackie, turning to Derrick. "It's from our cousins, Eugene and Poppy Stoneworth. They're fudging a little to say, 'teens.' Poppy is twelve, going on thirteen, just like I am, and Eugene is sixteen, the same age as Dulcie. I bet they're up to something. Hurry up, Dulcie!"

She unfolded the letter. "There's some other stuff in the envelope, but I'm not going to look at it 'til I've read the letter, okay?"

"Dulcie, you're stalling," said Jackie. "Read!"

Dulcie grinned at her impatient brother, cleared her throat, and read:

> *Dear Dulcie and Jackie,*
>
> *Last night Mom and Dad told us about a big surprise they've cooked up in cahoots with Aunt Hattie*

and Uncle Smith. Just wait till you hear what it is!

"YEA for surprises!" yelled Jackie. He jumped up, grabbed a wooden crossbeam and chinned himself a couple of times. "Keep reading!" he commanded.

> *With the war, and with gas rationed along with just about everything else, none of you Kentucky kin have gotten to visit our home in Tennessee. Now that the war's over, and Dad's home safely our folks invited your family to come for Thanksgiving. Aunt Hattie wrote back and said she and Uncle Smith couldn't because of the tests he will be having at Outwood Veterans Hospital. But they both agreed you two could come! Isn't that swell?*

Dulcie clasped the letter to her breast. "Mom, is it true? We get to go to Tennessee?"

Before she could answer, Jackie was back on his feet. "Eugene's not kidding is he? Are you really gonna let us go? Man, oh man! By ourselves? How are we getting there? When do we leave?"

"Settle down, Jackie," said Mother. "You're like a wiggle-worm in hot ashes! Yes, we plan to let you go, on certain conditions. Let Dulcie finish the letter, then we'll talk about the details."

Dulcie continued,

> *Included in the envelope is a map of Tennessee showing just where McMinnville is. Also, a couple of train tickets. You'll leave from Central City on the Wednesday morning before Thanksgiving, come through Nashville on the train that goes to Chattanooga. At Tullahoma you'll change to the train that comes here.*
>
> *In Warren County there are lots of nurseries. Our 50-acre nursery is tiny compared to some, but only we have the "Stoneworth Pears." By the way, Dulcie, Dad says he never can thank you enough for the*

18

*cuttings from the old pear tree you sent when we
bought the nursery. He told me to tell you the train
tickets are a token of our appreciation for your help
back then.*

"See, Honey," said Mother, "the Bible says if you sow abundantly, you'll reap abundantly. Why, you weren't more than ten years old when you fixed those cuttings to send Uncle Berk."

Mother turned to Derrick. "Back in the early '30s," she said, "my brother Berk discovered that our big pear tree was a 'sport' or mutation—the only one of its kind in the world! He thought it had commercial possibilities because of its firm, delicious fruit. He took cuttings from our tree to his home in Louisville and planted them in his back yard. When he bought the nursery in Tennessee, he moved them there, then wrote and asked us for more cuttings. Dulcie was just ten years old, but she took on the task. As a result—"

"Mom!" wailed Jackie.

"Oh!—sorry, Honey." She laughed and said, "I guess you'd rather finish the letter."

Dulcie read,

> *You'll love McMinnville and its fine, friendly people.
> You'll love our place, 'Stoneworth Hills' too. It's right
> on the Collins River. We're about six miles out in the
> country. Our house has nine rooms.*

"Wow!" said Derrick. "That's a whopper! I bet they've even got running water and electricity."

While Mother was telling the story of the "Stoneworth Pears," Dulcie had quickly read ahead. Now she paused a moment, and, adding just a touch of drama to her voice, continued.

> *Oh, yes, when you pack your duds for the trip, put
> in some old clothes. There's a monstrous cave on the
> back of our property. We want to explore it on Friday
> while you're here. How's that sound for adventure?*

Jackie jumped up with a big grin on his face. "Yeah, yeah, yeah! Nothing doing," he said. "You're trying to pull my old trick, but you're not smooth enough to fool me!"

As he spoke, he poked his chest with his right forefinger, then wagged it at Dulcie. "I'm onto you! You made up the part about the cave—it's not in the letter. You can't pull the wool over this boy's eyes!"

"It is, too. It's right here," said Dulcie. She nudged her mother with her elbow, and pointed to the page. "Isn't it, Mother?"

Mother nodded, then grinned, watching Jackie take the bait.

"Let me see!" he said, starting toward his sister.

"Oh, no you don't! No way!" Dulcie grinned and shoved the letter behind her back, then held up her left hand to ward him off. "It's my time to read—you just sit down and listen. Right, Mom?" She glanced at Mother, who watched the banter with a warm smile.

"You know the rules, Jackie. You dish it out, now you take it," Mother said firmly.

Dulcie took up where she'd been interrupted.

> *The cave has a huge entrance. You could drive a Sherman tank right in its mouth.*
>
> *There's a legend that Confederate soldiers hid out there during the Civil War. That's why they call it, "Rebel Cave." There's no telling what we might find in there. And tell Aunt Hattie not to worry about us. We'll be very careful. And, lucky you, you'll have your big, powerful cousin Eugene to take care of you!*

"That sounds just like Eugene," said Jackie, laughing. "But I still think you made up the part about the cave. You just—"

"Shhhhh!" said Dulcie, a finger to her lips. "There's more."

> *The good news is that the enclosed train tickets to McMinnville are free. The bad news is that they are just one-way tickets. You'll have to come up with the money for the trip back. Your folks insisted on that arrangement. They say you'll appreciate the trip more if you earn it. With just a month left before the trip, you'll have to hustle to earn that much, but they're sure you can do it.*

Eagerly awaiting your arrival, your handsomest cousin and his fragile little sister,
Eugene and Poppy

"Fragile, nothing!" said Jackie. "She may be prim and prissy but she's a trooper, and unless she's changed, she's tough as old shoe leather!" Jackie looked hard at Dulcie. "You did make up the part about the cave, didn't you?"

"Nope. It's right here, you Doubting Thomas. Just because you can't read a letter straight doesn't mean I can't. Now that I've finished, you can read it yourself." She handed him the letter, then unfolded the map.

"Look, Derrick!" Jackie exclaimed. "There really *is* a cave!" He held the envelope up to his nose, breathed in deeply and then handed the envelope to his friend. "Here, smell this!"

Derrick sniffed the envelope, then opened it wider, stuck his nose in and sniffed harder. "I don't smell nothin'," he said.

Jackie retrieved the envelope from Derrick and tilting his head back, stuck the envelope over his nose, shut his eyes, and sniffed dramatically.

"You don't? Man, oh man! I do. I smell adventure! That's spelled, A-D-V-E-N-T-U-R-E! Wish you could go, Derrick. I'll end up teamed with that little red-headed, spit-fire cousin of mine."

"I think we already got plans for Thanksgiving," mumbled Derrick sadly.

"Hush, Jackie!" said Dulcie. "They only invited us. But look at the price of the tickets!"

She frowned.

"They're $4.75 each way—where are we going to get that kind of money?"

"Mother, are you sure 'nuff gonna let us go—all by ourselves?" asked Jackie.

Mother nodded. "I admit I'm nervous about it, but Daddy says you're growing up. He thinks you're ready to see a little of the world outside of Muhlenberg County. We'll trust the Lord to take

21

care of you."

"Yea for Dad!" said Jackie. "Remember our trip to the zoo in Evansville, Indiana? That's the only time I've been out of Kentucky."

"I've never been out of Kentucky," said Derrick. "But I've been to Russellville—that's almost to Tennessee—and to Owensboro. Next time I go to Owensboro, I'm going to walk across the bridge to Indiana, so I can say I've been out of state."

"Maybe we'll all get to travel more," said Mother, "with the war finally over. But the issue you're facing now is where to get the money for the return trip."

"I've already got a dollar and seventy-five cents," said Jackie. He slapped himself on the forehead. "Oh, man!—if only I hadn't bought that Monopoly set from Al Buchanan for fifty cents!"

Dulcie pondered her plight. "I have three dollars saved to buy Christmas presents. Maybe I could use it for the trip, and make it up after we get back. But that's taking a risk."

"Would you kids like a refill of lemonade while you discuss high finance?" asked Mother.

"Sure, Mom!"

Just then the screen door opened and out walked Smith Delaney. "Did I hear someone say, 'high finances'?"

Before they could respond to their dad's question, another voice chimed in, "And did I hear 'lemonade?'"

Behind Mr. Delaney was a lanky, nine-year old boy with dark, tousled hair, his shirttail out, and his shoes untied.

All the children got to their feet, and Dulcie hurried over to hug her dad and then her little brother, Dalton. She smoothed the boy's cowlick. It immediately sprang back up.

"I take it you've read your letter," said Dad.

"Sure have!" replied Jackie. "Dalton, did you hear about our trip?"

Dalton scowled. "Yep. And it's a low-down rotten shame they didn't invite me," he muttered, then turned to his mother. "Mom, you got more lemonade in the kitchen? I'm *dyin'* of thirst!"

"I *have* more lemonade in the kitchen—let's go get it before you *die*, young man. And, if you survive, you can help me put the groceries away. Smith, you may have my seat on the swing. Maybe you have some ideas about how our would-be travelers can come up with some hard earned cash."

"That I do," said Dad. He eased down onto the swing. He raised his voice, ensuring that Mother could hear him in the kitchen.

"I was thinkin' that the quickest way would be to put an ol' still in the back of the smokehouse and run us some moonshine."

"SMITH!" called Mother.

"Daddy!"

Dad chuckled at the reaction of his captive audience. "I'm just pullin' your leg. I 'magine we'll have to do it the legal way." He seemed saddened by the thought.

Mother appeared in the kitchen door, hands on hips. "Smith Delaney, you stop teasin' these young'uns!"

He threw up his hands in mock surrender. "All right, all right. I'll behave. Actually, I did come up with a couple of ideas." Dad paused. "But first, I was thinkin' I might send a few miner's caps and carbide lights along for you to use in the cave. They're not as bright as flashlights, but they last longer and it's easier to carry extra carbide than batteries. Best of all, with the light on your cap, your hands will be free while you're explorin'."

Jackie jumped up and spun around. "Perfect! Wait'll Eugene sees 'em. He'll be tickled to death."

"As for the money, Jackie," continued Dad, "while I was in town, I saw Mrs. Billy Bridges. She said she'd sure love to have a bushel of those fine apples like you sold her last year, son. Wouldn't be surprised if she'd pay you seventy-five cents for the bushel if they're nice ones."

"That's great! I picked a whole bunch yesterday. I'll sort 'em, and shine 'em up good, and take her a basket of beauties."

23

"While you're at it, Jackie, take her one of the Stoneworth pears from the attic. They're not quite ready, but close enough. Suggest that when they've mellowed just a few more days, they'll be perfect. Wouldn't be a bit surprised if she takes a bushel of those, too."

"That's a great idea, Dad!" cried Jackie. "C'mon, Derrick, let's go shine some apples!"

"Hold on, son. That's not all. Don't you have some hulled walnuts in the smokehouse?"

"Yep—I mean, yes, sir."

"Well, as I was walkin' home, Mrs. Johnson came out on her porch and called to me. 'Mr. Delaney,' she said, 'does Jackie have any walnuts left from last fall?' I told her I thought you did. She said she needs some for baking. She don't have time to wait for this year's crop. I think you got a customer there, too."

"Boy, oh boy!" said Jackie, slapping his thigh with the palm of his right hand. "She paid me fifty cents last year and gave me a quarter tip! Hey, with money from the apples, that would give me a dollar and a half to go with what I already have. I'll be ahead of Dulcie." He looked at his sister, who was studying the map of Tennessee. "If Mrs. Bridges buys some pears, I'll be rolling in dough. I'll just about have the money I need for the trip back. If I hustle, I might even get enough ahead to lend Dulcie some. At a small rate of interest, of course."

Dulcie ignored him. "Look at this. According to the map, we'll go right through Murfreesboro. It's right there," she said, pointing to the map, "between Nashville and Tullahoma. That's where Grandpa Carver and Grandpa Stoneworth fought for the Union in the battle of Stones River. Just think, if they had been killed, we wouldn't be here—or at least we wouldn't be us, we'd be different—that's strange to think about, isn't it?" She paused, then continued. "Anyway, we'll be going right by that battlefield."

"Study up on that battle, Dulcie," said her father. "Then tell us all about it. But right now, we gotta figure how to get you some money for tickets. I've got an idea that might work for you, Honey."

"What, Dad?" asked Dulcie, folding the map.

"While I was at Radburn's store, Annie Radburn was fussin' about how bad she wants to fix up the store, especially the restaurant part. She wants to put up new drapes, with matchin' oilcloth on the tables. Harwell's not gonna be much help. He's purty stove up from the fall he took off the roof."

"Daddy, I see where you're heading! You're thinking she might hire me to help out, right?"

"Yep. If you go talk to her about it before she hires somebody else."

"I'll do it this very afternoon. I'm gonna go change out of my school clothes, then go up to the store. Oh, I hope Miz Annie hasn't hired anyone yet!"

"I doubt she has, Dulcie. I mentioned you might be willin' to take on the job while I was there. She's waitin' to hear from you."

Dulcie threw her arms around Smith's neck. "Thank you, Daddy!" she whispered against his ear.

As Dulcie started back into the house, Smith called, "Dalton, get Ol' Pride, and let's go for a walk. We'll check that safe-trap in the back of the orchard an' see if we've caught us a rabbit."

A few moments later, Dulcie glanced out of the bedroom window and saw man, boy, and dog starting on their walk. She reached under the bed and pulled out the notebook she used as a journal. Quickly she wrote,

> It's hard to believe that in just a month, if all goes well, Jackie and I will be in Tennessee.
>
> When I woke up this morning I never dreamed that by this afternoon there would be such an adventure waiting for me just ahead!

Dulcie closed the journal and reached down to pull off her school shoes, a pair of brown penny loafers. She looked at the flat shoes with pennies showing where she'd tucked them into a slot in the leather design across the top. She grinned.

"Better leave those pennies there! I may need 'em for the trip. If I take them out, I might spend them."

3

The Trip

"There's the depot," said Jackie, "and the train's already on the siding. Hurry! We'll miss it!"

"Hold your horses, son," said his dad. "They won't be leavin' ahead of schedule. We got plenty of time. They're takin' on water an' coal."

He parked the old 1934 Ford sedan, and they all climbed out. Dad opened the trunk and handed the suitcases and brown-paper-wrapped packages to the children.

Dalton dragged along behind the others. "I still say they should have invited me, too," he muttered.

"Aw, c'mon, Dalton," said Jackie. "Be a good sport. You're gonna have such a good time playing with Digger and the girls at Aunt Marva's, you'll never miss us."

"Girls!" Dalton grimaced. "They'll be dressin' *me* up like a *girl* again!"

Dulcie laughed. "Dalton, you should have forgiven us for that by now. You were only three when that happened. 'Sides, if we hadn't dressed you up like a girl, Mama would never have cut off

27

all your baby curls. You'd still be the prettiest *girl* in Muhlenberg County," she teased.

"Oh, I reckon I'd have gotten around to cutting his hair sooner or later," said Mother. "You just helped me make up my mind."

Mother's eyes swept over the suitcases. "I hope you packed everything. You did put in that jar of pear preserves, didn't you? You know how your Uncle Berk loves them!"

"I did, and I packed the tablecloth for Aunt Nan." Dulcie patted the neatly wrapped package.

"My goodness!" said Mother. "I can't believe my children are going on such a trip all by themselves—hundreds of miles away!"

"Just two hundred," said Jackie. "That's not so far."

"Here are your tickets," said Dad, handing a pair to each of the young people.

"Keep your eye on 'em," he said. "I'm mighty proud of how y'all worked to come up with the money for those tickets. Be a shame to lose 'em after all that work and not be able to get back home."

Dad's eyes twinkled. "Berk and Nan would just have themselves a couple more young'uns to feed, I reckon. We'd sure miss you!"

"Oh, Daddy," said Dulcie, "we'll hitch-hike or hobo our way back!"

"You'll do no such thing!" cried their mother. "Why, the very idea!—"

"C'mon, Mom, she's just kidding," said Jackie. "We'll hang on to those tickets, and come Sunday night we'll be stepping off the 8:05 train right here."

They were interrupted by the conductor's, "All aboard!"

"Look, Dad. It's Amos Frazier! He's a railroad conductor now!" Jackie said.

Dad turned toward the man in the navy blue conductor's uniform. His face lit up. "Alonzo, how are you, my friend?"

The conductor's dark face broke into a bright smile. "Mr. Delaney, it's good to see you, sir!"

Dad replied, "Children, this is *Alonzo* Frazier, Amos' brother. Alonzo, you know my Hattie. These are our children, Dulcie, Jackie, and our youngest, Dalton," he said, tousling Dalton's hair.

"Pleased to see y'all. You travelin' with me today?"

"Dulcie and Jackie are going to McMinnville, Tennessee, Mr. Frazier, to spend Thanksgiving with my brother Berk and his family," said Mother. "I must say, I feel much better knowing you'll be traveling with them."

"They'll be just fine. My, how you children have grown! 'Course, I don't reckon I've seen you since the Coaltown disaster."

The train whistle blew and the conductor glanced up at the station clock, then at Dulcie and Jackie. "We best be gettin' you on that train."

Mother hugged each of the children before letting the conductor guide them up the steps. He looked back at their mother and dad. "I'll watch out for 'em, and see they change trains at Tullahoma."

As the train began moving, Jackie and Dulcie hurried into the passenger car. They quickly slipped into a seat where they could look out and wave a last goodbye to the trio on the platform.

"Boy, oh boy," said Jackie, slapping his knee with his right palm. "We're on our way!"

"Isn't this nice?" said Dulcie, looking around. "We're already getting up a head of steam."

Jackie unfolded a map and looked at the route the train would take. "Yep, sure are. At this rate we'll be in Nashville in no time."

But Jackie's prediction didn't come true. In spite of its name, "The Dixie Flyer" would little more than get up speed before it would slow down to stop at the stations along the way.

"Dulcie, have you noticed what's different about being on a train from being on a highway?"

Dulcie thought a minute. "There are a lot of differences. It's more roomy, you can get up and walk around, and the railroad track is much more level. The hills have been cut through and valleys have been filled."

"Yep, and—hey, it's dark!" Jackie yelped. "We must be going

29

through a long tunnel."

Soon the train pulled out of the tunnel into the sunlight.

Jackie blinked his eyes at the sudden change from darkness.

Dulcie giggled at the comical look on his face. "The cars sure swing and sway! I hope I don't get sick to my stomach."

Less than an hour later, the train stopped at Springfield. It was well on its way again when the conductor paused by their seat.

"You young'uns doin' all right? "

"We're fine, Mr. Frazier," said Dulcie. "This is so much fun!" She gazed at his familiar face. "You sure do look like your brother!"

"S'pose I do, Miss Dulcie. Me and Amos are identical twins— like peas in a pod."

"Except we've never seen him in a nice uniform like you're wearing," said Jackie.

"No, I give up coal minin', but Amos stayed on. Sure wish he'd think about makin' the change. 'Course, things are better at the mines than they used to be. The United Mine Workers Union made a difference."

"I'm glad Mr. Amos stayed in the mines," said Dulcie quietly. "We probably wouldn't have our Daddy now if he hadn't. Daddy's told us many times about the part Mr. Amos played in the rescue at Coaltown. Daddy says he's a mighty good friend."

"Those are kind words, young lady. Amos 'bout thinks the world of your father, and he thinks your Mama is one of the finest ladies on God's green earth."

"They're pretty good, as parents go," laughed Jackie. "Say, I remember hearing Mr. Amos talking about your family. Didn't your people originally come from Tennessee?"

Mr. Frazier nodded. "That's right. Way back we did. My daddy's daddy come from Memphis. My granddaddy was a slave—" he looked at the floor, then raised his head and straightened his shoulders, "the slave of Genr'l Nathan Bedford Forrest."

"Oh my," said Jackie. "I've read about him."

30

"Yes, Mr. Jackie, Granddad Frazier was servant of Genr'l Forrest 'til he just couldn't stand it no more. He run away to Kentucky. When the Genr'l come to Greenville chasin' the Yanks, him and his men camped on the courthouse lawn. My granddaddy worked as a janitor in that very buildin'! He hid out in a closet in the basement. He knew there'd be no mercy if Genr'l Forrest caught 'im. After a while the Genr'l moved on to fight the Yanks at Sacramento. 'Course President Lincoln up and said we was all free. Then when the war was all over my granddaddy chose to stay in Muhlenberg County."

"Muhlenberg County is better because he made that choice, Mr. Frazier," said Dulcie quietly. "We know our family will always be indebted to yours."

"I guess we're all sorta beholden to each other," said the conductor, "one way or another. Guess I better get to back to workin'. Let me know if y'all need anything."

When the train reached Nashville, Dulcie and Jackie were able to see the capitol from a distance and were dazzled by the city. They got off the train briefly, walked through the impressive station. It was abuzz with people, many of them in military uniforms.

"With the war over," said Jackie, "it looks like a lot of servicemen are headed for home."

"Yes, or for new assignments," said Dulcie. She ignored the admiring glances, comments, and a couple of whistles from a trio of laughing sailors.

They stepped out onto the street.

"Just look at this place!" Jackie exclaimed. "Look at the size of these buildings! Man, oh man! I wish we could spend a day or two here."

"If all goes well, Jackie," said Dulcie. "I'll be going to school here at David Lipscomb College in less than two years. You can come visit and I'll take you all around."

Soon the two were back on the train and headed south. After a few miles the train slowed, then stopped. The conductor came through the passenger cars to explain.

"We're just out of Murfreesboro, and there's a truck stalled on the track. Soon as a wrecker pulls 'im off, we'll be on our way. Look over there," he said, nodding his head toward the scenery. "See the military cemetery? That's the graves of the soldiers who died in the Battle of Stones River."

"You mean the battle was fought right here?" asked Dulcie, excitedly.

"Sure was, Miss Dulcie. You can see the river right over yonder," he said, pointing through the left window of the car. "The Yanks took a stand right along the road over here and finally drove the Rebs back. If today was the first day of January in 1863, you might see your Granddad Stoneworth dug in along here somewhere, or chargin' across these fields fightin' the Rebs."

"That's right! He and Granddad Carver both fought at the Battle of Stones River," Dulcie exclaimed.

"Of course," added the conductor, flashing his warm smile, "if you had been here back then, you'd a wanted to keep your head down lest you get shot as Yankee sympathizers."

The rest of the way to Tullahoma, where they changed trains, Jackie and Dulcie talked about the events that had taken place in the area.

Dulcie gazed out at the passing countryside. "Jackie, during the Civil War there were soldier boys your age on both sides," she said. "Would you have joined up to fight?"

Jackie nodded his head. "Yep. If I had to. Don't think I would have liked it much though. Just think what Uncle Berk went through in World War II. It must have been awful hard being a prisoner of war."

"You know it was," said Dulcie. "I surely hope it didn't change him."

"Me, too! I hope he's the same happy, fun-loving Uncle Berk."

The trip from Tullahoma up the Highland Rim to McMinnville took more than an hour. As the train pulled into the station they spotted the Stoneworths waiting for them on the platform.

Dulcie grabbed Jackie's arm. "Look—there they are!" she said, pointing toward a tall man, his wife and daughter, and a large teenage boy.

Jackie peered over Dulcie's shoulder. "Wow! Is that Eugene? He's huge!"

Dulcie eyed their cousin. He was almost as tall as Uncle Berk, and heavier. "He sure has grown in the last four years."

"Bet he's a great fullback—or linebacker," said Jackie.

They gathered up their belongings and rushed to the door.

Uncle Berk swept Dulcie up in a bear hug and swung her around. "My goodness! Just look at you—you are the spitting image of your mother."

"My, how you've grown—Jackie, I can't believe that's you!" Aunt Nan said and kissed them both.

After the cousins had enthusiastically greeted each other, Aunt Nan began herding them through the station and out to the street, where they climbed into a long '38 Buick. Soon they were driving out of McMinnville.

"Since it's getting late, we'll head straight home," Uncle Berk told them. "You can see the town later. We want you to see our place in the daylight."

"The houses and farms look a lot like Kentucky," said Jackie peering out first one side of the car and then the other. "But we don't have fields of shrubs like those over there."

"Every one of the plants in that field is a variety of rhododendron. The next field is of dogwoods. This is a tremendous area for nurseries," Aunt Nan pointed out. "That's what brought us here."

As they passed a neat white church nestled in a grove of trees, Uncle Berk said, "We love Hebron Chapel. That's where we'll worship Sunday. In the distance you can see the top of Cardwell Mountain. Our place is on the northwest side of the mountain."

"That's Shellsford just ahead," said Eugene. "We cross the river here, make a right turn and follow River Trail to our place."

"Jackie," said Poppy, "we have two horses, Beauty and Bonnie.

Maybe you and I can ride on Saturday, if we're not too busy cave exploring."

"I like to ride horses," said Jackie, "but I can do that in Kentucky. I want to see that cave!"

"Maybe you can do both," said Aunt Nan.

"I'm excited about the cave, too," said Poppy. "We were too little to go in there before the war, and Daddy made it strictly off limits while he was gone."

Eugene pointed to a run-down house back in the trees on the left of the road.

"That's where the Snodgrass family lives. They're our not-very-friendly nearest neighbors."

"And just ahead is one of our county landmarks," said Uncle Berk.

"Aw, Dad!" said Eugene.

"There's no roadside marker up yet," said Poppy, giggling, "but this little dip in the road is called 'Eugene's Culvert.'"

"Let me tell it," Eugene interrupted. "That way it won't get all exaggerated." He sighed dramatically and then continued. "One Sunday afternoon about four years ago, friends came home with us from church. One of the kids double-dog dared me to crawl through the culvert. I... I sorta got stuck. Ever since, I don't much care for tight places. They give me the creeps."

"You sure told that quickly," said Poppy, laughing. "Took two hours to get you out. Daddy said he was 'bout to go in after you and butter your backside to grease you up good, and—"

"This next little bridge," Uncle Berk interrupted quickly, "is over Blue Hole Creek. It starts at a beautiful big spring above our house. You'll see it on the way up to the cave. We're almost to our turn. Our place is the last house on River Trail. It dead-ends a quarter of a mile ahead."

He slowed and made a left turn onto a lane leading up to a large farmhouse. Barns, greenhouses, and other buildings were scattered neatly behind the house. The lower half of the big house was of log, but the upper part, painted white, was of wood frame

34

construction. It was set among oak, elm and maple trees. On either side of the lane were acres and acres of nursery plants. A sign over the drive said:

Stoneworth Nursery
Fruit Trees and Ornamental Shrubs
Home of Stoneworth Pears

"Oh! This is just beautiful!" said Dulcie.

"The setting's one of the things that attracted us to the place," Uncle Berk said. "When we bought it, the only nursery stock was on the right side of the lane. We began developing the left side before the war. Nan and the kids expanded it while I was gone."

He drove the car past the house and pulled in by the back entrance.

"Look!" Dulcie exclaimed. "The porch on the back of the house looks almost exactly like ours!"

Aunt Nan smiled. "I think that's why your Uncle Berkley really fell in love with this property. The porch, the trees—it reminds him of the old Stoneworth place—your house."

For the next hour Jackie and Dulcie took a tour of the house and grounds and unpacked. Jackie was sharing Eugene's large upstairs bedroom, and Dulcie moved in across the hall with Poppy. Each room had a full bed and a half bed.

While Dulcie was unpacking, Poppy said in a voice large enough to be heard across the hall, "There's no railroad close by, Dulcie, but we'll want to be sure the doors are tightly closed, because the snoring over there will make you think a freight train is coming through."

She had just gotten the words spoken when Eugene said, "I hope you don't mind the door being open, Jackie. The girls across the hall will be too scared to sleep unless they know we're right here to rescue them if the boogey-man tries to get them."

Before the teasing could continue, Aunt Nan called them to eat. During the meal they discussed their plans for the next four days.

"We're looking forward to tomorrow's Thanksgiving dinner," said Aunt Nan. "What a difference from last year when your Uncle Berkley was missing-in-action in Europe."

"We didn't know he was in a German prison," said Eugene quietly.

"It was pretty scary," Poppy told them, "but Mama said he'd be home someday—and here he is!" Her enthusiasm lit up the room.

"I'm glad we're here to celebrate with you," said Dulcie, smiling.

"With your curly black hair and flashing Stoneworth dimples, it's almost like having your mother and your Aunt Marva here with us," said Uncle Berk.

Aunt Nan sighed. "It would have been wonderful if the whole Stoneworth clan could have come for our first Thanksgiving since the war ended," she said. "Since that couldn't happen, we've invited some friends to join us instead."

"Mr. Absalom Justice is one of the older members at Hebron Chapel," said Uncle Berk. "His wife died in March after a long illness. We invited him to come, and also his daughter, Julia Gunther, and her family. She's a homegrown McMinnville girl who worked for the U.S. Embassy in Germany before the war."

Uncle Berk passed a bowl of mashed potatoes to Jackie. "That's where she met and married her husband. Gearhardt Gunther is a scientist. They left Germany shortly before the war broke out. He worked at Oak Ridge during the war and is now with the Tennessee Valley Authority. They have twins, a boy, Erik, and a girl, Anna. They're about your age, Dulcie."

"Yeah, you'd better watch out, Cousin, or that tall, good-looking blond guy will sweep you off your feet," teased Eugene.

"Listen to who's talking!" said Poppy "Not any more than his tall, good-looking blond sister has swept Eugene off his feet." She giggled.

"Aw, cut it out, Poppy. She hardly knows I exist," argued Eugene.

"They're very attractive young people," said Aunt Nan, "but more important than that, they are nice kids."

"So nice, in fact," said Eugene, "that we've invited them to spend the whole weekend. They're even bringing clothes for exploring the cave."

"And you ought to see 'em ride Beauty and Bonnie," said Poppy. "They look so, so…elegant is the best way to describe it. They're so regal even the horses seem to hold their heads up high."

"Their Grandfather Gunther was a highly regarded German scientist," Uncle Berk told them. "He was pretty high up in the government over there. When Hitler's intentions became clear to old Dr. Gunther, he was able to arrange for Gearhardt and Julia to escape Germany with the children. But the grandfather and his wife just disappeared. Guess that was the price he paid to get his family out."

"Wow!" said Dulcie. "What a story the Gunthers must have to tell! I won't know how to act around aristocratic Europeans!"

Jackie stuffed a bite of biscuit into his mouth, chewed, then swallowed. "Well, I know what I'm going to do. I'm just going to be myself!"

"That's the way to be, young man," agreed Uncle Berk. "All of you just relax and have a good time. We want you to take some great memories back to Kentucky." Uncle Berk laid his napkin on the table. "Nan, thanks for a good meal."

"You're welcome," said Aunt Nan. "As you children help me clear the table and do the dishes, we'll catch up on family news. It's been a long day for all of us, and the next major item on the docket is a good night's rest. You never know what tomorrow will bring, but I have an idea exciting days are just ahead!"

4

New Friends

Dulcie lay in that clouded place between waking and sleeping. Everything around her felt strange. The bed wasn't familiar. Neither were the soft noises that whispered up the stairs. She began to awaken. *Where's the whistle from Black Diamond Mine?* The first sound of the morning was always the distant cage-elevator whistle at Drakesboro's Black Diamond Mine. *I wonder why they aren't blowing the whistle.* Disturbed by the thought that something bad might have happened, Dulcie rolled over and bumped into Poppy. The younger girl stirred, but didn't wake up. With a start Dulcie's eyes popped open and she glanced around in the semi-dark of the early morning. *You're not at home, you silly* ... *tly* laughed at herself. *You're in Tennessee! Lie* ... *anyone.*

, early morning sounds began to increase, heard the thunk of the back door closing. Nan moving around in the kitchen. The aroma of coffee brewing wafted up the stairs, then the smell of bacon frying. *I ought to be helping with breakfast,* Dulcie thought, slipping out of bed.

Before she finished dressing, Aunt Nan called up the stairs, "Rise and shine, kids. Roll out! Breakfast in fifteen minutes."

As Dulcie slipped into her shoes, Poppy sat up and stretched.

"'Morning, Cousin," said Dulcie. "Your mom says breakfast is almost ready."

"Good morning, Dulcie." Poppy finger-combed her thick, curly auburn hair. "Don't look at me! I'm such a mess! What'll I do with this hair?" she groaned. "Gimme half an hour and maybe I'll be ready for the world to see me."

Dulcie grinned. "I don't think your mother will give you that long. See you downstairs."

Soon the others gathered, and after a country breakfast of eggs, bacon, gravy, biscuits, and honey, the young people headed out to feed the animals and take care of other chores. As they did so, Eugene and Poppy showed the Kentucky cousins the operation of the farm and nursery.

"It's so pretty here," said Dulcie. They stood on the hillside behind the old homestead with the house standing below under a canopy of ancient trees. Beyond the front lawn were fields of nursery plants. They stretched out on either side of the drive all the way down to where it intersected the road that ran in front of the house. Beyond the road was the Collins River.

"We're gradually getting the place in shape," said Eugene. "It was pretty run down when we got here. Dad worked awful hard before he joined the army. While he was gone, Mom acted like every weed she pulled was one less Nazi for Dad to fight. Don't guess it did much good on the war front, but it kept her busy."

"And the hard work probably kept her from thinking as much about the danger Daddy was in," said Poppy. "Eugene pitched too, even if he was only twelve. I was eight years old when left, so I couldn't do much, but I tried."

"You sure did, Poppy. We all did, and it's finall

said Eugene.

"Now let's go see the results of *your* work, Dulcie," he continued.

"My work? I didn't do any—oh, you must be talking about the Stoneworth Pears."

"Yep," said Eugene. "You sent the cuttings, we grafted 'em, babied 'em along, and they've flourished. So you get a lot of credit for our most famous fruit tree."

The quartet of young people walked down the hill toward the lane.

Jackie bounded along, running ahead a little and then back to the other three. "Where's the thanks for my part?" he asked. "Don't I get any credit?"

"I didn't know you did anything—I thought you were too small," said Eugene, looking puzzled.

"I stayed out of Dulcie's way while she fixed the cuttings. That ought to count for something."

Eugene threw his head back and laughed.

"Hmmmph!" said Poppy. "They probably had you hog-tied on the back porch." She turned toward the house. "Hey, there comes the rest of our company!"

A 1940 Hudson sedan approached the opened gate and made the left turn up the lane. The cousins hurried down to meet the car. Uncle Berk and Aunt Nan came out of the house just as the auto came to a stop.

"Y'all come in," Uncle Berk called when the car doors opened.

An elderly man eased out of the front passenger side. A dark-haired younger woman who looked much like him followed behind.

That must be Mr. Justice and his daughter, Julia Gunther, Dulcie thought. Getting out from the driver's seat was a tall blond man. *Gearhardt Gunther,* she thought. *And the teens climbing out of the back are Erik and Anna, the twins. My, are they tall!*

Uncle Berk called Dulcie and Jackie over to meet the visitors. After they met the adults, he introduced Dulcie to Erik. Her heart

41

skipped a beat when she shook hands with the blond, wavy-haired young man and looked up into his sky-blue eyes. *Wow! Did I catch the flash of a dimple? Handsome!*

"You are the first Kentuckian I have ever met. I am glad to meet you," said Erik, with a definite German accent.

"And you're the most ... um, the tallest, uh ... well, at least one of the tallest guys I've ever met," she said, blushing fiercely.

He grinned, "Only 6 feet 3 inches tall, but they say I will keep growing for a while. And Anna is almost as tall," he said. He turned to his twin sister and introduced Dulcie to her.

I must look like a small shrub in a tall forest! Dulcie thought, "I'm so pleased to meet you."

"I'm glad to meet you, too," said the tall blond with the Dutch-boy hair cut. "I wish I had a cousin who says as many nice things about me as Eugene does about you!"

When the introductions were over, Uncle Berk said, "Let's go into the house. The cold snap the radio weatherman's been warning about is moving in. Temperature is dropping fast."

Aunt Nan and Julia Gunther shooed the children into the living room with the men, to await the finishing touches on the Thanksgiving meal.

The fire Eugene and Jackie had built in the fireplace after breakfast added just the right cozy touch to the room. Dulcie loved the spacious dining and living rooms. The hand-hewn logs were obviously part of the original house. Several additions had been made over the years. A beautiful quilt hung on a frame behind the couch. The young people sat on the floor around a coffee table working a giant jigsaw puzzle while the men discussed the aftermath of the war.

"It's terribly slow-going getting things back to normal," said Uncle Berk. "Things just aren't the same since the war. And I don't just mean the kids growin' up and the Depression being over."

"No, sir," said Mr. Justice, "it'll never be like it was. After World War I, we found things were different, but the changes are greater this time. This war moved folks to other parts of the country. And just look how many women took jobs in factories and offices—jobs that men held before the war. People are makin' more money than ever."

"Last night on the radio," said Mr. Gunther in his very correct, but heavily accented, English, "Lowell Thomas said that by next summer the average wage-earner in America will be making over $40 a week!"

"That'll be great for next year," said Uncle Berk, "but right now, I'd just like to see an end to the rationing of things we need to get on with our lives. What good is money, if you can't buy stuff. What good's my tractor if the government won't let me get enough gas, or tires, to use it?"

"When do you expect to see rationing end?" asked Mr. Gunther.

"Sir," said Jackie from the puzzle table, "the Secretary of Agriculture, Clinton Anderson, just announced that sugar will be rationed for a while longer, but rationing of shoes and some foods will end right away. And there's a possibility that gas rationing will end by mid-December."

"Son, are you sure?" asked Mr. Justice. "That would mean folks would be able to travel for Christmas—and that Christmas dinner might be more like in the old days."

"Yes, sir. I read it on the train coming down."

Uncle Berk chuckled. "If Jackie says he read it, that settles it—provided the government comes through with what Anderson announced. That boy has a photographic memory."

"Is that so?" asked Mr. Gunther. "I've heard of such."

"Absolutely." Uncle Berk answered.

"Could you prove it?" Mr. Justice asked.

"If it's okay with Jackie, we'll show you—would that be all right, Jackie? You willing to demonstrate your memory?"

"Yes, sir. I guess so—if I can keep working on the puzzle."

"Poppy, would you get us a newspaper from the storeroom?"

"Sure, Dad." She soon came back with a copy of the *Nashville Banner.*

"Here, Jackie," said Uncle Berk. "How about scanning the front page, the first page of sports, and the obituaries."

"Okay," said Jackie, reaching for the paper with his left hand. At the same time with the other, he stuck a piece of the blue sky into place on the puzzle.

"He speed-reads, but says he doesn't actually memorize, like most of us do when learning a poem or the scriptures," commented Uncle Berk. "Says he can actually see the page in his head once he's looked at it. And he doesn't forget it."

"It's not fair," said Dulcie. "The rest of us work like dogs trying to remember enough highlights to pass tests. He just takes the book to class in his memory and 'reads' whatever parts he needs to answer the questions. He's a real sideshow freak, but we're proud of him." She grinned.

"I'm finished, Uncle Berk," said Jackie. He handed the paper back to his uncle and dropped another piece into the puzzle.

"Okay. I won't bother with the main headlines—that's too easy—but what does the subhead on the second column say?"

"Vanderbilt Hospital to Expand."

"Third column near the bottom of page?" asked Uncle Berk.

"Centennial Park to Close for Remodeling."

"What front page subheads have I not asked you about?"

Jackie quoted five other headlines, including one about the Nuremberg War Crimes Trial, then said, "Anna, that piece goes in the left corner over there—the waterfall."

"Jackie, give us a column from the sports page," said Uncle Berk.

"Which one?"

"Bottom left."

"Neuhouser Picked by A.L. - Detroit Tiger pitcher Hal Neuhouser has been chosen the American League's Most Valuable Player for 1945 it was announced ... ."

"Bottom right," said Uncle Berk.

"'Vandy Faces Top Conference Foe. In the first basketball game after the Thanksgiving break, the Commodores will take on the conference-leading Kentucky Wildcats."

Mr. Justice and Gearhardt Gunther read over Berk's shoulder and shook their heads as Jackie continued until he had quoted the entire article—and found three pieces of the puzzle while he was doing so.

He next quoted the obituary of Gertrude Marie Ellis of Shelbyville, Tennessee and told about humorist Robert Benchley's death following a cerebral hemorrhage. When Jackie covered the death of Pulitzer Prize-winning novelist Ellen Glascow in Richmond, Virginia, Mr. Gunther threw his hands up and said, "Phenomenal, absolutely phenomenal!"

"It is astounding!" said Mr. Justice. "I've never seen anything like it! Young man, you have quite a gift."

"Thank you. That's just what it is—a gift. Mother says I shouldn't get the big head about it. Everyone has some gift. I'm not the artist Dulcie is. Eugene has perfect pitch and can sing tenor notes I couldn't hit on a pogo stick. And Poppy, she's just all-around special."

Jackie grinned and grabbed imaginary lapels, "So, as the Apostle Paul told the Roman Christians, we mustn't think more highly of ourselves than we ought," he said, "Each of us Stoneworth Teens has some special talent. Mine happens to be my memory."

"Well put, son. Well put!" said Mr. Justice, chuckling.

Erik frowned and rubbed his brow. "Why do you call yourself a 'Stoneworth teen'?" he asked. "I thought your last name was Delaney."

The four cousins looked at each other and grinned.

"That's easy to explain," said Eugene. "Our dad and Dulcie and Jackie's mother are brother and sister. Their parents were our Grandma and Grandpa Stoneworth. So, when we're together or writing letters to each other, we call ourselves 'the Stoneworth teens.'"

"Jackie and I," said Poppy, "aren't *quite* teens yet, but we get to be included."

"That's because we *mature* ones are so nice," teased Eugene. "Sometimes we refer to ourselves as, 'the Stoneworth cousins.' We're the Tennessee branch, and Dulcie and Jackie are part of the Kentucky branch. It's sort of like we have our own club, or something."

Erik nodded slowly, "I see," he said.

"Jackie," said Poppy, looking up from the puzzle, "I was just thinking. When you were talking about special skills, if you really knew Erik and Anna, you would have added, 'I can't toss my cap across the room and land it on the hall tree every time like Erik does. Or ride a horse with an English saddle like Anna.' You just oughta see —"

"Time to eat," announced Aunt Nan from the door of the dining room. "The puzzle will have to wait, kids."

5

Thanksgiving Dinner

Dulcie slipped to her aunt's side as the family and their guests walked into the dining room. "What a beautiful meal, Aunt Nan," she whispered. "And it smells so good!"

"Thank you, Dulcie. Uncle Berkley and I are so glad you and Jackie get to be here. I even slipped in a couple of Kentucky dishes so you wouldn't feel homesick. Since I know how much you love your mother's Christmas jam cake, I cheated a little and moved it up a month so we could have it as one of the desserts."

Dulcie gave her a quick hug.

When the family was seated at the big table with heads bowed, Uncle Berk prayed:

"Dear Lord, last Thanksgiving our nation was at war. Many of us were far from home, hungry, cold, and lonely. We had only our memories of meals such as this, memories of the warmth that comes from being surrounded by loved ones. We endured the uncertainty of whether we would live or die.

"There are thousands of empty places at tables this year, Lord, places that will remain forever empty because the men and women

47

who went to serve, but did not return. Our hearts break for their families. Comfort those families, Lord. Wrap them in your love. "For the shelter of this home, for the love within its walls, we are thankful. That the war is over, that bloodshed has ceased, that families are reunited, that peace prevails, we are thankful.

"We are thankful for the friends and family gathered at this table. We thank you for the food that nourishes our bodies as you nourish our spirits. And, above all, we are thankful for our Lord Jesus. In His name, we pray. Amen."

Following a hearty "Amen" chorus, the meal began.

When the meal was underway, Uncle Berk said, "Mr. Justice, you and Julia are the only people here who are natives of McMinnville. How long have your people been in this area?"

"It's the only place I've ever called home," said the elderly man. "My grandfather, Jonathan Justice, came here from North Carolina around 1810. He married Dixie Carnahan from Manchester, and they had seven children. My dad, their oldest son, was Jeremiah Justice. He married Eliza Duncan from Cookeville. She was my mom. I was born in 1860, just before the War of Northern Aggression. My daddy died in the battle at Chickamauga," he said, pausing to take a bite of turkey.

"Dad, remember we have Kentucky folk here!" Julia Gunther patted her father's arm, then turned to Dulcie. "Daddy and many of his friends still call the Civil War, the 'War of Northern Aggression.' You might be interested to know that the Rebel raider, John Hunt Morgan, married a McMinnville girl, Mattie Ready. At one time he made this town his headquarters."

"He was a Kentuckian who sided with the South," said Poppy to her cousins. "He even made a raid all the way up into Ohio, but he got caught. But he escaped and came back to Tennessee."

"Mr. Justice," said Dulcie, "Eugene and Poppy have been telling us about Rebel Cave. We're going to explore it. Do you think Confederate soldiers really hid there during the Civil War?"

"Sure do, young lady! Back in the late 1870s, when I was about Eugene's age, I was possum huntin' one dark night up on the mountainside. A sudden rainstorm come up, so me and my huntin'

48

buddies headed right into the mouth of Rebel Cave. When lightnin' flashed we could see the remains of an old military wagon. We tore a couple of boards off and made us a fire."

"Wow! Do you suppose any of the wagon is still there?" asked Poppy.

"I wouldn't think so. I 'magine we weren't the only hunters to take shelter there over the last seventy years—but you never know. There might be bits and pieces buried in the dry dirt."

"That wagon would likely have been left there in early summer of 1863," Poppy told them. "That's when the Union forces swept through on the way to Chattanooga."

"Can't say about that," said Mr. Justice. "You seem to know quite a bit about that war, Poppy. You been studyin' up on it for school, child?"

"Oh, no. It goes back to when I was just a little girl. I loved the stories Daddy and my aunts and uncles told about Great-grandpa Stoneworth and Great-grandpa Carver fighting for the Union. I started reading about it. When we'd go visit the family in Kentucky, I'd talk to people like Mr. Clarence Hunt. His daddy was a Union soldier when he was just thirteen years old. Pretty soon I was giving reports at school. And I've just kept reading, asking questions, and listening."

Erik asked, "Did you ever go way back in the cave, Granddad?"

Before he could answer, Anna asked, "Granddad, was anyone ever able to prove that soldiers of the Southern Army actually stayed in the cave?"

"I only visited the cave a couple of times, so can't tell you much about it. As far as I know, nobody ever proved the soldier boys were there, 'ceptin' for that ol' wagon we found. Mostly it's just an old legend. Some folks even say a McMinnville soldier boy hid out there after the Yanks overran this area."

"What's the cave like?" asked Anna.

"I remember that the entrance is big. As best I recall it goes a long way and there was water not far back. None of us boys spent much time around there. Close by are a couple of other caves, and they're a lot more excitin'. They got most of our attention."

"More caves? Really?" Jackie perked up. "Suppose we could we go see them, too, Mr. Justice?"

"Children," Aunt Nan admonished. "Let Mr. Justice eat his dinner! He's hardly had a bite."

"I can tell you a little about the other caves," said Mrs. Gunther. "My Daddy took me spelunking—that's cave exploring—a couple of times when we were both much, much younger."

"*You* went in a wild cave, Mom? Really?" asked Anna.

"I certainly did! But not *a* cave—*caves,* plural." Mrs. Gunther laid her fork down. "The first cave is Henshaw Cave. It's just around the mountain past the Stoneworth property line. It's not very big, maybe a little wider than this house. It likely goes back no more than a quarter of a mile. But it appears that during the War of 1812, and again during the Civil War, it was very important; the soil from its floor was mined for saltpeter—a form of nitrate."

"Sounds rather large to me!" said Erik. "Why did the soil contain nitrate, Mother, and why would anyone mine it?"

"Water working its way through the soil and rock carries nitrate into the caves," explained Mrs. Gunther. "And there are bats—"

"Bats!" exclaimed Dulcie, with a shudder. "I hadn't thought about bats living in these caves. Mice with wings—that's all bats are. I ... I just hate them." she declared vehemently.

"Bats never hurt anyone," said Mrs. Gunther, "and they catch lots of insects. Anyway, bats living in caves drop nitrogen-rich manure, called 'guano,' onto the cave floor."

Mrs. Gunther's hand flew to her mouth. "Oh my. I don't guess this is the best topic to discuss at the dinner table." She smiled. "Suffice it to say, the soil contains a lot of saltpeter."

"Mother," said Eric, "you still have not told us why they wanted the saltpeter."

"Oh yes, the nitrate can be combined with sulfur and charcoal to make gunpowder. The Confederate States were cut off from supplies from the North and Europe, so these works were very important. I imagine some of the wooden vats and other things used in the process are still back there in Henshaw Cave."

"Man, oh man! I'd like to see that," said Jackie. "But what

about the other caves?"

"Tell 'em about Higgenbotham, Julia," said Mr. Justice.

Mrs. Gunther put down her coffee cup and continued. "Higgenbotham Cave is huge! It's on around the mountain past Henshaw. It, too, has been known since the early 1800s."

"Known long enough," said Mr. Justice, as he wiped his mouth with his napkin, "that we used to take our girlfriends on trips in there when we was 'sparkin.' That's what we called romancin' the ladies back then. We even had big groups go in there for square dances. You should've heard the music a-ringin' off the walls!"

Mrs. Gunther smiled at the six enthralled young people. "Can you imagine toting musical instruments way back inside a cave? The entrance to Higgenbotham, unlike Rebel Cave, is small. You have to hunker down to go in. It opens up eventually, but going is tough for a long way. At least a mile or two, maybe more."

She took a sip of coffee. "You have to climb with just finger and toe holds at times, and at others you have to get down and crawl on all fours. There's even a cedar pole with limb stubs serving as a ladder at one place."

"Wow, that sounds exciting," said Poppy, "but isn't it awfully muddy? Who'd want to 'spark' with a muddy girl?"

Mr. Justice wiggled his bushy, white eyebrows up and down, and the whole crowd broke into laughter.

Mrs. Gunther continued, "It's actually quite dry. Finally it opens up and there's a huge flat room with a low ceiling. It's called 'The Ten Acre Field.' Not far from there is a room that goes up and up and up. As you climb the slope you make your way past what looks like giant chessmen. Let me tell you, Higgenbotham Cave is spectacular—but you kids will have to explore it another time. Mrs. Stoneworth says Dulcie and Jackie have to catch the train back to Kentucky after church on Sunday. You'll do well just to explore Rebel Cave by then."

"Of course, we ought to warn them," said Mr. Justice, "about the Ghost of Rebel Cave." A mischevous twinkle shone in his eyes, in spite of his effort to appear somber.

"Now, Dad," said his daughter, "don't you start any of that

scary nonsense.

"Just a little warning, so when they hear—"

"Dad!"

A grinning Aunt Nan pushed away from the table, stood and walked to the sideboard. "Ready for pumpkin pie?" she asked.

While they ate their desserts, in spite of Jackie's prodding about the Ghost of Rebel Cave, Mr. Justice changed the subject and told the young people about how McMinnville had become one of the nursery capitals of the nation. Soon, though, they turned to discussing their plans for exploring Rebel Cave the next day.

Erik Gunther looked at the other teens around the table. "Why not get a head start by going up to the cave this afternoon?"

"Yeah!" said Jackie. "Let's do it!"

Erik continued, "We could examine the entrance and see if we can find evidence of the old wagon—or any other signs that the Rebel soldiers really did hide out there."

Dulcie noted that Erik's face lit up and his blue eyes sparkled when he was excited. There was a trace of a dimple on his right cheek, and a slight cleft in his chin. She glanced away when he looked toward her.

"Great idea, Erik!" said Eugene. "I'll get a couple of shovels and a rake so we can dig around. Dulcie, you take a pad to sketch the entrance, and write down anything we find."

"And Erik could take pictures," said Anna. "He's one of the best photographers around. He has a Leica camera."

"*Ja*, that will be fine for today," said the twins' father, "since you'll be outside. It would not be wise to take such fine equipment deep underground. But should you locate anything of the old wagon at the entrance, pictures would record the find."

"If you're gonna look for what's left of that ol' wagon," said Mr. Justice, "look under the overhang on the right side, just inside the entrance. It's been eighty years since it was left there, so odds for findin' it ain't good. On the other hand, it's dry in there, so some of it might have been preserved. Good luck. Almost wish I could go along!"

Jackie patted his full stomach. "There's just nothing like an afternoon of adventure to top off a big Thanksgiving dinner."

6

The Wagon

Dulcie, Anna, and Poppy helped clear the table and wash the dishes while the boys did outside chores and hunted up the tools they'd need for the expedition.

"Anna, did you bring slacks to wear in the cave?" asked Dulcie as the girls dried the last of the dishes.

"I did. And a blouse and sweater and a pair of sturdy shoes."

Dulcie placed the last glass in the cupboard. "Me, too. And Daddy lent me an old denim shirt I can use as a jacket over my sweater to protect it. It'll keep me warm, but not be as bulky as a coat."

"That's a good idea," said Poppy. "I'll get one of Eugene's old shirts. There should be several packed away. Mom never throws anything out."

"Tomorrow I'll wear one of Erik's or my father's," said Anna. "Today, since we'll mostly check out the mouth of the cave for the old wagon, I should be fine in my sweater."

"At least you'll look like a girl," Poppy told her. "I'll look like

53

a tomboy, all bundled up in Eugene's old shirt. Guess I'll have to get used to it if I'm going to be a spee—what did Mrs. Gunther call a cave explorer?"

"Spelunker," said Jackie, as he, Eugene, and Erik came in the back door. "The people who explore seriously or for scientific purposes are called 'speleologists.'" Jackie nudged Poppy with his elbow. "We're ready to go—you girls still doing the dishes?"

"No, we're just discussing the new 1945 fall fashions for female cave explorers," answered Dulcie, laughing. "We're through here. Give us a minute to change. We'll be right back."

As the girls ran up the stairs, Eugene said, "Bet that'll be a long minute. Let's get the flashlights."

Jackie grinned, then scampered up the stairs behind the girls.

"Wait'll you see what we brought instead of flashlights!" he hollered back to Eugene and Erik.

Soon he bounded back down the steps carrying six miner's caps with attached carbide lights.

"Dad sent these. He said it would be easier for us to explore if we didn't have to carry flashlights. Good thing he threw in a couple of extras just in case we had problems with any of them. We have enough to go around."

The girls clamored down the stairs and joined the fellows.

Erik took a cap with its attached light and examined both closely. "How do they work?" he asked.

"We'll show you when we get to the cave," Dulcie answered shyly.

Within a few minutes the group was walking up a path that ran diagonally across the pasture. It led up toward the woods that covered Cardwell Mountain. Dulcie and Erik had army-surplus backpacks with the camera, film, a sketchpad, and other items needed to record any finds. Anna and Eugene each carried a shovel. Poppy had a pack with snacks and Jackie carried a canteen of water and a short-handled rake.

"Up the hill there's a huge spring—it's just this side of where the pasture ends and the woods begin," said Eugene, pointing ahead. "The spring is really a deep pool. We call it the Blue Hole. The cave is in the woods up beyond the spring."

Up ahead, Dulcie could see where the pasture flattened out and a stream ran from a depression down through a gully. On each side of the pool stood a huge oak tree with wide-spreading branches.

"Just look at those ancient monarchs," marveled Dulcie. "What a site for a house! You could call the place, 'Twin Oaks.'"

"Or 'The Two Sentinels,'" said Jackie, running ahead.

Poppy joined him in a race to the spring.

"Man, oh man!" yelled Jackie when he arrived at the pool. "This thing is as big as my school classroom—Come on! You gotta see it!"

The pool was large and shaped roughly like a pear sliced lengthways. The stem, pointing downhill, was a seven-foot-deep fissure where the small stream ran out and on down a little valley to the northwest of the Stoneworth home.

"Look how deep the spring is!" said Erik. "I can see why you call it 'The Blue Hole.'"

"It's so clear you can see the white rock walls way down under the water," said Anna.

"Yep, that's limestone, just like in the cave." Eugene pointed to the far end of the pool. "On the back side the water goes down, down, down until all you can see is blackness."

"We don't know how deep it is," said Poppy, "but Daddy says the water likely comes from one of the caves. In late winter, the water surges up. Then the pool rises a foot or two and the water rushes down the valley to the river."

"What a great place to swim," said Anna. "Should be quite a thrill to dive into the water from the high bank on the upper side."

"Quite a *chill* would better describe it!" said Eugene. He dipped his hand in the water and shivered dramatically. "The water temperature year-around is little more than fifty degrees—about the same as in the cave. I've been studyin' up on this stuff since I found out Daddy was going to let us go in the cave."

"Speaking of *cave*," said Jackie, putting on his best stage voice, "Rebel Cave awaiteth while we tarry and talk. As our good friend Willie Shakespeare sayeth, 'Action is eloquence. ... Make no delay, for, lords, tomorrow is a busy day.' So I say, 'Onward!'"

He swept his arm across his chest, pointed toward the woods and sprinted off in that direction with the rake held over his shoulder, javelin style.

Dulcie rolled her eyes and shook her head. She and the others started after him.

"Is he always like that?" asked Anna with a grin.

"He's always full of energy, if that's what you mean. And you never know what will come from his mouth." Dulcie laughed. "But you can be sure you'll frequently hear, '*hurry*.'"

Poppy ran to catch up with Jackie. The two rushed up a slight hollow into the woods and disappeared. Soon Jackie's echoing voice floated back to the four older teens, "IT'S HUGE! Hurry!"

Walking single-file along a narrow, overgrown path into the woods, they came to a slight opening. Ahead of them, Poppy and Jackie stood side by side inside a gaping hole in the hillside. The mouth of the cave dwarfed them.

"Welcome to our place, tardy travelers," announced Jackie, sweeping his arms wide to welcome the latecomers.

"This is enormous!" Erik said with awe. He slipped out of his backpack and opened it to get his camera. "Truly enormous."

"I just stepped it off with three-foot strides," said Jackie. "It must be about 45 feet wide and close to 30 feet high. A three-story building would fit in here! Or a whole Rebel regiment."

"Looks like they could have," said Eugene. "From what I've heard, though, it was just a few men. Like Mr. Justice said at dinner, nobody knows any details. But all the old-timers insist it was a Rebel hideaway."

Poppy pulled her pack off her shoulders. "We went back as far as there's light and there's no sign of a wagon. I'm disappointed."

"According to Granddad," said Anna, "the one he saw was on the right side not very far back. We should focus there, don't you think?"

"Sounds good to me," Eugene agreed, taking a shovel and heading that way. "Unless the stuff is mighty deep, I ought to be able to uncover it."

Dulcie glanced around the entrance. "Hold up a minute," she said. "Let's get organized. Mr. Justice said they built a fire using wood from the wagon—but look at all the ash piles. It appears there've been lots of fires here through the years. First, let Erik take a picture to show the site undisturbed. Then let's number the sites where we find ashes and carefully excavate each one."

Erik took the lens cap off his camera. "My plan is to take multiple pictures, including shots of each dig and some of the whole area."

"All right. I'll do pencil sketches," said Dulcie. "We can mark on them exactly where we find anything interesting. The rest of you work as two teams. Remove the dirt carefully and sift through it. Even something small might give us a clue. But first, let's decide which places to work."

Within a short time they found five locations on the right side of the cave entrance where bits of wood, charcoal, and ashes indicated fires had been built.

"This one looks the oldest. Let's call it 'Site One,'" said Eugene, looking at an area near the wall. "Anna, let's you and me start here. Jackie and Poppy, y'all start over at that spot farthest away—'Site Two.' That way we won't be in each other's way."

After about fifteen minutes of digging Eugene let out a whoop. "I've hit something metal!" He dropped to his knees and scooped away the dirt with his hands. "Aw, Phooey!" he said, pulling out a long brown object, "it's nothing but an old iron bar." He looked at it briefly and tossed it aside.

For the next half-hour the teams worked steadily, but found nothing of significance except two arrowheads.

"Well," Eugene asked, "what do we have from all that effort? Nothing except proof Indians used this place, too. Let's move to Sites Three and Four and save the fifth one for last."

"Why?" asked Poppy.

"It's the largest and freshest looking, so odds are good it's not very old," said Eugene. "I imagine 'possum or coon hunters likely built fires there recently. That ash pile likely won't offer us much."

Dulcie walked around the site that Eugene indicated. "I'm not sure you're right about that, Eugene. If you stumbled onto this place and wanted to build a fire, where would you likely start it?"

"Where another fire had already been, I guess. I'd probably use any scraps of wood that hadn't burned, and use the ashes as a base."

"Right," said Dulcie. "Site Five might be the best one yet."

"Yippee!" came a shout from Site Four, where Poppy and Jackie had just begun working. "Look what Poppy found!" cried Jackie.

Between her right thumb and forefinger, she held up a small, flat, dirt-covered disk.

The group converged on Site Four.

"Looks like a coin," said Poppy. She tried to rub off the dirt. "In spite of the soil being so dry, it's heavily caked."

"Go easy, Poppy," said Dulcie. "Be careful not to scratch it."

"Jackie, get the canteen," Poppy said. "I want to see what's on this."

Jackie ran for his pack and carefully poured a few drops of water on the coin lying in the palm of Poppy's hand. She rubbed it between her thumb and forefinger. Slowly a design began to emerge from under the caked-on dirt.

"Can you read it?" asked Anna.

"Yes, some numbers. Looks like a 6 or 8 and a 1 and a face. Jackie, pour a little more water."

He opened the canteen again and let a thin stream rinse across the face of the coin. Poppy held the coin in the palm of her left hand and using a circular motion, rubbed it with the first two fingers of her right hand. The dirt began to dissolve away. She turned the coin over, and repeated the process.

"You're getting there, Poppy! You're getting there!" said

Eugene. "Wow, look how shiny it is."

Poppy pulled the tail of her blouse out of her slacks and folded the cloth over the coin and rubbed. Then she pulled out the coin and held it between her finger and thumb.

"Rinse it off, Jackie."

He poured water on it and Poppy dried it on her blouse tail. It glistened. She turned it over.

Erik moved in closer. "Look! It's an eagle."

"It's an 1861, five-dollar gold piece!" gasped Poppy.

"Man, oh man," said Jackie, "a gold piece!"

Anna ran a finger over the face of the coin. "Look! It says, 'United States of America.' Would that be Rebel money or Yankee money?"

"'United States' means it would be Yankee money," Eugene told her. "But why would Rebel soldiers have left a U. S. coin instead of a Confederate coin?"

"I don't know why they left it," said Poppy, "but when I saw it was a gold coin, I knew it would be from the North. Rebels issued paper money, but they didn't mint any gold coins."

She bent her head over the coin. "Look," she said, "under the eagle it has a small 'O'— no," rubbing the coin with her thumb, "it's a 'C.' —Would that be for Cincinnati?"

"I have no idea," said Jackie, "but we can find out."

"At least we've found something," Dulcie told them cheerfully. "Poppy, you tuck that into your pack for safekeeping and then show me right where you found it. I want to make a record of where it was. Let's all get back to work. Who knows what might come in the next shovel full of dirt."

"Man, oh man! I guess so," said Jackie, as he and Poppy continued their work at Site Four.

"Five dollars!" he continued. "That's pretty good pay for a day's work. And it could be worth a lot more by now since it's so old."

The group worked with renewed enthusiasm after the find, but the next hour yielded nothing of significance at Site Three and Site Four.

Eugene and Anna abandoned Site Three and moved to Site Five, where Dulcie and Erik were working with a stout stick and the rake.

Eugene said, "You don't even have a shovel, but you've already moved a lot of dirt. You might as well call it quits. Don't you think so?"

"Not yet," said Dulcie. "You said this was the biggest site. That may be because it was started first. When you extinguish a fire in a place like this, what do you use?"

"Dirt. You throw dirt on it."

"Right. Looks like that happened here many times. Hand me that shovel. We may get to the 1860's level yet."

She began to dig with the shovel. Soon she felt the shovel hit something hard.

"That felt like metal," she told Erik and Eugene.

Eugene frowned. "I hope it's not another metal bar."

Poppy and Jackie hurried over just as Dulcie uncovered a metal bolt with a short piece of wood attached. The end of the piece of wood was burned.

"This," said Dulcie, "could be from the wagon!"

A thrust of the shovel a few inches away again struck something. When Dulcie moved the shovel still further away she had the same result. Something was there, but it didn't feel like metal.

"Pay dirt!" yelled Jackie. "All hands attack!"

Dulcie tossed the shovel aside and instantly six young people were on their knees scooping out dirt with their bare hands. They worked carefully to excavate the unknown object without damaging it.

"It's just a board." Dulcie felt disappointment sweep over her when she uncovered one end. "Oh rats! I was hoping it would be a wooden treasure chest, but it's just a loose plank."

She worked the other end free from the dirt on top of it. One end was charred black. She turned it over. On the bottom side, in faded letters were the words, "United States Ar" – the rest had been burned away.

"This is it!" said Eugene. "It's got to be part of the wagon." He took the board from Dulcie and turned it over and looked at the lettering on the end.

"It's marked USA, not CSA. And the coin we found is marked USA. Could the legend be wrong about which soldiers hid here?"

Erik picked up the shovel and leaned on it. "We have a mystery. Let us work fast. It will be dark soon. Perhaps we will find additional clues."

The team rapidly completed the dig at Site Five. They found additional pieces of metal and wood from the wagon, including what looked like the partially burned hub from a wheel, and one charred wooden spoke. Without doubt, a wagon had been abandoned there. But nothing else was found to solve the mystery of who left it.

An exhausted, yet happy, group of young people trudged their way out of the woods and down the hill in the waning light.

"I was hoping we'd fine more clues," Jackie said, kicking at the tall grass beside the path. He grinned and shrugged his shoulders. "Anyway, I can't wait 'til we go back tomorrow!"

"Me neither," said Poppy brushing at the dirt on her pants. "But just look at me! I'm such a mess! I'll never look decent again."

"I have little doubt, young lady," said Erik with a warm smile, "that you will be an even more horrible mess when we come out of the cave following tomorrow's explorations."

Dulcie saw Erik flash a grin and a wink at their cute little companion. A flush of emotion swept over her.

That night Dulcie wrote in her journal:

> *Erik is so nice. Even to the little kids. What a guy!*
> *Maggie, you can have Arnie. I think I like them a little*
> *taller, a little blonder, and a little sweeter.*

7

The Cave

It was Friday morning, and after an extra-hearty breakfast, the six cave-explorers-to-be climbed the hill to Rebel Cave.

"It's amazing how easy it is to get up in the morning when there's a cave to explore!" said Dulcie.

"Sure is easier than getting up to go to school," Eugene agreed.

Dulcie continued, "I was so excited, I woke up before daylight, and couldn't go back to sleep. I was thinking about Poppy's $5 gold coin—if we could find a hoard of those, we wouldn't have to worry about money for college!"

"It's not *my* gold coin," said Poppy. "It's *our* gold coin. We agreed that we'd share equally everything we find."

"I'd sure hate to see that nice, near-perfect coin cut into six pieces," Jackie said, with a dramatic sigh.

"I didn't mean cut the coin into six pieces, goon-child!" said Poppy. "We'll share equally the *value* of anything we find."

"Hold on, Poppy," said Dulcie with a grin. "'Goon-child?' Derogatory name-calling is—what's the word, Erik—*verboten*?"

Erik nodded. "Yes. Forbidden or unacceptable."

"Awwww! I was just kidding," Poppy refuted.

"And I thought it was a compliment!" said Jackie. "Hey, did I feel a rain drop?"

"You certainly did," said Erik. "Let's run!"

Soon the group was under the shelter of the huge cave overhang.

They walked a short distance into the mouth of the cave until they came to a large flat rock. They set their packs on it to finish arranging their gear for the trip on into the cave.

"I'm going to record this as the 'Living Room Rock,' said Dulcie. She began sketching on her pad. "It's flat and big enough to build a living room right on top of it."

"These carbide lamps certainly are strange looking," Anna remarked. She took a brass object about five inches high off the miner's cap and held it up. The lamp had two roughly equal-size cylindrical chambers connected together, one on top of the other. On one side of the top chamber was a reflector like the one on a flashlight, except it was larger, flatter, and had no glass lens. "Dulcie, yesterday we had enough light from the outside, so we never got to use these," said Anna. "How do they work?"

"They're pretty simple. I've watched Daddy clean and repair them all my life. He showed me how to use them a long time ago."

Dulcie unscrewed the lower chamber, filled it with small, dry lumps of carbide, and screwed the sections back together. Then she filled the upper chamber with water.

"Turn the control on top just a little to the right—clockwise," said Dulcie. "That lets water drip onto the carbide. The reflector on the top chamber has a little stem, sort of a nub, in the center. Listen and you can hear a hissing sound — that's gas coming out the small hole in the middle of the stem. The water dripping on the carbide releases the gas. If you wet your finger and put it in front of the stem, you can feel the gas escaping."

"Whew! I can smell it!" Poppy wrinkled her nose.

"Sure, you can," said Dulcie, "but I wouldn't breathe too much of it. Now, let's light the lamps. Hold the lamp with your left hand and cup your right hand over the reflector with your fingers pointing upward. Create a pocket. Make it tight so the gas will build up between your hand and the reflector. You'll create a spark by spinning the little wheel on the side of the reflector. Feel it under the pad of your hand?"

Nods and affirmative answers indicated they did.

"Okay, sweep your hand quickly across the wheel and away from the reflector," Dulcie told them, "like this—" She flicked her hand across the wheel of her lamp. A bright spark jumped from the little wheel, and with a sudden 'Pop!' a small flame sprang from the center of the reflector. "Watch how the flame gets bigger when I open the water flow control a bit. Now, try to light yours—it may take a couple of tries, but you'll get it."

Soon all six carbide lights were burning brightly. After they reattached the lamps to the metal clips on the front of the cloth miners' caps, they gathered their packs and made their way into the deepening darkness.

"These lamps certainly don't give much light," said Erik.

"Daddy said they wouldn't seem to be very bright," said Jackie, "but as we get away from daylight and our eyes adjust, they'll be fine. Especially in smaller passages."

Eugene patted the belt at his waist. "That's why I have my faithful old flashlight clipped on here. If we need a spotlight, it'll reach quite a distance."

"Wow! Look at the size of that rock!" said Poppy. They moved to the left to avoid a rock blocking the right side of the cave. "It's as high, and as big, as our kitchen. And there's still space above it. I'm glad I wasn't here when it broke away from the ceiling!"

Anna shivered. "Don't say that! It gives me the heebie-jeebies!"

"Look," said Eugene. "Someone built a fire way back here."

Behind the big rock there were ashes, partially burned sticks, and a pile of wood someone had left behind. Eugene studied them. "Hunters, probably, or ancient cave men. Maybe we can investigate later."

As the group made its way deeper into the darkness, the ceiling lowered and the passage swung to the right. Soon the floor began to drop. They could no longer see light from the entrance. But a rushing noise came from further back in the cave.

"Water!" exclaimed Dulcie. "Mr. Justice said there was water when he was here more than seventy years ago. It's still down here!"

Eugene unclipped the flashlight from his belt and swept its beam ahead. Thirty or so feet in front of them and a dozen feet below, a pool of water stretched the full width of the passage. On the right, a small waterfall poured into the pool from a large hole in the wall near the ceiling. On the left, the water ran over a lip of stone, and down into another passage.

"Uh-oh!" said Erik. "It looks like this may be the end of the expedition! Unless, that is, we are ready for a cold swim."

Anna disagreed. "Maybe not. It could be just a wade—perhaps it's not deep."

Dulcie turned to her brother. "Jackie, would you go back to that last fire site and bring one of those long sticks we saw there?"

"You bet!" he said, turning back.

The floor of the cave dropped quickly toward the water, and they carefully made their way down the rocky slope. When they reached the edge of the pool, Dulcie pointed to a formation hanging from the ceiling on the other side.

"Shine your light over there, Eugene," she said. When his light hit the formation, she continued. "That thing hanging up there that looks like a large icicle is a stalactite. The stumpier one, which looks like it is coming up from the floor to meet it, is a stalagmite."

Anna looked upward. "Yes, I've read about them in books and magazines, and seen pictures. But these are the first real ones I've seen."

Dulcie continued, "Mammoth Cave is the largest cave in the world. It's not far from where we live in Kentucky. When I was in eighth grade, my class went there on a field trip. The guide told us an easy way to remember which formations grow up and which ones grow down."

"How?" asked Erik.

"The guide said if the stalactites are *tight*, they won't fall, and that if the stalagmites keep growing, they *might* reach the stalactites and create pillars."

"That's corny," said Eugene, "but I guess it'll help me remember which is which."

Dulcie, Erik, and Anna walked over the rough stones to the right side of the passage nearest the place where the water was pouring into the pool from an upper level.

Anna knelt and touched the stones of the floor. "Look at this. It looks like someone once built something here—or started to."

Stones had been arranged to provide a somewhat flat, platform-like area. A large, very soggy, rotted timber lay on one edge. The end was wedged under rocks.

"I can't imagine what anyone would have built back here," said Dulcie. "Whatever it was, it was abandoned long ago."

They stood on the flattened area trying to decide its purpose when Jackie returned with a 7-foot-long pole.

"Here ya go, Erik, catch it," he said, and tossed it to the tall young man.

Erik grabbed it in the middle and turned toward the water. "I am a strong swimmer. I will wade in and check it out."

"I can't swim at all," said Dulcie. "It had better be shallow."

Erik slowly waded out, checking the bottom with the pole. "Brrrrr! It *is cold*." Soon the water was to his knees. "Oops! I have bumped something." He plunged his hand under the water, felt around and pulled out a piece of coiled metal tube. "Looks like an old copper pipe," he said, as he stepped toward the edge of the pool. "Stand back and I will toss it on the rocks. We can look at it later." He turned back into deeper water, probing the uneven bottom with the pole.

"Careful, *mein* brother," Anna warned, as he waded to where he was again knee-deep. Then he reached forward and probed with the stick—only to have it go almost out of sight under the water. He backed up.

Over the next few minutes, Erik checked the water at a number of locations.

He finally turned to the group on the shore and said, "It appears to be at least 6-feet deep at any point from wall to wall—and no telling how much deeper beyond where I can reach. There is little current now, but I imagine it would be a torrent during a rainstorm. I guess this is as far as we go." A look of disappointment spread across his face.

"Hey, look at me!" yelled Jackie.

All turned in the direction of his voice. They had been so focused on what Erik was doing that no one had noticed that Jackie was climbing along a ledge on the left wall above the pool. He was now halfway across the pool and standing directly above the edge of the water.

"Jackie!" yelled Dulcie. "You get back here before you fall in!"

"Aw Sis, don't be a worry-wart! This ledge is more than a foot wide most of the way to this point. And here it's at least 6 inches wide. Try it! No, wait. Let me be sure I can get all the way across."

"Jackie! —" Dulcie called threateningly.

It did little good to call him back. He eased carefully along the ledge with his back to the open space and water, chest toward the wall, arms slightly spread, hands against the rock face of the wall.

Dulcie's heart pounded in her throat. *Lord, please keep him safe!* she prayed silently.

"All you gotta do," Jackie called to them, "is lean against the wall a little, keep your eyes on the ledge, scoot one foot forward, then the other. It's easy as pie—almost. It's a little tricky right in the middle, where the ledge is narrow, but there's a place you can hold onto—sorta like a crack or crevice you can stick your hands in and get a good grip."

Soon he was on the other side. With a wave of his arm, he said, "Well, c'mon. There's adventure waiting. Let's go!"

"What do you think?" Dulcie asked Erik as they made their way toward the ledge. "Should we try it? I don't think we should risk doing anything really dangerous."

Erik's eyes swept across the ledge and out over the pool. "I suppose, should anyone fall in, the water will break the fall and we can pull them out. The greater danger would be a fall onto the rocks—but the ledge is wide over to where it is above the water, so there should not be a problem."

"I doubt we'll find clues back there about the Confederate soldiers—or whoever they were," said Anna. "But it would be a shame not to see what's over there."

Poppy moved toward the ledge. "I volunteer to go next."

"Eugene?" Dulcie looked questioningly at her cousin.

"Let's give it a go. We didn't expect it to be like walking down the street back in Drakesboro."

"That can be dangerous enough when the miners are on strike," Dulcie said. "Oh, all right. Just please be careful. I don't want to have to explain to any of our parents. Let's just be extra careful."

Looking up at the tall, blond young man beside her, she said, "Erik, you're shaking. You okay?"

He grinned. "I am soaked almost to my waist, and standing still has let the cold penetrate. Once we're moving, I will warm up and dry out. I will be fine."

"You sure?" Anna asked worriedly.

"Sure. Poppy, you go ahead, then Anna —she's a strong swimmer, too—then Eugene. Dulcie, you follow him and I'll be the caboose."

"C'mon, cousin!" yelled Jackie to Poppy. "Spread your arms, lean against the wall and don't look at the water. Remember to get a good handhold in the crevice at the narrow place, and focus on your feet and the ledge. C'mon, you can do it."

"Okay! Here I come!"

Anna followed, then Eugene. Within a few minutes they were all safely on the other side.

"You made it! I knew you would," Jackie crowed as he grabbed

Dulcie in a bear hug. "I'm proud of you! As Willie Shakespeare once said, 'Just screw your courage to the sticking place and we'll not fail.' And his cousin, Mark Twain, further commented, 'Courage is resistance to fear, mastery of fear - not absence of fear.' Sis, you are the very epitome of such—"

"Oh, hush, you nut!" Dulcie interrupted, with a grin.

"That response reminds me," said Jackie, "of a statement by another literary personage whose name I shan't reveal: 'Derogatory name-calling is *verboten*—forbidden and unacceptable.' But enough verbiage—Onward! The cave awaits."

The six young people turned from the pool and walked into the darkness.

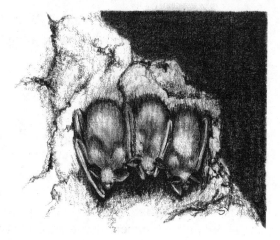

8

Probing the Darkness

"Wow, crossing that ledge was some experience," said Anna as the group moved away from the pool.

"Yeah," agreed Eugene, "and none of you had as much hangin' out over the pool as I did." He chuckled. "You skinny people had it easy."

"I'll admit my knees were shaking," said Dulcie. "I was scared."

Jackie patted her arm. "Yeah, but you made it, Sis. Now you're an experienced 'ledge walker' and since you've done it once, you can do it again."

"I guess we'll have to if we want to go home tonight," retorted Anna. She dug into her pocket and pulled out a pack of gum.

"Anyone want a piece of Juicy Fruit?" She held out the package.

Dulcie shook her head at the offer. "Let's not talk about going back across," she said shakily. "We'll have to face that soon enough. Right now, let's explore!"

"Yea, for exploring!" cried Jackie. He turned and ran up the slope.

"Hold up, Jackie," Dulcie called. "When we get to the top of the slope, we should plan what we're going to do."

"Good idea," said Erik.

When they came to a flat area where the cave was only about twenty feet wide, Eugene said, "Let's stop for a minute." He was puffing slightly.

Erik and Dulcie, Eugene and Anna, Poppy and Jackie, seated themselves on three flat rocks that made a horizontal triangle on the ground.

"Looks like we have found ourselves a council chamber," Erik said, grinning. "What plans do you have in mind, Dulcie?"

"This is a new experience for all of us," Dulcie replied. "I think it'll help if we agree on some ground rules."

"Makes sense to me, but we'd better make 'em '*under*ground' rules," said Jackie, with a chuckle.

"Okay, wise guy," said his sister. "First, I think we should stay together—no running ahead. If we decide to break up to explore side passages—and we've all seen plenty of those—we should always have two or more go together."

"And there should be no practical jokes, like hiding and pretending to have disappeared," said Poppy, nudging Jackie with her elbow.

"Or hiding and jumping out to scare people," Anna interjected.

"Any other suggestions?" asked Dulcie. She was jotting notes in her notebook.

"If anything we decide to do makes you uncomfortable or scared, you should speak up," said Eugene.

"And, if we don't reach the end, we should turn back before we get too tired," Poppy added.

"Yep," agreed Jackie. "The trip back will probably seem longer than the trip in—and we promised your folks we'd be back no later than seven o'clock tonight."

"I've got my wrist watch on. I'll keep an eye on the time," offered Poppy.

"And I have a pocket watch," said Erik. He pulled the watch

out of the bib pocket of his overalls. "I am glad it is waterproof. I forgot all about it when I was wading back there at the pool."

After they discussed other additional suggestions, Dulcie read them back, then asked, "Everyone agree to these?"

When they had unanimous approval, Dulcie said, "I've been making sketches, and I'm drawing a rough map. I marked this spot, 'The Council Chamber.' Things will be easier to remember later, if we have reference points we can identify."

They picked up their gear and moved on. After a short climb, the passage again leveled off, and soon the floor was covered with dirt. Easily visible were a number of footprints.

"Well, rats!" Eugene cried in disappointment. "We obviously aren't the first explorers back here."

Erik knelt down and peered at the prints. "I wonder if any of these were made by our Confederate soldiers."

"Or, Yankee soldiers— according to the coin we found," said Anna.

Dulcie shook her head. "It's amazing to think that footprints left almost a century ago could still be here."

"Sure they would," said Eugene, "unless other people trampled them."

"Look up here," yelled Poppy, from the front. "It splits!"

The cave forked, with the left branch slightly larger than the right.

"Hey, Dulcie," said Poppy, "list this as 'Point of Decision,' because here we'll have to decide which passage to follow."

"Yeah," Jackie agreed, "and how about something original for the two forks—like 'Right Branch' and 'Left Branch.'"

"That's brilliant, Cousin," Poppy said sarcastically. "But I guess those names will work until we've checked them out. Maybe something we see will suggest something better."

"Well, which way do we go?" asked Dulcie. "Any preference?"

Anna looked down. "Footprints show most people have taken the larger passage, the one to the left. Only two pair of footprints go to the right."

"That settles it," said Jackie. "We should, of course, like Frost, Robert, not Jack, take the road less traveled by. Let's go right."

Eugene shrugged. "Suits me. If there's nothing exciting on this side, we can always take the other fork when we get back."

"Speaking of getting back," said Dulcie, "we should have a way to make sure we don't get lost. If we aren't careful we could get turned around and become confused."

"Yeah," Eugene said thoughtfully. "We should have brought string and tied one end outside. By unrolling it as we go, we could follow it back—I read about that in a book."

"I doubt that would work, Eugene," Erik disagreed. "It would slow us down too much. Besides, how long would the string have to be? They say Higgenbotham Cave is several miles long. This one might be as big. Can you imagine carrying so much string?"

"What we need," Anna told them, "is a way to show which passage to take to get out."

"We could stack rocks like scouts do," said Poppy, "with a rock beside the pile to point the way."

"Or lay out rocks in an arrow pointing the way to go," suggested Jackie.

"Where there is a dirt floor, we could mark an arrow in the dirt," said Erik.

"Wait!" said Dulcie. "Watch this—it's something Daddy showed me once."

She took her miner's cap off her head and opened the water control on top of the carbide light. The narrow flame increased until it extended more than two inches beyond the reflector. Walking to a large rock near the center of the passage, she held the point of the flame against the rock as she swept the lamp to the left. The flame left a black carbon mark half an inch wide. At the left end, she made the point of an arrow. "There, when we come back to this spot, this arrow will tell us the way out."

"And if we do that every time we reach a fork," said Jackie, "there's no way we'll get confused and miss the way."

Erik frowned. "Let us do that only if necessary. As a

74

photographer, I know how awful it is to see a beautiful scene all marked up with names and messages."

Dulcie agreed. "We'll only mark the way with the carbide lights if we can't use less permanent ways to show the way out. And we could put our arrows on a rock we could turn face down when we come back."

"Hey, I have an idea," said Jackie. "We could make a trail with Anna's chewing gum papers. The yellow outer wrapper would show up well, and the tinfoil inner wrapper would really shine. The gum—"

"Forget it, my little brother!" Dulcie disagreed. "We're not about to scatter trash all through the cave. All right, let's get going! Head on up the right fork, Jackie, Poppy. We're right behind you."

Soon the trail turned steeply upward. Jackie and Poppy found themselves challenged to find toe holds and handholds close enough together to be able to climb. Gradually, though, they made their way.

"Dulcie," called Poppy, glancing down at the group struggling up the steep slope, "show this as, 'The Matterhorn.'"

"I'll be sure to do that as soon as we get up this mountain," Dulcie replied, looking up past Erik, who was climbing above her. "Oooo! This is scary!" she said.

Erik reached a wide ledge, stopped climbing, and reached his hand down to pull her up next to him.

Poppy and Jackie finally reached the top of the climb and followed the passage into a room with a very high ceiling. Erik and Dulcie were a short distance behind them.

"Look, Jackie," cried Poppy, "our carbide lights don't even reach the ceiling!—and what's that smell?"

Jackie stopped, pointed his light upward, and then swung it from side to side as he brought it downward, trying to see across the room. Without looking down he took a couple of steps, then stopped abruptly.

"Look at the floor, Poppy! We're walking in something!"

They looked down. Jackie was almost ankle-deep in a dry,

grainy, brownish substance.

"What is it, Jackie?" asked Dulcie, who had just walked up behind him.

"Don't know. Hurry, Eugene, bring that flashlight!" yelled Jackie.

Eugene came puffing up.

"First, point it up there!" Poppy told him, pointing upward.

Eugene swung the light toward the ceiling. Something moved.

"Bats!" screamed Poppy. "Thousands of them!"

"NO!" Alarmed, Dulcie stepped backwards. "NO!" Waves of revulsion and fear engulfed her. Her heart pounded and faintness swept over her. She reached out blindly for support and connected with Erik. He grabbed her and held on.

"It is okay, Dulcie, it is okay," he whispered softly. "They will not hurt us! They are hibernating."

Her knees almost buckled. She felt Erik's arms tighten around her fear-frozen body.

"Hang on, Dulcie. It's all right," said Jackie, squeezing his sister's hand.

She caught her breath and said, "I know they won't hurt us— I know with my head," she paused, "but my heart takes a while to catch up with my head." She breathed deeply again. "I … I'll be okay now." She stepped away from Erik.

Eugene's light continued to sweep the colony of bats on the ceiling. "I know all about bats. From spring to fall they sleep here in the daytime, fly out at night, wipe out trillions of mosquitoes and other insects, then fly back in at daylight," he said. "We see them at dusk pouring out of the cave like a small black cloud. But we haven't seen them for weeks. Erik's right—they've started their winter hibernation. That's why they're just hanging up there."

Erik commented, "This colony must have been here for centuries. Just look at the floor." He kicked the surface with the toe of his shoe.

"Bat manure!" yelled Jackie. "That's what I've been standing in? I've been walking in bat manure!"

"NO!" squealed Poppy. "I've got it all over my shoes!"

Anna laughed, stepping back and stomping her feet. "We all do. It's dry, almost powder. It'll come off as we walk."

"Look at it," said Eugene, his flashlight sweeping over mounds of the nitrogen-rich compound. "Looks sort of like heaps of grains of rice. That stuff would be fantastic for fertilizer at our nursery, if we could just get it out of here."

"Let's just get *us* out of here," Poppy insisted. "I sure don't want to wade across this mess. Let's go try the other fork."

"Wait, come look at this," called Erik from a small chamber to their left. He squatted in a little grotto where the ceiling was too low for him to stand up. His lamp lit the ceiling. "These little fellows must be outcasts," he said, pointing at a cluster of three bats clinging upside-down to the ceiling.

Dulcie waited outside the small room, but the other four joined Erik. Soon they were on their knees looking up at the bats just inches above their heads.

"Aren't they amazing?" said Jackie.

Poppy reached out to touch one, but hesitated. "Look at their large ears. Just think, by bouncing squeaks off the walls they can listen for the echoes and make their way through total darkness."

"Yeah," said Jackie, "and when they leave here there'll be thousands of these little critters flying out at the same time. How in the world can one bat recognize the echoes of his squeaks with millions of other echoes bouncing around?"

Shaking her head, Poppy told him, "I don't know, but they're sure special creatures."

Jackie reached up a tentative finger and gently stroked the bat nearest him. The sleeping bat ignored him. "Dulcie, you gotta come see this! C'mon in here, Sis. You just gotta see this."

"No, thank you, Jackie. I'll be just fine without getting closer."

"You really should, Dulcie," said Erik. "They will not hurt you. You know that—and you have had time for your emotions to catch up with your knowledge."

"Later, maybe," she said.

"Dulcie, do come look at them," Erik plead softly. "We are leaving and you may not get another chance. They would make a fine subject for you to write a school paper about. You should make some sketches—for our record—you are our team artist."

Dulcie hesitated, then reached into her pack for her sketchpad. She stooped and crawled, trembling, into the chamber. Looking up at the bats, she shuddered. "Oh, except for their flat faces, they really *do* look like ugly mice with wings! They really do!"

Jackie looked at the bats and then back at his sister. "But they're not, Dulcie. They're not mice. They're bats. They eat insects, and do a lot of good. It'll be great to have a sketch of them."

Dulcie bit her lip, and began to draw.

Jackie turned to the rest of the group. "Why don't the rest of you head back down to the Point of Decision? And you can check out that little side passage just before the last climb. We'll finish this and meet you in a little while."

"You sure you'll be okay?" asked Erik.

Dulcie flashed him a weak smile. "Sure, we'll be fine. But if Jackie and I aren't there in half an hour, send a rescue party." She laughed softly.

It took her only ten minutes to complete the drawing. As they started down the slope, Jackie, who was just behind his sister, said, "Dulcie, wait a minute."

She turned toward him and found Jackie standing slightly up slope, his face almost on a level with hers.

"Sis, that was just about the bravest thing I ever saw. I know how scared you were, and I'm … I'm proud of you. Just wanted you to know!" he blurted out.

She hugged him tightly and said, "Thanks, Jackie. That means the world to me. Someday I'll get over this mouse thing of mine."

"Sure you will," he said. "You know, hugging's not easy when you have an open-flamed carbide light on your head. You could scorch somebody."

Within a few minutes, they joined the rest of the group at the Point of Decision.

9

Westminster Cathedral

"Anyone need to rest before we head up the left fork?" asked Eugene, as the group got together at Point of Decision. "Dulcie, what do you think of 'The Bat Belfry' as the designation for the right fork? Is that okay?"

"I guess so," she answered. "That's certainly what it is." She penciled in the name on the rough map.

"I don't need rest," responded Jackie, "but I'm starving. Think we could eat?"

"It's already 12:45! Can you believe it?" asked Poppy, looking at her watch. "Time is flying! Still, I don't think you'll collapse from hunger any time soon, Jackie."

"Ah," Jackie responded, "it seems I recall Willie Shakespeare once quoted Napoleon as having said, 'An army marcheth upon its stomach.' And as far as General Jackie Delaney, namely myself, is concerned, 'tis time and past, to break our fast."

"Oh, you nincompoop." said Poppy, laughed. "Even I know Shakespeare lived long before Napoleon, and couldn't have quoted him."

79

"A trifling technicality, my dear cousin," responded Jackie. "You sadly underestimate the genius of Shakespeare."

"All right. Enough of that," said Eugene, with mock exasperation. "Let's go a little further and stop at the next good place we find. Agreed?"

There were no dissents, so the explorers moved on. Jackie and Poppy led the way with Dulcie and Erik close behind. Anna and Eugene brought up the rear. The passage soon narrowed, then made an abrupt left turn.

When Dulcie and Erik reached the turn, they heard Anna call behind them, "Wait a minute, please. I want to see this."

Dulcie looked back, and saw Anna slip sideways into a tall narrow passage to the right that the others had missed. Eugene pulled in his stomach and squeezed himself through the slit behind her. A moment later, Anna's squeal of delight echoed out of the crevice. Eugene stuck his head back into the main passage and bellowed, "Whoa! Come back here—you gotta see this!"

Dulcie turned and called to the others, then waited for them to return. When she slipped through the narrow opening, her mouth dropped open. Anna and Eugene were standing in a small circular chamber. It was magnificent!

Jackie followed Dulcie into the room and looked up. "Man, oh man! There must be a million stalactites hanging down! Just look at them!"

Anna stood gazing at the sparkling stalactites. "Look at that ceiling!" she whispered.

The roof of the room was flat, and just a bit higher than the living room ceiling at home. It bristled with innumerable stalactites as slender as pencils, and of varying lengths. Most were less than ten inches long, but some twice that. They ranged in color from medium-brown to pure white. Drops of water clung to the tips of some. The right wall was moist and covered with flowstone—a mineral coating left behind by water trickling slowly down its surface. In the center of the rock cascade, a vein of pure white stone flowed from top to bottom.

"Wow!" Poppy cried softly. "Wow! I … I can't think of anything to say!"

"Can you believe it?" said Eugene. "Anna checked as she came in and there were no tracks ahead of us. We must be the first ever to see it. The very first!"

Erik stared in wonder. "If only I had my camera! I want to remember this." His eyes roamed from one stunning formation to the next, then turned to Dulcie. "Let us eat right here. That way we will have a little more time to see it all."

"Sounds good to me," Eugene agreed. "Anna, you have the food—"

Anna slipped out of the backpack and parceled out the bologna and cheese sandwiches.

"Sure wish soda pop came in something other than glass bottles so we could bring them along," said Eugene. "Guess a drink of water from our canteens will have to do."

"Not necessarily," said Anna. "You didn't notice the water trough over by the 'Crystal Niagara.' That's what I'd like to name the stone cascade over there."

Anna waved her sandwich in the direction of the vein of white rock. "To the right side there's a horizontal groove that water collects in and then trickles out the right end."

Jackie walked over, found the spot, leaned over, and took a drink. "Good stuff!" he proclaimed.

Erik turned to Eugene. "You said no one has ever been here before. Just think—all this beauty has been here for ages and ages. But until Anna walked in here with light, it had been in total darkness. No one had seen it. No one—ever!"

The six friends each looked around in the dim light.

"If I was a preacher," said Eugene, "I'd probably be able to come up with a sermon out of this."

Erik laughed, then turned to Dulcie. "You have been sketching the room while we have been eating. What did you name it?

"'Anna's Diner.' Is that okay?—If not, I can change it."

Anna turned to Dulcie, her face beaming with delight. "Do

81

you mean it? A room in a cave named for me?"

"Sounds good to me," Eugene answered, smiling at the attractive young lady.

"You are the one who found it, Anna," suggested Erik, "so I suppose it is appropriate for us to name it for you."

Silence descended on the team as they ate, until Dulcie spoke up quietly.

"I'm embarrassed about the way I acted in Bat Belfry," she said. "I know it probably seems silly to you, but there's a reason why I get so stupid about mice... and now bats, too, I guess."

Jackie interrupted. "You don't have to tell 'em, Dulcie. It's not important."

"It *is* important, because her fear bothers her," said Erik. He turned to Dulcie. "But you do not have to tell unless you really want to."

"Actually, I think I'd like for you to understand."

"I already know about it, Dulcie," said Eugene. "Mom and Dad told me."

Dulcie nodded. "I was three when my daddy died. Mother had it pretty tough. She was expecting Jackie, and trying to keep everything from falling apart. Once in a while, when there was no one else to leave me with, she would leave me with our Grandmother Crowe, my dad's mom. She ...." Dulcie swallowed hard.

"What did she do to you, Dulcie?" asked Erik gently.

Dulcie's eyes focused on the wall. "When she wasn't pleased with me, ... with the way I acted ... she ... she punished me."

"How?" asked Anna.

"Sometimes she slapped me, or locked me outside of the house. But the worst was when she locked me in her cellar. It was just a little dirt room, under the kitchen floor, but it was pitch black. She told me bad children were eaten alive by rats and mice, and since I wasn't good, they'd eat *me*. She'd leave me in that cellar 'til I was hysterical. I could hear the mice scurrying around on the shelves behind the canning jars. I know now, that to make me think rats were trying to get in, Grandma scratched the door or the floor with something, maybe a stick. It scared me senseless." Dulcie choked rising sobs.

"How cruel! That's absolutely horrible!" exclaimed Anna. She put her arms around Dulcie. "That woman was sick, sick, sick!"

"She really was, I know that now. My mother came home one night and found me locked in a closet. That's how she found out what Grandma was doing. That was the time Grandma told me the devil would get me."

Dulcie blew out a breath. "I... I wasn't nearly as scared of the devil as I was of those mice, though," she said.

Poppy looked sympathetically at her distraught cousin. "I'm so sorry, Dulcie. Mama and Daddy didn't tell *me*."

"I am sorry, too," said Erik. "No wonder you react as you do."

"You said earlier that bats look like winged mice," said Anna. "You're right."

"Don't they though!" Dulcie smiled shakily. "But I think I'm actually doing better. At least I stayed and sketched the three bats in the Belfry. As I told you earlier, my head knows they won't hurt me. But oh, it does take time for my feelings to catch up."

Dulcie brushed the tears from her cheeks. "Speaking of *time*, we'd better finish eating, and get moving if we're going to see much more before we have to head home."

She smiled at the others, then added quietly, "Thanks for listening."

"Thanks for telling!" said Anna.

Soon the team was underway again with Jackie and Poppy leading the way, as usual. After about an eighth of a mile the ceiling began to lower, but the level of the floor stayed the same.

Jackie called to the group, "We're gonna have to crawl for a while."

"But the passage goes on," added Poppy. "And there are tracks going and coming."

She and Jackie ducked down and walked in a squat for a short time, then dropped to crawl on hands and knees. The taller teens

83

followed, but lagged behind as the smaller pair scrambled forward.

"Follow right behind us," said Jackie, pausing to look back. "It's a belly-crawl just ahead—very wide, side-to-side, but narrow, top-to-bottom. Then it looks like it may open up. At least we're crawling in dirt, not on bare rock."

"We're gonna be hauling water for weeks to wash this mess off," Poppy complained. "Sure wish we had running water at our house!"

After some distance the low passage ended and Jackie and Poppy, side by side, crawled out into a large room.

"Jumping Jehosaphat!" Dulcie heard Jackie exclaim. "Wait till you see this!" He looked back into the crawlway and called, "Hurry!" Then he said to his companion, "Poppy, check it out over to the right— I'm going on across. Look at the size of this room! Hey! Listen to that echo!"

Dulcie and Erik, on their stomachs side-by-side in the crawlway, were almost to the point where the passage opened up.

"Erik, I've just got to stop for a minute," said Dulcie, panting. "My side is hurting—need to catch my breath. I'll just lie here for a moment."

She laid her head sideways in the dirt and tipped her head so she could look into the room ahead. Erik did likewise. In the distance Poppy's and Jackie's lights moved about, casting eerie shadows.

Poppy circled the room to the right, and Jackie made his way among towering stalagmites until he reached the other side of the large circular room. He explored the area, then positioned himself where those coming from the crawlway could see his light.

Erik stretched his arms out ahead of him and rolled his shoulders. "I have been using muscles I did not know I had," he said. "We are going to be sore tomorrow."

They lay still for another moment, then scuffling and straining sounds behind them let them know Eugene and Anna were catching up with them.

"Man! Whoa!—this one's really tight. I'm not sure if I can …

yeah, just—barely—made it!" said Eugene.

Dulcie looked back. He was gasping for breath. Sweat ran down his reddened face. His body filled the passage, top-to-bottom.

"You're getting there, Eugene," Anna encouraged. "Keep plugging away."

Oh dear, thought Dulcie, *'plugging' might not be the best choice of words.*

"You're almost there, Eugene," she called back. "It widens where we are, and then opens up. Keep coming! We'll get out of your way."

Dulcie turned to Erik. "I'm okay now," she said. A moment later they crawled out of the low passage. "Wow! What a room!"

Getting to his feed, Erik's eyes widened. "Huge!" he exclaimed. He reached his hand to Dulcie and helped her stand upright. As they were dusting themselves off, Eugene and Anna crawled out into the room and got to their feet.

"We ought to call that—" Eugene huffed, and leaned forward with his hands on his knees. He breathed deeply and began again— "Ought to call that, 'The Misery Bellycrawl.'"

He straightened up and stretched his arms upward. "Part of the time my belly was in the dirt and my back was scrubbing the roof. Memories of 'Eugene's Culvert' sure came flooding over me. My heart was pounding."

He paused, caught his breath, then shouted, "Wow-weeee! Would you look at that!" He had flipped on his flashlight and was pointing the beam toward where Poppy stood on the sloping right side of the passage. "It looks like my little sister is standing on a hillside among giant chess pieces."

"Say," said Anna, "yesterday my mother told us about the formation in Higgenbotham Cave that looks like chessmen. They must be like these."

"And look at Jackie, way over there," Anna pointed.

They looked at the tiny light that seemed to wink at them from across the immense chamber. Eugene flashed his beam at the younger boy. It wouldn't reach. The vast space dwarfed them.

"Just look at those kids," said Erik, shaking his head. "They are something!"

"Come on over here," yelled Jackie. "The footprints go on – but I want to show you something."

Poppy angled toward them as they crossed the room. "Have you noticed the ceiling?" she called. "I can just barely see it with my light, but it's beautiful."

Eugene's light showed that her remark was an understatement. The stalactites hanging from the ceiling were small compared to the large "chessman" stalagmites growing up from the floor, but they were numerous and greatly varied. Where the ceiling sloped toward Jackie, the stone surface seemed to flow downward like irregular stage curtains. Fluted drapes of varying shades, from brown to cream to pure white, followed the contour of the ceiling and then the wall.

"Wow!" said Poppy. "Look at Grandma's drapes!"

"That's a good name for them," Dulcie said with a laugh. She stopped, got her sketchpad out, and sketched rapidly. "I'm calling this room 'The Rotunda of the Chessmen,'" she said, nearing where Jackie waited.

"If you'll follow me," Jackie informed them, "you may change your mind about the name for this huge chamber." He walked perhaps forty feet, then pointed to the wall. "I could barely make it out with my light, but look at that—what does it look like?"

Hanging from the ceiling, about thirty feet above the floor, was a row of long stalactites. At the top they were massive and fused together, but about a fourth of the way down they separated into perhaps a dozen separate stalactites that ended two to six feet from the floor.

"A pipe organ!" said Anna and Erik, almost in unison.

"And wait till you hear this!" said Jackie. "Listen!" He tapped one of the formations with his knuckle. It gave off a clear, vibrant tone.

"Wow!" gasped Poppy, "Wow! Wow! Wow!"

"Line up on either side of me with your backs to the wall," instructed Jackie.

They did as he requested.

"Sis, I think you know what comes next."

Dulcie hummed a note, then began to sing in a rich, full soprano voice, "Amazing Grace, how sweet the sound .... "

Poppy quickly supplied the alto part, Jackie the baritone, and Eugene pitched in with the tenor. Erik and Anna listened, stunned. The acoustics in the room were magnificent, with every surface seeming to contribute its part. After the last word was sung, the room continued to reverberate for a full three-count or more.

The group stood in awed silence.

"Jackie, you're right," Dulcie whispered. "Let's christen this, 'Westminster Cathedral.'"

"How did you learn to sing like that?" asked Anna. "How can four voices make such full harmony? That was magnificent!"

"It truly was," Erik agreed.

"With the Stoneworths, singing begins in the womb," Dulcie told them, blushing in the darkness the moment it dawned on her that she had said something so intimate in front of the boys. Walking back to where they had joined Jackie, she continued. "In our family mothers sing to their babies even before they are born. Then they sing to the newborn. It never stops. Children in our family learn to sing along with learning to talk. Whenever we're all together, we sing. And, of course, we all sing in church. Singing is just a part of who we are."

"I've never heard anything more beautiful—both the singing, and the idea," said Anna.

"Just wish we'd had Uncle Berk along to fill in the bass. That would have made it perfect!" Dulcie answered.

"Erik and Anna, you hang around this bunch," said Jackie, "and you'll be joining in before you know it. But now," he swept an imaginary cavalier's hat off his head, and bowed low, "I've got something else to show you. Something *important*."

10

The Message on the Wall

Jackie led them to a point near where he'd been standing when they first came into the huge room. He dropped to his knees and pointed to prints on the dirt floor.

"These footprints go through that opening in the stone drapes," he said, pointing to his right. "They lead into a small walking passage—I mean, one high enough that we can walk upright in it."

Dulcie sighed. "That'll be a relief. After Misery Bellycrawl, I'd like to be vertical for a while."

She looked at Erik. "What time is it? We should turn back soon."

Erik pulled his watch from the bib of his overalls. "Already 2:39," he said. "We do need to head out before long. There will be plenty to see on the way back."

"Yeah, I know one spot," said Jackie. He winked at Poppy. "But can't we go just a little further?" He pointed his light into the passage. "Whoever we're following kept going. We've come this far—don't you want to see if we can go as far as they did?

89

We may not have another chance to do it."

"That's true," agreed Eugene. "I guess if we make up our minds not to take side trips into new passages on the way out we can go a little further now. When we come back tomorrow we'll have more time to check leads nearer to the entrance."

"I'm willing to go on," said Dulcie, "but let's only give ourselves fifteen or twenty minutes more."

Jackie wrinkled his nose and scowled. "Aw—okay. But don't start counting time yet. Look at these footprints. Four sets go in, four sets come out. See? There are two sets of boot tracks, a large pair and a smaller pair." Jackie pointed to each set. "Over there's a pair of tennis shoes, and those appear to be regular work shoes. See? There's a hole in the right sole."

Poppy nodded. "Looks like you got it figured right, Sherlock."

"That's not all," said Jackie. "I've been checking them since we first noticed the prints. When the sets of tracks overlap, the boots are underneath. Always. Sometimes the tennis shoes are on top, other times the work shoes are on top. But boot prints never cover the others, and notice that the boot prints aren't as sharp, as distinct."

"And exactly what does that tell us?" asked Eugene.

Jackie glanced up at him. "The four people didn't travel together, Eugene. The boot-wearers came in first. Their footprints are older. The 'holey shoe guy' and the 'tennis shoe guy' followed the boot fellows, and now we're following all of them."

"Makes sense to me," said Erik. "If we are going to follow them, we should get started."

Dulcie stretched and bent to loosen the kinks in her tired muscles. "All right, let's get moving," she suggested.

The group headed into the passage. They had to go single-file, but the walking was easy. After about a quarter of a mile, the passage opened into a room.

"Here's a room about the size of the nursery office," Poppy called over her shoulder to the others who were following. "Look! There's writing over there!"

Where the wall sloped toward the low ceiling, written in black letters were the words,

THE END –
Sgt. P. Burton·C.S.A.
Pvt. J.Littlejohn·C.S.A.
July 18, 1863

Poppy jumped up and down and squealed. Dulcie and Erik grinned, and Anna's mouth dropped open. Jackie, for once, stood still momentarily and just stared.

"There *were* Rebels in this cave," exclaimed Eugene. "That settles it for sure!"

"Man, oh man, oh man!" yelled Jackie, coming out of his trance. "We proved it! I knew we'd do it! Aren't you glad we didn't turn back?"

Dulcie slipped out of her backpack and snatched out her notebook and pencil. "I'm going to copy this down just as it's written."

She jotted the words down quickly, then studied the original writing on the wall.

"I... I think one of the soldiers might have been illiterate."

"How can you tell, Dulcie?" asked Eugene.

Dulcie frowned and bit her lip. "I can't, really," she said. "I'm sort of guessing, but it wasn't uncommon back then."

She pointed to the writing. "See how both places where it says *C-S-A* look almost identical? In fact, all the handwriting looks like one person wrote it."

Poppy lightly touched the date on the wall with her fingertips, and did some quick mental math. "Just think, eighty-two years, four months and five days ago, two Confederate soldiers stood

91

right here in this room."

"Look," said Eugene, "you can see where the writer walked back and forth printing the message. Poppy, step back. Let's leave his boot prints just as they were when we came in."

"Good idea," agreed Dulcie, reaching out to guide Poppy away from the prints.

Erik, pointed at the tracks beneath the message. "Notice," he said, "that the one who did the writing is the one who made the smallest of the boot tracks we have been following."

"Yep," said Poppy. "The soldiers must have thought this was the very end of the cave."

Anna murmured, "Don't you wish we could know who they were and what happened to them? I wonder if they had children and grandchildren. If they did, I bet they told them all about their adventures in this cave."

The group stood in silence, looking at the inscription, and at the prints in the dirt below them.

Dulcie took off her cap and checked the carbide lamp.

"Hey, look over there!" Anna pointed to the side of the room where they had come in. On the wall by the entry someone had used a carbide lamp to write two names:

R. SNODGRASS — USA

T. Tesh — USA

Oct. 3, 1945

"Oh, NO!" Poppy cried. "Don't tell me that Rothal Snodgrass has been here!" She stomped her foot.

"Aw, for Pete's sake," grumbled Eugene. "What were those two doing poking around on our property? And just last month!"

"Who's Rothal Snodgrass?" asked Jackie.

"Just about the biggest weasel in Warren County," Poppy told them. "A real animal! Tad Tesh is his tag-a-long—and he's almost as bad."

"Rothal tries to make life miserable for Erik and Anna every chance he gets," said Eugene. "It just about drove him crazy when they both made the basketball teams. And he even tried to talk the football coach out of letting Erik play."

"He hates us because we were born in Germany," said Erik. "We don't speak the English language perfectly."

"As if he does!" protested Poppy.

"How could he be so mean?" Dulcie exclaimed. "What were you supposed to do about the war? Uncle Berk said you weren't even *in* Germany during the war!"

Eugene shrugged. "It doesn't matter. Rothal's just plain bad news. They're our closest neighbors, and we've tried to be friendly. But friendly doesn't work with those folks. Well, it might with Ruthie, his sister. She's so shy, though. Acts like she's scared of her shadow. But I can't say anything good about the rest of 'em."

"Sounds like the Snodgrasses are sorta limping along through life," said Dulcie. "My mother says if you see someone limping, you can be sure they're either hurting or have been crippled someway."

Dulcie looked down at her hands, then back up at the others.

"When I see Daddy limping along it... well, it makes me proud. That limp is his badge of courage. Seven men are alive because of our dad." She gazed down the passage. "It's true, we don't always know what's behind other folks' pain."

"Hey!" came a muffled shout from across the room. "Over here!"

A hand beckoned from a small opening in the wall near the floor. Then the hand withdrew and Jackie peeked out.

"P. Burton and J. Littlejohn were wrong!" he said, grinning. "The room you're in isn't the end of the cave. I just checked it out. C'mon in and follow me! It's kinda like crawling' under a

93

bed, only narrower. You go about fifteen feet and it dips down and is almost filled with dirt. It's tight but we can scoop it out and keep going."

"Jackie Stoneworth Delaney! We agreed that none of us would wander off!" exclaimed Dulcie. "What do you mean going in there by yourself?"

"I didn't really go anywhere—I could still hear your voices. I coulda called you if I got stuck, or something'—" Jackie's voice trailed off. "Sorry. I won't do it again," he said. "But we can keep going if y'all are ready to dig a little."

Eugene shook his head. "Can't try it today. We agreed we'd head back before now. So come outta there."

"Oh, all right," grumbled Jackie, crawling out of the hole. He reached back to pat the wall above the small opening. "But there's a big cave back there—I could feel the air surging past me. It turned the flame on my light sideways. Someday—"

Eugene grinned. "Save it for later, 'tator. Now, let's head back. We should be out by dark."

Dulcie placed a hand on Eugene's arm. "Wait, our lights aren't going to make it without fresh carbide," she said. "Let's service the lamps."

"Yeah, that's a good idea," agreed Eugene.

"Girls, we'll fix ours first—be sure you don't spill the spent carbide," said Dulcie. She reached in the pack for the can of carbide. "Put it in the empty container we brought, and we'll take it out of the cave. The stuff is very poisonous."

Dulcie pulled her cap off her head. "Guys, keep your lights burning so we can see, then you can refill yours."

Soon the girls' lights were burning brightly, and the boys repeated the process.

"Hey, Erik," said Eugene, "while you have the carbide lamp off your cap, how about giving us a cap-tossing demonstration?"

"Okay," said Erik, gripping his miner's cap by its bill just below the clip where the lamp would normally sit. "I need to get used to the weight and balance. The metal lamp holder makes this heavier than most caps and affects the balance."

He flicked the cap back and forth several times then said, "See the three stalagmites over there? I will aim for the middle one."

He leaned forward, and holding the cap with his right hand, brought it to his stomach, then quickly extended his arm and flipped his wrist. The cap flew through the air and landed on the five-foot high stalagmite.

"Bingo!" said Jackie, hurrying over to get the cap.

"Do it again!" he said, handing the cap back to Erik.

After Erik made three more hits and one near miss, each of the others made a few attempts. They had little success.

"Hey," growled Eugene, seeming aggravated by his failures. "I thought we were in a hurry. We've been here almost an hour."

"Let's go," said Dulcie. "First, though, be sure your carbide light is securely fastened to your cap."

"Yes, Mother," Eugene teased. "Well, get going. I'll guard the backside—just in case the Ghost of Rebel Cave or a speleomonster tries to attack from the rear."

"What kind of monster?" asked Poppy.

"Speleomonster—cave monster," said Eugene. "Yesterday Mrs. Gunther said 'speleo' means cave in Greek. Speleomonsters are those rare monsters that live in caves. They're rare because there are so few cave explorers to devour. But never-you-fear, Big Eugene is here. I'll fend 'em off. 'Course, if you hear a blood-curdling scream, run for your lives—I'll be in mortal battle on your behalf. Remember me fondly."

"Yep, he's a Stoneworth," said Jackie nodding his head solemnly. "Has that wild story-telling imagination." His face split into a grin. "One good thing—when the speleomonster finishes eating Eugene, his appetite should be satisfied and while he takes his after-meal nap, the rest of us will escape. Onward!"

The six young people rushed across Winchester Cathedral then dropped on their stomachs and snaked through Misery Bellycrawl. The smaller pair took advantage of their size to emerge from the long crawl quite a bit ahead of the others.

When Jackie and Poppy got back to their feet, he called back to the others, "Poppy and I will make a quick check of a passage just ahead on the left. We saw it coming in. We'll hurry."

"Don't you go far," yelled Dulcie, "and don't take any chances."

It took several minutes for Eugene to make it through the crawl. Once through, the group walked slowly so he could catch his breath. By the time they got to the opening the smaller duo had disappeared into, Poppy was back at the main passage and was excitedly beckoning to them.

"Jackie's waiting—Gotta see this! He promised he wouldn't move an inch."

Dulcie shook her head and Eugene started to protest, but Poppy had turned and was hurrying back down the narrow passage. The others followed. Soon it opened up and they found themselves staring down a slope into a wide canyon. Halfway down its side sat Jackie on a boulder looking back over his shoulder at them. His light winked at them from the distance.

"Eugene, shine your light over there," he called, his voice echoing in the huge chamber. He pointed across from where he sat.

When Eugene's spotlight flashed on the floor and wall beyond Jackie, Erik gasped, "Snow! It is a snow bank!"

Jackie was prepared for their reaction and tossed a small pebble at the white mass. It hit with a sharp click and bounced off what was obviously solid rock—pure white stone.

The group stood in momentary silence until Anna exclaimed, "Every where we turn in this cave, there's something more wonderful to see!"

No one answered.

Jackie rejoined them and soon they were back in the main passage heading out.

"We just must get back tomorrow to explore 'Poppy's North Pole Passage,'" said Dulcie. "That 'Snow Bank Room' is unlike anything we've seen! But now we need to hurry. Oops, I'm beginning to sound like Jackie." She chuckled.

Anna's Diner was too much to resist, though, and they stopped to admire it again. There was another delay when Erik discovered a small passage tucked behind the Crystal Niagara. Finally, they tore themselves away with promises to add "Erik's Hideaway" to the next day's agenda.

They hurried past the Point of Decision and the entrance to Bat Belfry. Soon they stood by the side of the huge black pool.

"We've got up a good head of steam," said Eugene. "Let's not rest here; let's get right on across the ledge. Head over in the same order we've been going: Poppy, Jackie, Dulcie, Erik, and Anna. As always, I'll bring up the rear, in case there's any problem."

"But don't rush," said Dulcie. "Take your time, and play it safe. Watch your footing."

Poppy walked onto the ledge with confidence, hugged the wall and scooted along.

"Stay about a yard behind the person in front of you and keep moving," yelled Eugene.

Dulcie carefully edged along the narrowest part of the ledge. *What a great day!* she thought. *Could it have been any better? I can't imagine doing anything that would be as much fun.*

She focused on the small shelf under her feet to find the surest footholds. At the same time, she groped with her fingers in the crevice just above shoulder level. Something soft brushed against her hand! Glancing up, she saw beady eyes staring back at her! A cave rat scurried across the back of her knuckles and disappeared into the crevice. Dulcie snatched her fear-scalded hands from the crevice, screamed, and toppled backward into space, arms thrashing.

The flame of her carbide light went out as she plunged under the surface of the icy pool. *Help me!* she pled silently, holding her breath and fighting futilely for the surface. The backpack and wet clothing dragged her down into blackness.

11

The Clue in the Smoke

From the ledge above the pool, Erik shouted to Anna, "Take this!" Snatching the miner's cap off his head, lamp and all, he flung it to his sister. Anna clung to the wall with her right hand and with the other grabbed the cap in midair. Erik jumped feet first into the water beside where Dulcie had disappeared.

"Run, Poppy!" yelled Jackie, almost hysterically. "Got to help Dulcie!"

He leapt the last three feet from the ledge onto solid ground, then scrabbled down the rocky slope to the edge of the water.

In the dim light, Dulcie, coughing and splashing desperately, broke the surface of the water and then went under again. Erik came up for air, and dived back down.

Jackie, frantic, ran back and forth over the rocks. "Help them!" he screamed. "Lord, please, don't let there be an undertow!"

He ran for the pole that Erik had used earlier to check the depth of the pool.

Across the water, Eugene slid down the rocky bank and beamed his light across the surface. Anna, on the ledge, clung facing the pool and added the light of her lamp and Erik's to the others. Even with the lights, the water was still pitch-black.

Finally, Erik and Dulcie surfaced, his left arm clamped around her body. Using his other arm and powerful leg strokes, he struggled against the frigid water. Slowly they edged toward Jackie and Poppy, who shouted encouragement.

Dulcie choked and sputtered as Erik held her head above water.

"Grab the pole, Erik!" Jackie yelled. "Grab the pole!"

Jackie braced his feet against a large rock beside the pool. Poppy clutched him from behind and held on.

Erik swam closer, reached up, and grasped the end of the pole with his right hand. He pulled himself and Dulcie to the edge of the pool. There they gained their footing and staggered up onto the rocks.

Shouts from the ledge and the other side of the pool told them that Eugene and Anna had seen the rescue.

Jackie threw his arms around Dulcie. "You made it! Oh man! Are you all right?"

Dulcie laid her cheek against Jackie's head, shivering. "I... I think so," she gasped.

Jackie and Poppy helped her slip off her sodden backpack.

Dulcie slumped down in a soggy heap. Her mind was in a fog—a jumbled confusion of fear, relief and cold. She trembled uncontrollably, coughing water from her lungs.

Jackie knelt down beside her and wrapped his arms around her again.

She felt the warmth of his embrace, his cheek against hers. He trembled almost as badly as she did.

"You must have swallowed a lot of water, Sis. You sure you're okay?" he asked.

"I think so. ... thanks to Erik. I ... I'd never have made it without... ." Her body shuddered violently.

Erik stood bent at the waist, leaning down with his hands on his knees, trying to catch his breath.

"Hey, you are fine now, Dulcie," he said between deep breaths. "That is what counts! But you lost your cap and light—you do not look quite right without your miner's cap," he teased gently.

"Here's yours, Erik," said Anna.

She joined the others, placing his cap with its still-burning light on his wet head, and then hugged him. "I can't believe you both came back up with your backpacks!" She laughed shakily, trying to make light of the situation. Then she burst out, *"Ach, Danke Gott in Himmel!* Thank God in heaven!" she repeated in English. "You two gave us a scare."

"I'm *so* sorry," said Dulcie, blinking tears. "Such a fuss over something as silly as a rat!"

"It's all right, Dulcie," said Anna, squeezing her hand. "Guess what? I know right where your cap and carbide lamp are."

"Me too," said Dulcie grimly. "Under the water over there. And they can *stay* there, as far as I care." She paused, then continued, "I *did* tell Daddy I'd take care of them. Maybe we can fish 'em out with a pole tomorrow."

"What do you mean, you know *right* where they are, Anna?" asked Jackie.

"Eugene and I were shining our lights on the water. I was on the ledge almost directly above the spot and saw bubbles coming to the surface. Even though the flame is out, gas under pressure in the lamp is still spewing out. When Eugene gets back, he can shine his flashlight over there and show you."

"When he gets back? Where'd he go?" asked Poppy with alarm.

"Once we saw Dulcie and Erik were safe," said Anna, "he followed me across the ledge. He hustled out to start a fire by Kitchen Rock. You know, where we saw the wood piled up? He said you'd both catch your death of pneumonia if you don't dry off before we walk back home in the cold."

"Yep, and that's what you'll need to do," said a voice from behind them. "I ran all the way to the entrance. It's about quit raining," said Eugene, "but it's really chilly outside the cave. I

101

built a good fire. You ready to warm up?"

"One minute, Eugene," said Erik. "Anna says gas from Dulcie's lamp is bubbling up below the ledge. Shine your flashlight in that direction. Let's see if it is still coming up."

Eugene's light soon illuminated the spot where telltale bubbles floated up through the water.

"I'm already wet," said Erik, starting for the pool. "I might as well go back in and get it now." He took off his cap and laid it on a rock.

"Wait, Erik. Please don't!" Dulcie begged.

Anna agreed. "Wait till tomorrow, Erik! We'll get it then."

Already waist deep in water, he turned to face them. "'Never put off until tomorrow what you can do today.' Tonight the escaping gas shows where the lamp is, but tomorrow it won't. I might as well get it now. Hold your light right on the spot, Eugene."

Without hesitating, Erik turned and swam with strong strokes to the spot where the bubbles were surfacing. He took a deep breath and dived for the bottom.

Dulcie prayed silently, eyes gazing intently at the spot where Erik had gone under. *I don't care about that old cap and light, just keep him safe. Please, please keep him safe.* She held her breath.

After a long forty seconds, Erik popped to the surface and held up Dulcie's cap. The carbide lamp was still attached to the front. A cheer went up, and a moment later they applauded when, grinning, he climbed up the rocks to where Dulcie stood. He put the dripping cap on her head. The two grabbed each other in a tight bear hug, and held on for a moment.

Suddenly the enormity of what happened overwhelmed her. "Thank you, Erik," she said quietly. "You saved my cap—and my life."

If Erik noticed how her lip trembled, he didn't let on.

Dulcie whispered, "I'll never forget it."

Erik tugged the bill of her miner's cap gently. "And now you will die of exposure, since I got you soaking wet again."

102

He grabbed her hand and pulled her toward the passageway.

"Let us find that fire Eugene built."

The dry wood made a great fire. By the time the young people got there, the roaring flames reflected off Kitchen Rock, bounced off the ceiling, and lit up the area close by. They took off their caps and turned off their lamps, lining them up on a rock close by. For the next half-hour the explorers discussed their day's discoveries, and ate what food was left in Anna's dry pack. Dulcie and Erik became vertical human rotisseries, soaking up heat as they rotated slowly in front of the fire.

When the soil became warm a short distance back from the fire, the two took off their shoes and socks and stood barefooted. Jackie and Poppy hung the socks on sticks close to the fire.

"Dulcie, while you are toasting yourself," said Anna, "will you help me get some of this Civil War stuff straight? We're studying the Revolutionary War in American History at school, but this is more interesting. I feel like we have a connection to it now that we've found proof that the soldiers were really here. I want to know more."

"I am totally in the dark, and I do not mean cave-wise," said Erik, with a grin, "about some of the things you say!"

"Like what?" asked Jackie.

"Well," said Anna, "words like, 'Rebels,' 'Rebs,' 'Yanks,' 'Feds,' 'Confederates,' and 'Union.' I'm confused."

"Me, too," said Erik.

Dulcie turned to Poppy. "You're the Civil War expert. Why don't you give it a shot?"

"The main thing to keep in mind is that there were only two parties at war," said Poppy. "The North was made up of states that wanted to keep all the United States of America together—all of them, whether they wanted to stay or not. So the North is sometimes called the *Union*—they wanted to stay united. And they wanted to free the slaves. They are called the Yanks or Yankees. To remember that nickname, you might think of them as trying to 'yank' the country back together."

"But other states, here in the South," said Jackie, "depended on slaves to keep their plantations and farms going. They thought the Union should mind its own business. They rebelled against what they felt was unfair treatment by the North. Since they *rebelled*, they were called Rebels, or Rebs, for short."

Poppy continued where Jackie left off. "The southern states got together a union of their own—except they called it a 'confederacy'. So you have the Confederate States of America, the C.S.A. in the south, and the United States of America, the U.S.A. in the north."

"And don't forget," said Dulcie. She stopped turning to face the group, "that the soldiers of the North are sometimes called Federals or Feds."

"If that's not confusing enough," said Jackie, "both sides are sometimes called by the colors of their uniforms. The North known as 'Blues,' the South as 'Grays.'"

"So the soldiers who hid in here were Grays, Confederates, Rebels, and Rebs, right?" asked Anna.

"Hey, you got it. Now just keep it," said Eugene. He threw another armload of wood on the fire and sparks flew upward.

"That should be plenty, Eugene," said Erik. "We should not need the fire much longer. I am about dry—how about you, Dulcie?"

"I am too. In fact, I'm ready to put on my socks and shoes. Toss me my socks, will you, Jackie? They'll be toasty even if my shoes aren't completely dry."

She sat down on a rock and put on her shoes, then knelt down to look in her still-damp pack, which sat steaming in front of the fire. "I'm sure glad I use a pencil for sketching. My sketchpad is soaked but I can see the writing and drawings. I'll get a new pad tomorrow and copy everything."

"Hey!" Anna interrupted, gazing upward. "Look at the smoke. It rises, scoots along the ceiling, and goes *into* the cave. I would've thought it would go *out* of the cave."

The group looked at the smoke curling up from the fire. It

scudded along the ceiling and back into the cave.

"That's an easy mystery to solve," said Jackie. "We had an atmospheric low and the air in the cave rushed out. Now, a high is moving into the area, so the air is pushing back in."

"That would explain it," said Erik.

But it wouldn't explain that! thought Dulcie, looking at the wall at the far end of Kitchen Rock. She walked over and picked up her cap and lamp and opened the water-flow control. She picked up a stick from the fire and brought the burning end to the nozzle of her lamp. With the characteristic "Pop!" the gas lit. She put the cap on her head.

"Stir the fire, Eugene, I want to check something."

She walked toward the wall.

Eugene took a long stick and stirred the fire. Sparks flew and rose with the smoke, but Dulcie wasn't looking back into the cave. She pointed to the right wall of the chamber.

"Okay, who wants to help me find out why some of the smoke is disappearing *through* that wall over there?"

They scrambled for their lights and caps.

Dulcie crossed the dirt floor, which gradually sloped upward until it reached the wall of the cave. There the wall was about four feet high, from floor to ceiling. Smoke was disappearing near the top of the wall.

The space got lower and Dulcie dropped into a "duck waddle." Glancing back over her shoulder, she saw Eugene was right behind her.

"Dulcie, that wall doesn't look natural," said Eugene.

"Hey! Look at the wall—it's man-made!" said Jackie, scampering past Eugene to Dulcie's side.

"Yep," she answered. "It sure is! Now that we're up close, it's obvious."

"Why in the world would anyone build something like that back here?" asked Poppy, peering over Jackie's shoulder.

"Obviously they wanted to *conceal* something—something important," said Erik.

"Like what?" Poppy asked.

"Like treasure!" Jackie shouted.

Anna grimaced. "Or themselves. What if they hid out in there and died. What if *there are bodies* back there?"

Dulcie reached up and tugged at one of the carefully stacked rocks on the top of the wall. "Let's find out."

NBF

12

Through the Wall

"This wall wasn't designed by an engineer," Erik said.

"No, and it's not exactly the Great Wall of China," said Dulcie. As she pulled steadily, the top rock came away in her hands. She handed it to Eugene.

"Pass that back—make a chain over to the right. Put the rocks in that little depression over there so they won't be in our way."

"Whoever built this wall must've thought no one would pay any attention to it," said Eugene, eyeing the makeshift barrier. "It's almost hidden unless the light is right on it."

Dulcie nodded. "If I hadn't seen the smoke drifting back this way, I wouldn't have noticed it at all."

She ran her fingers along the crevice where the rock wall met the ceiling.

"There's a bit of a crack up here. See how the shadows from

107

the rough ceiling hide it? That's where most of the smoke was going."

She continued to remove the stones and pass them back. The opening quickly got larger.

"Can you see anything in there, Sis?" asked Jackie.

"Yes, I can see a room that angles to our left—almost parallel with this passage. It's about eight feet or so wide. But I can't see anything in it."

Dulcie, on her knees, leaned against the wall and peered into the hole. The wall shifted slightly.

"Oh!" she said, leaning back. "The wall's not very stable now that we've started taking it apart. Don't crowd me. If it collapses, I'll need to be able to get out of the way."

Eugene tried to look into the empty chamber. "Nothing in there? Oh, drat!" he said. "I thought for sure we'd find Blackbeard's Treasure!"

"You dunce," said Poppy. "Blackbeard was a pirate! There's not an ocean anywhere close. We might find Confederate General Braxton Bragg's hoard, but not Blackbeard's."

"Let's open the wall enough for Poppy and Jackie to crawl through, if they're game," said Dulcie.

"If we're game? Yea for that!" said Jackie. "We'll reconnoiter the place."

He passed a rock back to Poppy.

"Oh, such big words you use," said Poppy, grinning and tossing the rock onto the growing pile. "But can you spell it?" She clapped the dirt from her hands, and brushed the dust from the front of her blouse. "Of course you can. You saw it in a book somewhere and can just read it off the page in your head."

Jackie shut his eyes, and tapped the side of his head above the left ear. He said, "Yep—I got it. R-E-C-O-N-N—"

"Hush!" said Dulcie, chuckling. "Stop showing off and come on over here. Poppy, too. I think you can get through now."

She turned to the older teens. "They can check it out for us while we enlarge the hole. We'll all go in if they find anything."

The two youngsters hurried to the hole, while Eugene squatted to the right of the opening and Dulcie to the left.

"Poppy, you go first," suggested Dulcie. "Eugene will steady you as you go through the hole. Then wait for Jackie just inside the opening. Crawl over the bottom row of rocks, but don't bump the right side as you go through. I think it's the most unstable."

Poppy pulled her miner's cap down over her head and slipped through the small opening. When she was safely out of the way, Jackie followed.

"Got good news," called Poppy. "It's high enough to stand up in—at least for me."

"And there are a lot of tracks," said Jackie. "All of them made by the fellows with the boots. That would be our new Rebel friends, P. Burton and J. Littlejohn."

Jackie's voice faded as he and Poppy moved away from the opening. Eugene positioned himself right outside the hole.

Anna whispered to Dulcie, Eugene and Erik. "What if... What if the soldiers realized they were behind enemy lines and cut off from their unit? They could've been so scared and hopeless, that they closed off the wall from the inside, then killed themselves!"

"Oh, Anna! How awful!" said Dulcie, her eyes huge. "If they did, Jackie and Poppy will find their skeletons!"

"Yes, or in this dry atmosphere, their mummies!" said Erik.

Dulcie shivered at the thought.

"Yipppeeee!" came a faint shout from the other side of the wall. It was Jackie. A split-second later, Poppy's higher-pitched voice joined in. "Yeeaaaa!"

"I don't think they found mummies," said Dulcie, with a grin.

"What is it?" bellowed Eugene, sticking his head into the opening. "What'd you find?"

"Boxes, two long wooden boxes!" shouted Jackie, running back toward the opening.

Anna's hands flew to her cheeks. "Caskets!" she gulped.

"I'm going through," yelled Eugene, pushing his head and shoulders through the small hole. His right hip and leg caught against the false wall.

"NO! Eugene! It's coming down!" shouted Dulcie. "Look out!"

The crunch and rumble of rocks crashing together rolled through the room as much of the upper part of the wall fell inward. Dust filled the air. Deathly silence followed the collapse.

Dulcie, Anna, and Erik frantically scrambled into the void where the wall had been. Eugene, face down, struggled to crawl from under the fallen rocks. The trio dragged the stones away from Eugene's legs, pulling them to the side. Jackie materialized out of the darkness, followed by Poppy.

Coughing and groaning, Eugene got to his knees. He held his right shoulder with his left hand and flexed his right fingers.

"You okay, Eugene?" asked Poppy.

He nodded, his face grim.

Poppy gently brushed the dust from Eugene's face and hair.

"What happened?" she asked.

Eugene shrugged. "Dumb! I was just dumb! What happened? —I tried to get through the wall before the hole was big enough," he said, moving his right arm back and forth to check the shoulder.

"Didn't break anything, I guess. Feel like I've been run over by a freight train, though."

"Well, we are all through now," Erik said, rocking back on his heels. "And it did not take nearly as long," he continued, "as it would have if we had moved those rocks one by one."

He gestured toward the opening. Rocks lay helter-skelter where the wall had been. Only a small part of the far end remained intact.

"Erik's right," said Anna. "The Stoneworth method of wall removal is much more efficient!" She blew out a breath. "Eugene, I'm *so* glad you're not badly hurt."

"Do you feel like going with us to check out the find Poppy and Jackie made?" asked Dulcie.

"You'd better believe it!" said Eugene. "I wouldn't miss that!"

"You'll need this," said Poppy, picking up his cap and light from where it had tumbled when he fell forward in the dirt.

Eugene stood up and brushed the dirt from his pant legs.

"Let's go," he said, pulling his cap on.

Soon the group was making its way up the narrow dirt-floored passage. Jackie stopped them and pointed to the floor.

"See those boot prints?" he asked. "They were made by Sergeant Pascal Burton and Private Jason Littlejohn of the Confederate States of America."

"Wait a minute," said Dulcie. "We don't know their first names. Only the initials P. and J. were on the wall in the Inscription Room."

"Oh, but they told me!" he responded smugly. "And that's not all… just wait till you see! We're almost there."

He pointed at the ceiling.

"Look at that big opening up there—that's what caused the draft that sucked the smoke through the wall."

The passage leveled off and hooked to the right. The floor changed from dirt to loose flat rocks. Against the right wall were two long wooden boxes. Between them was a short, squat one with a rope handle on either side. On each box one word was stenciled: "Wider."

"Look!" said Poppy, pointing to the wall above the boxes. In black letters was a message:

DO NOT DISTURB!

These boxs and contens are Proprty of C.S.A. and Soley for Genrl Nathan Bedford Forest. Left for him by, Respctfuly—

Capt'n PRATT FENNER-CSA-Marietta, Ga.
Sgt. PASCAL BURTON-CSA-McNarvl. Tenn
Pvt. Jason Littlejohn-C.S.A.-S. Hook, Tenn.

July 24, 1863

"Two of these are the men whose names we saw earlier," said Eugene. "And the new one is their officer."

"Whoever they were," said Erik, "they must have been proud to be Confederates. They took the time to write CSA after each name."

"Right," said Dulcie. "Notice that the same person did all the writing except the names and hometowns. It looks like Private Jason Littlejohn did the writing."

"Sergeant Burton had a bit of trouble with his letters," said Poppy.

"Where in the world is South Hook, Tennessee, Eugene?" asked Anna. "That was Private Littlejohn's home. You've lived here longest—do you know where it is?"

"Never heard of it," Eugene said.

No one had, but Jackie drummed his forehead. "Hold on a minute. I'm checking a map of Tennessee."

Dulcie rolled her eyes, sighed, and grinned. She put her right forefinger to her lips and said, "Shhhhhhh! He's looking in the atlas in his head."

"I got it!" he said. "No wonder I couldn't spot it on the map. We thought the 'S' stood for 'South,' but it doesn't. Private Littlejohn wasn't from *South* Hook, he was from *Sandy* Hook, Tennessee. It's a little town south of Mt. Pleasant, near Columbia."

"You're joking! You made that up, right?" asked Anna.

"Nope. Check it out on a map—a paper one, since you can't see this one," said Jackie, tapping himself on the head and grinning.

Erik stood directly in front of the inscription. "Whoever wrote that message could not spell correctly," he said.

"That's true," said Poppy. "He even left an 'r' out of General Forrest's name. Remember what Dulcie said yesterday? Eighty years ago many people couldn't read and write, and spelling wasn't standard as it is today."

"Spelling! Geography!" said Eugene, "Forget that stuff. I wanna get into those boxes!"

"Yea for that!" said Jackie. "But how? They're nailed shut. We need a crowbar, or a claw hammer. We don't even have a screwdriver in our backpacks."

Dulcie, examining the boxes, said, "Looks like this one's been pried open, then nailed shut again."

"Could we use a rock to pound the boards off?" asked Poppy.

"I don't think so," said Eugene. "We need some kind of lever."

"Hey, I got it!" said Jackie. "Remember when we were digging for the wagon yesterday? Eugene found that old iron bar near the mouth of the cave. I'll go get it."

With that, he hurried down the passageway and out. The others sat down on the boxes to wait.

Poppy sat fidgeting on the box. Her eyes returned again and again to the writing on the wall. "Do any of you know about General Nathan Bedford Forrest?"

"Seems I've heard the name," said Dulcie, "but that's all." She read the inscription again. "The Confederate soldiers sure wanted him to have these boxes."

"I know a lot about him," said Poppy. "He was the most feared man in all the Confederate Army—by friend and foe!" Poppy stood up and gestured broadly. "Some historians say he was one of the greatest cavalrymen of all time. Nothing terrified the Yankees more than knowing they were facing Forrest and his raiders."

"Tough guy, huh?" said Eugene.

"Yep, he was!" said Poppy. "They say he personally killed thirty enemies. He was wounded at least four times—once he was shot and the bullet stopped near his spine but he kept on fighting. And they say he had twenty-nine horses shot out from under him."

"Surely he did not! You're making it up, Poppy," said Dulcie. "C'mon 'fess up."

"No, it's all the truth. I promise!"

"Why have we not heard more about him, if he was so great?" asked Erik.

"Well, for one thing, he was on the side that lost," said Poppy. "For another, he was an easy man to dislike."

"Why?" asked Anna.

"He was ruthless," answered Poppy. "Before the war he was a big-time slave trader. It infuriated him that the slaves might be freed. He hated colored people as much as Hitler hated the Jews."

"Oh, my goodness!" said Dulcie, glancing at the twins. Neither Erik nor Anna commented, but both blushed and dropped their eyes.

Poppy's face flushed the same color as her auburn hair. "Sorry," she muttered, then continued. "After the war Nathan Bedford Forrest became the first Grand Wizard of the Ku Klux Klan—those people who tried to terrify the ex-slaves."

"Yes," said Dulcie, "and any white people who tried to help them."

"I can't believe decent people put up with such things," said Eugene.

"Well, they did," said Poppy. "And that's not all—"

"Wait a sec," said Dulcie, snapping her fingers. "I just remembered where I heard that name. As we came down here on the train, the conductor told us his grandfather had been the personal slave of General Forrest. But his grandpa escaped and came to Muhlenberg County, Kentucky —Jackie will remember the details. The conductor's twin brother, Amos Frazier, is a friend of our family."

"You have acquaintances who are descendants of African Negro slaves?" asked Erik. "In Germany, we were taught that they are an inferior race."

"No, Erik. We have *friends,* not just acquaintances," exclaimed Dulcie with feeling. "If you knew the Fraziers, or the Bards or any of our other friends with African ancestors, you'd realize how wrong Hitler was with his ideas that the Negroes are inferior."

"Even General Forrest came to realize he was wrong," continued Poppy.

"His story doesn't end on such a bad note," she said. "In his

114

last years, he changed his life completely. He even tried to shut down the KKK, and to get himself appointed to chase down and prosecute the worst of their lawbreakers."

"Are you kidding?" asked Dulcie.

"No. In fact, at the end of his life, he worked as hard to help colored people as he had persecuting them. And they came to his funeral. Hundreds and hundreds of former slaves came to show their respect."

"Wow," Dulcie shook her head. "Sounds like he *completely* changed. Can you imagine? I bet some old friends became bitter enemies when he walked away from his old life!" She stopped abruptly. "Shouldn't Jackie be back by now? It's not *that* far to the entrance."

"He is probably having a hard time finding the metal bar," said Erik. "It was just tossed aside. If he does not come back soon, I will go check on him."

Dulcie bit her lip. "Maybe we shouldn't have let him go alone. Remember our agreement? No one was supposed to go off by themselves."

"I'm sure he's all right," said Anna, placing her hand on Dulcie's arm. "Now, what do you think we'll find when we get these boxes open?" she asked.

"One guess is as good as another, I suppose," said Dulcie. "Blankets or uniforms, maybe?"

"I wonder why the boxes have the word 'Wider' on them," said Erik. "Does that mean anything to any of you? Do you know what it means, Poppy?"

"Must be a name. Wider, Wider, Wider," she muttered. "I should know who that is …" She walked back and forth. "Let's see, General Wider, Lieutenant Wider, Private Wider, Sergeant Wider, Raider Wider. It doesn't ring a bell. If only I had a photographic memory like Jackie!"

"Speaking of Jackie, I'm gonna go find that kid," said Eugene. "I agree with Dulcie—he should have been back by now."

"I will go with you," said Erik.

"Nah," said Eugene, "you stay here and protect the females in case the vengeful Ghost of Rebel Cave shows up."

He adjusted the flame of his lamp, pulled his cap down on his head, and lumbered back down the passage.

"I'll have you know, Patrick Eugene Stoneworth," a grinning Dulcie shouted down the passageway, "we *females* can handle any old ghost you can!"

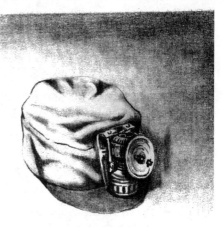

13

The Encounter

It hadn't taken Jackie long to reach the entrance of the cave. He had hustled back through the rubble of the false wall, rounded Kitchen Rock, and headed toward the entrance overhang.

Once he got there, he searched the area where he thought Eugene had thrown the metal bar. Suddenly, he stopped. He smelled something. *Cigarette smoke!* Jackie looked into the darkness beyond the entrance and saw someone silhouetted against the night sky. The person ducked into the shadow of the cave wall.

"All right, come out," Jackie called. "We got you spotted."

Two figures moved out of the shadows and came toward him. One of them flipped away a burning cigarette butt, then turned on a flashlight.

"Don't look like no 'we' to me," said the larger of the two strangers. He moved closer and turned the flashlight directly into Jackie's eyes.

"Looks like just one person, and he sounds like a Yankee. A Yankee pip-squeak, at that," the young man sneered, swinging the light from side to side as if to make sure Jackie was alone.

He was a stocky older teen. His companion, lighter by forty pounds, peered over his shoulder. He snickered, too. They got to within about eight feet of Jackie and stopped. Jackie used the skill he knew best. He tried talking his way past the bigger boys.

"I'm not a Yankee, I'm a Kentuckian. I'm Jackie Delaney."

"Well, Kentucky's north, and north is Yankee," jeered the stocky youth. "I'm thinkin' we ought to fix you up a bit. Send you home to show the Yankees how we feel about havin' strangers invadin' our territory."

"Hey, fellows," said Jackie, "I'm not invading your territory, I'm—"

"I say you are. This here's my daddy's cave. We seen you in here yesterday afternoon. Diggin' and pokin' and messin' around. An' you're back here tonight with them Nazis! We ought to—"

"Hold on, you!" said Jackie, through gritted teeth. "First of all, this cave is on my Uncle Berk's property," he snapped. "You're the one's trespassing. Second, our *friends* aren't Nazis! You get yourselves outta here in a hurry or I'll … I'll …."

"You'll what? Ha! There's a lot *you* could do!" the stranger snarled. "There's two of us, and we're men. There's one of you, and you're just a kid." He raised his fist. "I'll teach you to smart mouth me!"

Jackie stepped back. When he did, he stepped on something hard. He glanced down. There in the dirt lay the iron rod. He stooped, snatched it up and swung it in a vicious arc that cut the air and stopped the bully in his tracks.

"I may be a kid, but … but … " Jackie stammered, "one crack of this iron bar will split your skull wide open like busting a ripe watermelon."

Rothal winced.

Jackie swished the bar through the air again. Then, mustering his strongest baritone voice, he said, "Now, you two back out of here. All I have to do is yell one time. There's five more of us in shouting distance. You may be able to bully one little kid, but you'll never take us all!"

Jackie drew back the iron bar in a stance that would have made Babe Ruth proud.

"Let's git," whispered the skinny youth.

The bully clenched and unclenched his fists, uncertainty written on his face.

"It's six agin' two, and with him armed ...." his companion whined.

"Yeah, yeah. All right, we're goin', this time," said the bully. "But this here *is* my daddy's cave! We'll get you, you ...." Curse words filled the air as the pair moved through the darkness toward the entrance.

Jackie took a couple of menacing steps forward as though to follow them. They disappeared into the darkness outside the cave entrance. Once they were out of sight, Jackie relaxed his stance, and looked at the ground. In the dirt was a footprint showing a hole in the sole of the right shoe, and there were tennis shoe prints. Jackie grinned. He had come face-to-face with the fellows who had made the footprints they had seen back in the cave—he had chased the bad guys off!

He turned and walked back into the cave.

Suddenly, a rock whizzed by his head. Another smashed into his right shoulder. He yelped, grabbed his shoulder, and dived behind Kitchen Rock. Raucous laughter faded as Rothal Snodgrass and Tad Tesh hurried down the hillside outside the cave.

Jackie waited a moment, then eased past the big rock to where he'd dropped the iron bar when the stone hit him. He picked it up and hustled back into the darkness. In fact, the passageway was too dark! Jackie took off his cap, shook the light and turned up the water flow of the carbide lamp. It flickered a little more brightly. Tugging the cap firmly onto his head, he carefully made his way back into the cave. Just as he reached the opening through the wall, a light came bobbing toward him.

"There you are!" said Eugene. "Man, we were worried about you! Hey, no wonder it took so long—your light's about out."

"Yep. Took me forever to find the bar without good light," he muttered. "Guess I should'a thought about that before I took off by myself. Sure was glad to see you coming." He handed the piece of iron to Eugene. "Think this'll do?"

"Hey, look at this," yelled Eugene as they trotted up to where the others were waiting. "Just what the doctor ordered. Let me at those boxes."

Dulcie breathed a huge sigh of relief when Eugene and Jackie appeared.

"Pretty exciting, huh?" said Jackie, watching Eugene pry at a board on one of the large boxes. "Who knows what we'll find in there." His voice was flat.

Dulcie, standing to one side, watched Jackie. He was too quiet, not his usual self. *Why isn't that boy crowing about being the hero for finding that bar? What's going on with you, Little Brother?* she wondered.

"You okay, brother-mine?" she asked, walking to his side.

"Fine." Jackie ducked his head, and brushed her aside to get a closer look at the box. "I just need to put fresh carbide in my light. That's all."

Oh Jackie, there is something wrong. Dulcie was sure of it.

With a loud screech, the nails came away from the frame of the box, and one end of a plank pulled free. Eugene slipped the lever along the board and pried again. Erik took hold of the board, pulled, and away it came. Eugene stuck his hand inside and started to feel around.

"Stop, Eugene," yelled Poppy. "It might be booby-trapped!"

Eugene laughed. "Hey, this is from the Civil War, not World War II! But hold on a second."

He reached for his flashlight.

"There are newspapers on top of whatever's in here."

He pulled a yellowed paper out and handed it to Dulcie. "I think there's a—Hey, look in here! It's a gun! A Civil War rifle! Let's get these other boards off."

"Man, oh man!" said Jackie, "I can't believe it—hurry!"

While the boys worked to open the box, Dulcie stood to the side. "Listen to this old article:

Philadelphia, May 23, 1863.

Former Ohio Representative Clement Vanlandingham, in a recent speech at Mount Vernon, Ohio, called on our nation to rid itself of President Lincoln in order to end hostilities with the rebelling states. 'If it is necessary to impeach the president, then impeach him,' insisted Vanlandingham, 'but the war must end.'"

"There are more guns!" exclaimed Eugene, ignoring her and lifting a rifle from the box. "Just look!"

Dulcie quickly laid the newspaper aside and soon the six teenagers of the 1940s sat on the floor of Rebel Cave, each cradling a rifle from the 1860s.

"Man, oh man, oh *man*!" said Jackie, running his hand up and down the barrel of his rifle. "Look at these beauties. Wow! They're perfect, not a speck of rust."

"Oh my goodness!" exclaimed Poppy. "These are *Spencer* rifles. Spencers!—the legendary seven-shooters that opened up Middle Tennessee and the South to the Yanks."

"Seven-shooters?" said Erik. "What do you mean?"

"The guns would shoot seven times before being reloaded. They were the first repeating rifles ever used in warfare. And the battle happened at Hoover's Gap, not far from here!" Poppy answered.

Dulcie watched Poppy as she spoke. The little girl's eyes sparkled, and her slender hands gestured gracefully. "How I envy your confidence and the way your words flow, Miss Poppy!" she said. "You'd better grow up to be teacher, or a writer, or both."

Poppy grinned, and then continued, "Look at the gun's stock—the shoulder piece. There's a hole there for a tube of cartridges," she said.

"And we have a whole box of these guns, right here!" said Eugene. "Must have terrified the Rebs to face 'em."

"Yes sir!" said Poppy. "The Rebels had a saying, 'Them Yanks have a gun they can load on Sunday and shoot all week.' Of course they couldn't, but compared to one-shot muzzleloaders, Spencers were a fearsome weapon."

"I'm glad you got so interested in all this, Poppy," said Anna. "I can't imagine knowing so much about a war."

"War is terrible," said Erik quietly, "but they happen. If we fail to learn about them, we will not be able to avoid the same stupidity in the future. People around here still carry the scars of the Civil War. And we will never get over what happened to our family in Germany. Our grandmother Gunther was at Dach ..."

Anna nudged him with her elbow and coughed softly. He flushed a deep red and changed the subject. "Do you suppose the other box also contains rifles?"

"Let's find out," said Eugene. "Erik, would you do the honors?" He handed him the pry bar.

Soon they found the second box held a dozen more guns.

"Appears to me," said Eugene, "that there were originally 12 guns in each box. The first box has 3 missing—this one's full."

Poppy, squatting on her knees, traced the stenciled name on the boxes with her finger—'Wider.' Spencer seven-shooters—YES! Now I remember!" she said. "*WIDER!*—on these boxes they misspelled the name—it should be 'Wilder'—not 'Wider.' Sure, that's it! Wilder was a Union officer from Indiana. He borrowed money from a bank back there to equip almost 1,500 of his infantry brigade with these guns! Just think, we have seven-shooters that were intended for Wilder's troops. Wow!"

"Could this be true?" asked Erik. "Could these be such guns? They are like new!"

"It is true!" Poppy responded. "It just has to be."

She turned to Anna. "May I have a piece of your gum? It's so dry in this passage."

"Of course," said Anna. She dug the pack from her pocket and passed the Juicy Fruit around. Stuffing the package back in her pocket, she asked, "Why doesn't someone open that smaller box? It's our last chance for Blackbeard's Treasure." With a giggle, she glanced at Eugene.

"My turn," said Jackie. He picked up the pry bar.

Dulcie noticed that he winced when he bore down on the lever. He changed the pry bar to his left hand. A moment later he peered into the box.

"And look what we have!" Jackie exclaimed. He lifted from the box a tin tube. "We've got a whole box of tubes," he said.

"I'll bet each of those tubes contains seven bullets," said Dulcie.

"Yep," said Jackie, making a quick count.

Poppy reached for one of the tubes and turned it over in her hands. "Pity the poor Reb with a muzzle-loader who could shoot only two or three shots a minute. His enemy could insert and shoot as many as three of these 7-shot tubes in the same amount of time!" she said.

"Astonishing!" said Erik. "In less than sixty seconds Wilder's 1,500 men could hurl some 30,000 bullets at a charging line of soldiers!"

"No wonder our friends Fenner, Burton and Littlejohn wanted this hoard saved for General Forrest," said Jackie.

"Good night!" said Poppy. "I just looked at my watch. Do you have any idea what time it is? It's almost 8 o'clock!"

"Oh no!" said Dulcie. "Uncle Berk and Aunt Nan will think we're lost or that there's been an accident. We've gotta go."

"Let's take one rifle each," said Eugene, "and we'll each take one of those... what do you call them?"

"Cartridge tubes, I guess," responded Jackie.

Erik said, "One gun and one cartridge tube. That sounds good. Tomorrow we can bring a horse and the sled and get the rest—"

"No," interrupted Jackie. "We should take 'em all out tonight." Dulcie saw his sober expression.

"Look, Jackie," argued Eugene, "we're tired. It's late. They've been safe here for 80 years. Ought to make it another twelve hours.

Dulcie saw Jackie narrow his eyes and slightly shake his head. His jaw was set. *Uh-oh! He gets that 'Smith Delaney look' when his mind's made up. He won't budge,* she thought.

There was no sparkle in Jackie's eyes when he said, "Tonight. They go tonight."

"Okay, Jackie," said Dulcie, "level with us. What's going on?"

He shrugged and hesitated, then he recounted his run-in with Rothal Snodgrass and Tad Tesh. He skipped the rock throwing and said, "I'm worried that they might be waiting to waylay us."

"Jackie, that's not all. What else happened?" asked Dulcie. "They hurt you, didn't they?"

Jackie bit his lip, looked at the floor, and nodded. Then he told them the rest of the story.

"Those stinking cowards!" said Erik, his eyes blazing and fists clenching. "Two almost grown men, who would back down from a twelve-year old. Not ignoring the fact, my warrior friend," he smiled at Jackie, "that you would be a formidable foe armed with that piece of iron. But that they would stone you! … They are cowards. They would not think of facing the six of us."

"But they wouldn't hesitate to slip in here once we're gone," said Eugene, "and take anything we leave behind."

"We *had* better take it all tonight," said Dulcie.

"Erik, you get one end of the full box, I'll get the other. We can carry it without a problem," said Eugene. "The hardest part will be the low area by the opening into this passage. When we get these to the house, we can come back and get the rest."

"No, wait. Let's take them all out now," said Dulcie, turning to Anna. "I think you and I can handle the lighter box, don't you?"

"Sure," said Anna, "but that leaves Jackie and Poppy to carry the box of bullets, and with his shoulder…."

"Don't worry about my shoulder," said Jackie. "We can handle it even if I use only one arm, right, Cousin?"

"Of course we can," said Poppy. "Especially since our box has a rope handle on each side. Let me at it!"

14

The Shower

Water dripped from the trees outside the cave.

"Looks like it's been raining pretty hard," said Eugene. The tired team slogged down the hill. "I'm glad it's just a light drizzle now."

"One good thing about carbide lamps is that a little rain won't put them out," said Dulcie. "Dunking them all the way under is another story." She grimaced.

Heads down against the rain, the teens showed the effects of their long day. They were wet and chilled to the bone. Their muscles knotted under the strain of carrying the heavy boxes. Silently, the weary troops made their way through the orchard.

"Look!" said Eugene, nodding his head down the path.

Two figures climbed the hill toward them, each carrying a lantern.

"Mom! Dad!" shouted Poppy. "Yippee! Wait till you see what we have."

"You kids all right?" yelled Uncle Berk.

As they approached, Dulcie saw Aunt Nan's fearful eyes search through the darkness for each child. The mud-covered, bedraggled teens looked at each other in the lantern light, then back at the anxious adult and grinned. She shook her head, took a deep breath, and blew it out. The worry lines smoothed from her forehead.

"Looks like your excursion was successful. What do you have there?" she asked.

All six teens started talking at once.

"Wait, wait, *wait*!" Aunt Nan held up both hands and laughed. "All right, now, one at a time. Eugene?"

"We'll tell you all about it, Mom, but could we wait 'til we get to the house? These boxes are awful heavy. Dad, will you give Jackie and Poppy a hand?"

A little later the strange procession made its way across the back yard toward the screened-in back porch. Poppy, relieved of the load by her father, hurried ahead to light the way with his lantern. Jackie insisted on continuing to carry the box, so Aunt Nan walked behind, and lit the path from the rear.

"Poppy," said Eugene, "will you get the door? I can't open it without letting go of this box."

Poppy pulled open the wood-framed screen door at the end of the porch and held it wide.

Nan called from the back of the procession, "Take those boxes to the far end of the porch. Watch the tub of water! I figured you'd need baths."

They carried the boxes into the long, room-like porch and set them on the floor.

"What in the world do you have in there?" asked Uncle Berk. "Gold bars from Ft. Knox?"

The exhausted teens headed toward the door leading into the kitchen.

"Wait!" exclaimed Aunt Nan. "Sit down on the floor. Don't go in the house all caked with mud!" She opened the kitchen door. "I have hot chocolate on the stove. You tell Berkley what

126

happened while I reheat the chocolate. I'll listen from the kitchen."

Jackie and Poppy flopped down on the floor of the porch and leaned against the wall. Dulcie and Anna sat on one of the boxes, while Eugene and Erik stood at either end of their box.

"I don't think I can walk another step!" said Eugene. "Dad, will you please get me the crowbar?"

Uncle Berk walked to the other end of the porch and raised the hinged seat of a built-in bench. He reached inside and pulled out the long metal bar and handed it to his son. Eugene quickly pried open the box, pulled back the newspapers, and lifted out one of the guns.

"Sir," he said, presenting the weapon to his father, "you are now in possession of a Spencer repeating rifle from the Civil War."

"Eugene, this is a prize!" said Uncle Berk, looking awestruck. "I've never seen anything like it! It's in mint condition. Nan, come look at this!" he called.

He smelled the gun barrel. "It's never even been fired. My! Do you have any idea what it's worth? Quite a lot, I'd say. And you have a box of them? This whole box is full?"

"Two boxes full, or almost full, Daddy," said Poppy. "Twenty-one guns, in all."

"Oh gracious!" said Nan, stopping in her tracks in the doorway when she saw the gun. She was carrying a tray with six cups of hot chocolate and a plate of sandwiches. "Where did you find them?"

Just then a blast of wind hit the house, and rain pounded the roof.

"Wow! Listen to that downpour," said Erik. "I am glad we got back when we did!"

Eugene grabbed a sandwich off the plate his mother was

127

passing to the teens. He nodded around a bite, swallowed and asked, "All right, who's going to tell our story?"

Erik smiled at Dulcie. "Since you started us on our final adventure, Dulcie, you tell what happened."

Dulcie began the story, but over the next fifteen minutes five other young people chimed in. Occasionally two or three talked at the same time. Between wolfing down bologna sandwiches and drinking steaming hot chocolate, they filled in details.

"Who would have dreamed of anything like that?" said Uncle Berk when the story ended. "This is unbelievable. Absolutely unbelievable!"

"You know what else is unbelievable?" asked Aunt Nan, who answered herself before anyone could respond. "How absolutely filthy you are!"

"Oh, for a good hot shower like in the locker room at school," said Anna.

"Or even a cold one," said Erik.

"Someday maybe we'll have running water," said Nan," but tonight we'll have to settle for the wash tubs. I … I guess you could rinse the worst of it off in the rain."

"Yeah!" said Jackie. "We can't get any wetter than we already are. It'll be cold, but we can handle it."

He and Eugene raced to the yard. Poppy and Anna followed a little more slowly.

Nan nudged Uncle Berk with her elbow. "You go get the other wash tub and take it around to the front porch for the boys. I'll heat more water for a final scrub when the kids come back in," she said. They both headed into the house.

"May I help you to your feet, fair maiden?" asked Erik. He extended a hand to Dulcie.

She looked down at herself and then back up at him. "I'm probably the *unfairest* maiden you've ever seen," she said, grinning. "But someone had better help me up. I just want to wrap up in a quilt and sleep for a month!" She took his hand and let him pull her to her feet.

"Erik, you *did* rescue this damsel in distress. Thank you." Dulcie's heart skipped into quick rhythm when he gently squeezed her hand.

"I'm glad I was there, Dulcie," Erik said. "I ... I think you're pretty special." A faint flush colored his cheeks in the lantern glow. "We'd better get going."

Together, they went out the door.

Under the cold, pounding rain, with much squealing and bellowing, the adventurers scrubbed off pounds of mud.

Poppy bent forward and let the rain beat down on the back of her head. "Rain water's supposed to make your hair soft. Mine should be about as soft as it gets!" She giggled from under the cascade of auburn curls.

"Boys, you head for the front porch now," Nan directed from the door. "Berkley has a tub of hot water for you. Girls, I've got yours ready here on the back porch. Come in this way."

A short time later, the two cousins, dressed in warm pajamas and robes, sat on their bed in Poppy's room. Dulcie put her arm around the small girl, and said, "What a trooper you are, Poppy! You were wonderful today!"

"I think we're quite a team, the six of us," said Poppy.

"We are!" agreed Dulcie. She turned to Anna and looked her up and down. "It's just not fair that you are still so beautiful after what we've been through!"

"Beautiful?" the tall blond made a face. "I sure don't feel beautiful. I feel old and creaky."

"I just hope I look as good when I'm 'old and creaky' like you," giggled Poppy.

Anna fell backward on the bed, feet still on the floor. "Dulcie, can you believe we just met yesterday morning?"

"It can't be!" exclaimed Dulcie. She tied her robe. "It seems like Thanksgiving was ages ago."

"Did you say, 'Thanksgiving'? When was that—last

February?" joked Poppy.

Dulcie laughed and slowly stood up. "Oh, I hurt!" She rubbed her lower back and bent to touch her toes.

"Guess I'd better rescue my note pad from that soggy pack. Tomorrow I'll copy it on a new pad. You two can help me remember anything I missed. I could use a nudge or two."

"Speaking of remembering," Poppy said through a huge yawn, "why didn't you mention to my parents Jackie's run-in with Rothal Snodgrass?"

Dulcie hesitated. "Well, for one thing, it's my brother's story to tell. He didn't mention it, so I didn't either. And I didn't want to worry your parents."

Anna rolled onto her side and tucked her feet under the quilt. "I know what you mean. Erik and I sort of have an agreement not to tell our parents all the stupid and hurtful things other people say to us. It just upsets them. Especially our father."

Poppy twirled an auburn curl around her finger. "I understand that. I don't tell every little thing, either, but Jackie said Rothal threatened him before he left the cave. Don't you think that's serious enough to tell?" she asked.

"I guess you're right," said Dulcie. "But I think we should tell the guys we're going to talk to your parents."

The other two nodded their agreement.

Dulcie heard Nan moving around in the kitchen and slipped down the stairs. She found her aunt in the kitchen, washing the cups they had used for the hot chocolate.

"Aunt Nan," she said, "we're pretty stiff. Do you have any liniment?"

"Sure do!" She walked over to a closet, stretched up on her tiptoes to reach a high shelf and came down with a large bottle of a brown liquid.

"When your Uncle Berkley came back from the war, he was in pretty ragged shape, after all he'd been through. When he'd overwork around the place here, he'd be as sore as all tarnation. So we kept a good supply of liniment on hand."

She handed the bottle to Dulcie. "Rub each other down with that and it ought to help a lot. You'll smell like an old horse, but you'll feel better."

"Thanks, Aunt Nan," said Dulcie as she took the bottle. She hugged her aunt, and climbed back up the stairs. She stopped by the door to the boys' room, tapped lightly with one knuckle, and called, "Jackie?"

"Yeah?"

"I'm leaving a bottle of liniment by the door. Rub it on that shoulder—in fact, all you guys rub it on. Aunt Nan says it'll cure what ails you. When you're through, put it back out in the hall and we'll use it, okay?"

"Okay. Thanks, Sis."

A little later the girls retrieved the liniment from the hall and rubbed it all over their aching joints and muscles. Dulcie and Anna crawled back into their beds. Poppy turned down the kerosene lamp, blew it out and crawled across Dulcie to the far side of the double bed.

"That stuff may be good for what ails us," she said, giggling, "but whew—it reeks! I sure hope it evaporates during the night."

"Or kills our sense of smell," said Anna with a laugh.

Suddenly Poppy sat straight up in bed. "Dulcie, how much do you think those guns are worth? Daddy said it could be quite a lot."

"No idea. But they're in perfect condition and, as antiques, should be worth something."

"Like what?" asked Anna.

"I dunno," said Dulcie, "maybe twenty-five dollars apiece."

"Wow! Do you think so?" said Anna, raising up on one elbow. "We have twenty-one of them!"

"And we have that box with all the bullets in those special

tubes," added Poppy.

"Together, they could be worth more than five hundred-and-twenty-five dollars!" said Dulcie.

"We'd each have a start for a college education with *that* kind of money!" exclaimed Anna.

"Yeah," said Poppy. "I could put my part in the bank and let it draw interest until I graduate. That would add up." She flopped back down on the bed and curled into a ball.

Dulcie yawned and snuggled deeper into her pillow, then glanced toward Anna in the other bed. She raised up on her elbow.

"Where do you want to go to college, Anna?" she asked.

"Maybe Middle Tennessee State in Murfreesboro. Or maybe Peabody, in Nashville, since I want to be a teacher. How 'bout you?"

"I'm thinking about David Lipscomb College in Nashville," answered Dulcie, lying back on her pillow with fingers interlocked behind her head.

The rain had stopped and breaks in the clouds let moonlight filter into the bedroom through the lace curtains.

Dulcie continued, "Lipscomb's a fine school with an excellent reputation for the quality of education it provides. It's only a two-year college, though, so I guess I'd continue at Peabody."

"Hey! Maybe we could be roommates when you get to Peabody," said Anna.

"Wouldn't that be fun!" Dulcie replied. "What about you, Poppy, where do you want to go?"

"To *sleep!*—That's where *I* want to go! With you two talking and that ruckus across the hall, I'll be up 'til dawn," she muttered against her pillow.

Sure enough, the boy's whooping and laughter made it obvious that they weren't ready to wind down.

"Sounds like they're chasing Rothal Snodgrass and Todd Tesh off the mountain!" said Anna.

Just then a male voice boomed from halfway up the stairs. "Turn it off, fellows!" called Uncle Berk. "You boys are running on nervous energy. Lie still for five minutes and you'll be asleep. It's after midnight, and we've got work to do tomorrow, Eugene."

"Aw, Dad! Couldn't we sleep in for once? After all, tomorrow's Saturday."

"Son, you know as well as I do that chores have to be done on Saturdays, too. Tell you what, though—if you get to sleep in the next five minutes, maybe I'll compromise and let you sleep till eight."

"Yea for eight!" said Jackie.

"That sure beats the usual 6 a.m. wake-up call," said Eugene.

"It's a deal. G'night, Dad."

After further "good nights" were exchanged up and down the stairs and across the hall, all got quiet.

A couple of minutes later, Anna whispered, "Dulcie, you asleep yet?"

"Uh-uh."

"You think the guns are really ours?"

"We found them on Uncle Berk's property," said Dulcie. "Technically, they're his, but since we found them, he said we should divide them evenly among the six of us."

"It's so hard to believe that we found such treasures! And I'll bet there are other secrets in Rebel Cave for us to discover."

"I know! My heart says, 'I can't wait,' but my body says, 'Forget it for now!'" said Dulcie.

"I agree with both sentiments!" said Anna. "So let's get some sleep. Looks like Poppy's out already."

"Yep. Good night, new friend and fellow adventurer," said Dulcie.

"Good night, Dulcie."

Clouds covered the moon again and darkness filled the room. The wind picked up, and an exhausted Dulcie listened to its sound and the creaking of the old house. When she heard Anna's breathing slip into an even rhythm, she quietly scooted out from under the covers and lit the kerosene lamp. Turning the wick down low, Dulcie knelt by the bed, pulled her out her suitcase, unlatched it, and drew out a notebook and pencil. She began to write.

What a day it has been! I wish I could describe Anna's Diner and Westminster Cathedral. They're so magnificent. And so is the Snow Bank Room.

I almost drowned! Thank goodness Erik was right there. I wouldn't have made it without him. I just know I wouldn't.

We never dreamed of finding the guns. I guess we didn't really know what to expect. Certainly not Jackie's run-in with those creeps. I'm so thankful he wasn't badly hurt.

What a day! And I can't wait to find out what happens tomorrow!

Dulcie laid the pencil on top of the notebook and pushed both under the bed, then blew out the lamp and climbed back into bed.

Soon all was quiet—other than the usual country night sounds, and the gentle snores of six extremely tired young people, and two greatly relieved parents.

15

The Surprise

A rapping on the bedroom door brought Dulcie swirling slowly toward wakefulness. She snuggled deeper into her pillow. *No! Go 'way,* she thought. The knock became louder.

"Sis, wake up!" called Jackie. "Come on, Dulcie. There's a surprise waiting for you!"

Dulcie started to stretch, but pain screamed through her body. *Oooh!* She attempted to turn over. *Ow, ow, OW! I can hardly move!* Her tight muscles rebelled with each effort to change position. *Every inch of me is sore! That's my surprise!*

"C'mon, Dulcie, roll out!" called Jackie.

"Hush! I can't even roll *over*, much less roll *out*," she replied with a grimace. But she did slowly roll over, slip her feet off the bed, and sit up.

"What's the noise?" asked Anna, starting to sit up—"Ouch!" She pushed herself into sitting position on the bed and leaned down to rub her stiff legs. "I'm a little bit sore," she said.

"A little bit? A *little* bit?" repeated Dulcie. "I'm so sore I can hardly breathe. If you're a *little* sore, be glad you're in shape from playing basketball."

"Even basketball won't get you ready for cave exploring," Anna replied, with a laugh. "But I know if you'll stretch gently, you'll loosen up."

"Hey!" Jackie snickered behind the closed door. "What's all the groaning? Got a torture chamber in there? The female half of this team must be soft."

Dulcie mumbled, "Give us a few minutes to wake up. We'll see who's soft!"

Poppy began to moan. "I don't think I can move anything but my eyeballs!" She opened her eyes and blinked them rapidly. "Oh no, they hurt, too!"

"How about your ears, Poppy?" said Dulcie. "You slept right through Jackie's wake- up call."

"Had my head under the pillow. I was dead to the world."

"I heard him," said Anna, "like he was a million miles away. But I couldn't get up even if I wanted to."

Dulcie rubbed her sore shoulder. "I thought that horse liniment was supposed to help," she said.

"Maybe it did," said Anna. "Think how we'd feel if we hadn't used it."

The girls slowly began dressing and moving around the room, getting ready for the day. Within a short time, the stiffness and soreness let up a little, and they decided to face the world.

"I'll bet those beasts across the hall are as sore as we are," said Poppy, "but will they admit it? Not likely!" She found a pair of clean overalls in her bureau drawer and slowly drew them up over her stiff legs. "Go on downstairs. I'll be down as soon as I finish torturing myself into my clothes."

"Okay, see you at breakfast," agreed Dulcie. "What time is it, anyway?"

Poppy looked at her wristwatch, stared at it, shook it, held it to her ear and looked again. "You won't believe it. It's 10:38!"

"You kidding?" exclaimed Anna. "I never sleep this late!"

Poppy laughed. "You did today."

"You've never done what we did yesterday, either," said Dulcie. "I can't wait to get back into the cave."

"Yeah," agreed Poppy, "I thought we'd be underground again by this time." She bounced on the bed a little. "If we don't get a move on, we won't have time to do much more exploring."

Dulcie and Anna exchanged doubtful looks at the thought of cave exploring anytime soon. They eased down the stairs one careful step at a time.

"Morning, Aunt Nan," said Dulcie. "Where are the brutes? Their door is wide open, but there's not a soul in sight."

"Hi, girls," said Aunt Nan. "The boys came down rather slowly this morning. Said they were going to go loosen up their kinks. I think they headed to the barn to finish the chores your Uncle Berkley started earlier."

"Sounds like they're as sore as we are," commented Anna. "Even Erik must have found a few new muscles."

"I have a feeling," said Aunt Nan, "Eugene felt guilty about leaving everything to his dad while he slept in. But they won't be gone long. Berkley already had things pretty well under control. If you'll set the table, we'll be ready to eat a late breakfast by the time they come in."

Poppy came down the stairs and helped Anna and Dulcie lay out the silverware, plates, and cups.

The phone rang just as the girls finished setting the table. Aunt Nan went to the wall phone and lifted the receiver off the hook.

"Poppy," Dulcie remarked, "you have a phone, but no electricity."

"Uh huh. That's not unusual out here in the country. We need a phone for the business. One of these days, we'll have electricity on this side of the river, too."

Dulcie heard Aunt Nan say, "Yes, Hattie, they're doing fine. Had quite a day yesterday—. Oh, that would be great— of course! No, Dulcie's right here. All right, then. Bye."

Aunt Nan turned to her niece. "Honey, it's your Mama." She

handed her the receiver. "Speak right into the mouthpiece."

Dulcie leaned toward the phone. "Hi, Mom, is everything okay? Is Daddy all right?"

Then she heard her mother's voice; it was faint but understandable.

"Everything's fine, Dulcie. Daddy's about the same. Can you hear me okay?"

"Pretty well. You sound far away but I can hear you."

"I'll speak up. Everything's great here. The hospital put off Daddy's tests for a couple of weeks, but he's doing fine. How are you and Jackie?"

"We're great. Wait'll you hear! We'll tell you all about it tomorrow when we get home. Where are you calling from, Mr. and Mrs. Sumner's or Radburn's store?"

"We're at the store," Hattie replied. "The reason I called is that Mr. Shaver was here when we came in to get groceries. He asked about you. Wondered if you made the trip safely and if you planned to be back for school on Monday. I told him you'd be home tomorrow."

"Mom, why would he ask that?"

"Well, it seems there's been an accident and the high school won't have classes Monday and Tuesday."

"An accident? What happened? Was anyone hurt?"

"Everyone is fine. Night before last there was some kind of explosion in the closet where Mr. Ross stores the chemicals for his science class. There was a small fire, but mostly it's because the explosion left awful fumes."

"Do they know what caused it?" asked Dulcie.

"Mr. Shaver suspects a prank by some of the boys got out of hand. They may have mixed a bottle or two of chemicals that didn't get along with each other, but took a while to react. Anyway, Mr. Shaver is afraid the fumes may be poisonous."

"So there'll be no school the first two days of next week?"

"That's right. There's some smoke damage but the big thing, according to Mr. Shaver, is the smell. School's closed until

Wednesday to air it out. So, if you want to stay, you can come home on Tuesday."

"Really?"

"That's why I called."

"But what about Jackie? The grade school wasn't affected, was it?"

"No, but when I mentioned that to Mr. Shaver, he just laughed and said, 'Jackie could miss a month and still keep up.' He offered to work it out for Jackie with his principal."

"Mom, that's wonderful! Jackie will be tickled. I am, too! Mom, you won't believe what happened yesterday —. Oh, my goodness! This call must be costing a fortune! It'll have to wait until Tuesday, when we get home."

"All right, Honey. We'll be at the train come Tuesday afternoon. I sure miss you."

"I miss you, too, Mom. We love you. Give Daddy our love."

"Love you both, Sweetheart. Bye."

"Wow!" exclaimed Poppy. "Did I hear what I think I heard? Do you and Jackie really get to stay till Tuesday?"

"Yep! If it's okay with Aunt Nan and Uncle Berk."

"Sure it is," said Aunt Nan. "Your mom cleared that with me before I gave you the phone."

A sly look crossed Dulcie's face as she hatched a plan to tease her brother. "You know, I owe Jackie a little something for being such a loud and annoying alarm clock this morning." She grabbed one of Anna's hands, and one of Poppy's. "Don't tell him about Tuesday yet—don't even tell him Mother called. I'm going to have a little fun—*innocent* fun, of course!" The other girls nodded conspiratorially.

"Dulcie, what about your dad? Is he okay?" asked Aunt Nan.

"His limp is getting worse. He tries not to show it, but sometimes I can tell he's hurting. He's going back to Outwood Veteran's Hospital for tests. He hasn't been able to work much lately. Of course they don't say much in front of us kids, but I'm sure money is tight. I know they're concerned about paying for my college education. And if the government doesn't cover Dad's treatment or surgery—I don't quite know what we'll do."

Aunt Nan shook her head. "With the Good Lord's help, I'm sure it'll all work out. I'll never forget how quickly Smith and your mother helped us out so we could buy this place. Your dad's a good man."

Uncle Berk and the boys banged through the back door. Jackie was leading the way, as usual.

"Hey, Sis, glad you're finally up. Let's you and me have a little foot race. Say, down to the front gate and back. It's less than a half mile, round trip. You know, get the old blood circulating."

"Little Brother," Dulcie responded, "even if you kept up with me going down the lane, you'd be so tuckered out, you'd have to crawl back."

"Just for that," said Jackie, "we'll race after breakfast, and the winner will—"

"Hold your wagers, gang," interrupted Uncle Berk. "I have something to discuss with you. Maybe it will even change your plans for this afternoon. Right now, let's join hands and thank the Lord for our food and this day's blessings. Then I'll tell you about a phone call I made this morning."

Once the meal was underway, Berkley said, "I called a friend in Murfreesboro who has quite a collection of Civil War relics."

"Dad!" Eugene half-choked on a bite of food. "You didn't tell him about our guns!"

"Of course not, Eugene," said his father. "I asked how often certain guns are available, and what he had on hand. He told me about several—mentioned he had a Spencer repeater that belonged to his great-uncle. It's in fair shape, though the rear sight's missing. Said he doesn't want to sell it, but had an offer of $75 for it."

Jackie scraped his chair back quickly, jumped up, and said, "Twenty-one times $75—wow! Man, oh man! That's ... that's $1,575 for our twenty-one guns! And they're perfect. Not even

140

counting the cartridge tubes! It could amount to $2,000 or more!" He dropped back down in his chair and put his arms on the table.

"What a start for my college fund!" said Dulcie.

"Mine, too," said Anna.

"And just think," said Uncle Berk, taking a sip of coffee, "I paid $750 for this whole farm with all the buildings, equipment, cattle, horses and the start-up nursery. 'Course, that was during the Depression. Prices have gone up since then."

"Yep, sure have," said Jackie. "The *Nashville Banner* says the average cost of a home in America is up to a whopping $2,000."

"So, all together," said Erik, "our find could be worth the price of a house. Amazing!"

"Sure is," said Uncle Berk. He spread a spoonful of blackberry jam on a hot, buttered biscuit. "As I told you last night, we'll divide it evenly among the six of you, since you all played a part in finding the guns. However, we need to be sure we know the going price. I won't have anyone taking advantage of you."

"I want to keep one of my rifles," said Eugene, reaching for the gravy bowl.

"I do, too," said Erik. "These guns are a part of history."

"Decisions like that can wait till we find out what they're actually worth," Uncle Berk told them. "I thought we might load in the car this afternoon, take one gun and a cartridge tube and go to Murfreesboro and see what we can learn."

"Yea for Uncle Berk!" yelled Jackie.

"But if we go to Murfreesboro, we won't get to go caving this afternoon," said Anna. "I was really looking forward—"

Dulcie cut in. "That's okay, Anna." She glanced sideways at Jackie who was devouring a second helping of scrambled eggs. "We can go to the cave right after school on Monday. I can have our cave clothes washed and everything ready. Do your homework in study hall and when you get off the bus you can change—"

"What are you jabbering about?" asked Jackie, laying his fork down and looking mystified. "We can't go caving Monday. We're going home tomorrow—Sunday."

Dulcie said, "Oh, Jackie, that's right! I forgot. You weren't here when Mother called. She said there was a chemical fire at the high school. It's nothing serious, but *my* classes are dismissed until Wednesday. That means *I* don't have to leave till Tuesday."

She looked sadly at Jackie. "Of course, the explosion didn't affect the grade school, so they'll have classes as usual."

All color drained from Jackie's face. He stammered, "Dulcie, you mean … a fire … and you're gonna stay, but I … I …."

Turning to his hostess he said, "Aunt Nan, she's kidding isn't she? Mom didn't really call, did she?"

"Yes, she did, young'un," Aunt Nan answered solemnly.

Dulcie saw the misery in her normally bubbly brother and she couldn't take the joke any further.

"Oh, Jackie, I get to stay and you do, too!" She grinned at him. "There really *was* a fire. High school is dismissed until Wednesday. Grade school is going on as usual, but Mr. Shaver said you can stay. Said he'd fix it with Mrs. Lindsey." Dulcie turned to the others. "She's the grade school's principal."

"Man, oh *man*!" shouted Jackie. "What a relief! We get to stay—hot diggity dog!"

"Good deal!" said Eugene, with Poppy, Erik, and Anna chiming in their approval.

"I guess that settles it," said Uncle Berk, laying his napkin beside his plate. "We're off to Murfreesboro. I hate using that much gas with rationing still on, but how often does something like this come along? We might even have time to run by Stones River Battlefield. Are we agreed? Murfreesboro today, church on Sunday, next cave trip, Monday after school—agreed?"

"Agreed!" shouted six excited teenagers.

Dulcie got up, poured Uncle Berk, Aunt Nan, and Eugene more coffee and started to refill the milk glasses when, through the window, she glimpsed a car turning up the lane toward the house.

"Someone's coming," she said, watching as the car, an emblem on its side, stopped at the edge of the drive by the front porch. "Um … Uncle Berk, why would the sheriff be coming to call?"

16

The Challenge

Footsteps clomped across the wooden front porch. The knock was loud and insistent. Uncle Berk opened the door and greeted the two men standing there, one in uniform, the other in a pair of dirty overalls.

"Good morning. What can I do for you?"

"Good morning, Mr. Stoneworth," said the officer. "I'm Deputy Sheriff Jim Edwards. I believe we met at the Warren County Fair. You know your neighbor, Dwart Snodgrass?" he asked, pointing to the man behind him.

Uncle Berk held the door open, and let the two men pass in front of him into the house. He looked at the tall, beefy-looking man who followed the officer. "Yes, we've met. Y'all have a seat." Uncle Berk pointed to the couch, then took a seat himself. "Is there a problem?"

He paused and called back toward the dining room, "Honey, bring a couple of cups of coffee. Cream or sugar for either of you?"

"Don't go to any trouble, Mr. Stoneworth," said Deputy

Edwards. "This won't take long."

In the dining room the group at the table continued eating, but very quietly. From Dulcie's position, she could see the guests, as well as Uncle Berk.

"Hate to take up your time, Mr. Stoneworth," said Deputy Edwards, clasping and unclasping his hands, then gesturing toward the other visitor.

"Mr. Snodgrass brought up a matter that needs tending to, and I'm the only one around to handle it. Sheriff Thompkins is outta town, an' Judge Harrington ain't in, seein' it's Saturday. So here I am. Or I should say, here we are."

"And what matter might that be?" asked Uncle Berk.

"Trespassin' on my property!" blurted out Dwart Snodgrass, before the deputy could speak. "My cave, to be exact! Them young'uns o' yourn have been messin' around my cave. I won't stand for it—not for another minute!"

Eating at the breakfast table stopped altogether. Aunt Nan's and the teens' expressions turned to shock. Dulcie saw Uncle Berk lean forward and look piercingly into Snodgrass's eyes.

"Now, wait just a minute. You're not talking about Rebel Cave, are you?"

"Shore am. Been in my family since it was called 'Raccoon Hollow Cave' back before the War of Northern Aggression. I woulda sold it to you for $100 if you'd asked. But for them kids to go in there, an' start haulin' stuff off—that don't set right with me! I'm takin' you to court. Don't aim to have no d—dad-blamed bunch of Yankees marchin' in here and takin' advantage of our Southern hospitality!"

"Mr. Snodgrass, let me make a few things clear," said Uncle Berk, counting his points off on the fingers of his right hand. One, we're no more Yankees than you are. Two, we don't take advantage of our neighbors. Three, Rebel Cave is on *my* property, plain and simple. Four, nobody is going to tell me or my guests what we can do on my own place."

Deputy Edwards cleared his throat nervously. "Mr. Stoneworth, you obviously claim Rebel Cave, but Mr. Snodgrass came to me with an official-looking old deed. We stopped down yonder at the corner of the property and sighted up through the woods, and best I can figure it, the cave's his."

Uncle Berk got to his feet, and paced in front of the two other men. "Well, it's not. Before I bought this place in 1937, I trekked over every inch of the property line with Mr. Anderson, the previous owner. I know where the corners are. The cave is well inside my lines."

He walked around the rocker and placed his hands on its back and looked at the two men.

Dulcie took a deep breath. It seemed that no else around the table was breathing.

"All I know, is you got rooked!" Mr. Snodgrass sneered. "I can guess what Anderson done. He took you across the bridge over Blue Hole Creek and went on down the road toward my house. I bet he pointed out the rock that juts into the Collins River, and said it was the startin' place. I reckon he took you up the hill from there. You got rooked, Mr. Stoneworth." Snodgrass grinned. "Just plain got rooked."

He reached into his hip pocket and pulled out an old deed and passed it over to Uncle Berk.

"Take a look at that," he said, jabbing his gnarled finger at the bottom of the page.

"See where it's describin' the lay of the land?"

Uncle Berk looked and nodded.

"The property begins at a rock on the bank of Collins River ten paces *up* the river from where the Blue Hole Creek empties into the river. That's *this side—yore side* of the creek, Mr. Stoneworth. Not the other side. You git yourself down there this afternoon, an' step off ten paces up river from that branch. Even if you take ten little mincey, cheatin' steps, you sight up the hill from that point. If you got one eye and half sense, you'll see the cave up there on the mountain is well to the left of that line. On *my* property."

145

Uncle Berk stared at the deed. "Jackie," he said, "would you come take a look at this?"

Jackie eased into the living room. Uncle Berk held the deed where the boy could see it. Jackie stared at it for a couple of moments, nodded his head and said softly, "I got it, Uncle Berk."

"That kid your attorney?" asked Mr. Snodgrass, then snorted and roared with laughter.

Uncle Berk ignored him, looked at the deed again, then handed it back.

"Stoneworth," Snodgrass said, tapping the deed, "this here deed is dated June 12, 1825. For a hundred and twenty years that land's been in my family. Ain't never changed hands, ain't never goin' to. It's mine and I'm aimin' to keep it."

"I don't know much about this kinda thing," said Deputy Edwards. "But we did take a look and it appears he's right. I'd just as soon stay out of it, but, like I said, there wasn't anyone else. I had to draw up a temporary restrainin' order. When the sheriff gets back, him and the judge will look into it."

Uncle Berk shook his head.

"Yeah," Snodgrass snickered. "Judge Harrington will know all about it. His granddaddy and mine used to have a moonshine still back there by the stream in that cave. Our families go way back."

Erik nudged Eugene with his elbow, and whispered, "Remember the foundation rocks and the old copper pipe we found by the pool? That must be what he is talking about."

"Well, I don't know what to make of it," said Uncle Berk. "But we'll get to the bottom of this."

"I'm sure you will," said the deputy. "In the meantime, I'm required to give you the restraining order. It prohibits anyone from going into the cave."

"Oh, no!" said Jackie, from the dining room, then clamped his hand over his mouth.

"And that ain't all," said Mr. Snodgrass. "Tell 'em about the rest of what it says. Just in case anybody's got any big ideas."

Deputy Edwards shot the other man a look of disdain, then turned to Uncle Berk. "You'll see that you're further restrained from disposing of any items, of any sort, that you, your family, or any others, including your guests, have removed from the cave."

"What that's gittin' at," said Snodgrass, "is whatever it was your young'uns toted out of my cave last night, is mine! You ain't to take nothin' else outta there or off of this here place."

"You don't have to tell me what the order means, Mr. Snodgrass," said Uncle Berk. "I can read it. I'll respect it until the proper authorities lift it. Then we'll see who owns what."

"In the meantime," interrupted Mr. Snodgrass, leaning forward and raising his left eyebrow. "I ain't made up my mind yet whether to file assault charges agin' the boy who attacked my son last night." He smiled meanly.

Uncle Berk walked around the rocking chair and sat down again. "What assault?" he asked.

"My boy, Rothal, and a friend of his seen your young'uns trespassin'. They went to check it out, an' one of your kids tried to run 'em off."

"Let's see if I have this straight," said Uncle Berk. "One of my boys tried to run your son and his friend out of the cave? Which one was it?"

"Musta been that little 'un. Rothal said it weren't Eugene, or the Nazi boy."

In the dining room, Erik jumped to his feet, eyes blazing, but Anna grabbed his arm. Dulcie stood up, stepped in front of him and whispered, "Shhhh, let Uncle Berk handle it."

The angry young man sat back down clenching and unclenching his fists.

Uncle Berk didn't respond to the slur, but Dulcie could see the set of his jaw.

"Yep, I reckon it was the youngest boy. Coulda killed Rothal. Tried to brain 'im with an iron bar. Way I see it, he musta snuck up on 'im. Like I said, I ain't decided yet about filin' charges—but we got a witness."

Uncle Berk rubbed his hand over his chin. "Look, I don't know anything about this, but I'll get to the bottom of it. And fast."

He flashed a look toward the dining room, then to the officer.

"Deputy Edwards, I'll fully cooperate in any investigation. So will my family and my guests. And we'll comply with the restraining order. I understand why you felt it necessary to issue it. I'll be in to see the sheriff or Judge Harrington on Monday."

"I'm sure you will, Mr. Stoneworth," said the officer. "I appreciate that."

Uncle Berk again stood up. "Mr. Snodgrass, I'd appreciate it if you'd get on your feet. I want to look you in the eye, and clarify a thing or two. And I want this officer of the law to witness what I'm about to say to you."

Dwart Snodgrass slowly got to his feet and glared down at Uncle Berk.

The deputy arose also, and put one hand on his billy club.

"Mr. Snodgrass," said Uncle Berk quietly, "understand this loud and clear. There are no Nazis in this house. Nor have there ever been. I know the Nazis. I fought them all across Europe."

He unbuttoned the first four buttons on his shirt, and pushing it aside, bared his left shoulder.

"These scars came at the hands of Nazis. There are more on my other shoulder, and my back. Friends died in my arms and by my side in German prisons."

"Well, I –uh I…. Now I guess yer gonna … uh, … drag out that little medal they give you an' … uh …." stammered Mr. Snodgrass.

"My medal doesn't enter into this discussion, but I'm not through yet," said Uncle Berk.

He re-buttoned his shirt.

"I was blessed to come home from the war. But I didn't come home to be insulted by the likes of you. I won't have my guests insulted by you, either. I came home to be a part of a nation where we respect each other—no matter who we are or where we come from. I will show that respect for you when you show yourself to

148

be respectable. I will welcome you again into this home when you rise to where you can judge a man by who he is, not based on some cockeyed, lame-brained, half-witted bunch of prejudices."

Uncle Berk continued, "I'll work things out regarding the property on the basis of the law. I don't intend to take advantage of you, but get one thing straight, neighbor, I don't intend to be walked on by you either. Put that down as fact. Period."

Uncle Berk crossed his arms on his chest and stared into the shifting eyes of the larger, stocky man. No one in the living room spoke. No one in the dining room breathed.

The deputy broke the silence. "Would you like to say anything before we leave, Mr. Snodgrass? We've delivered the restraining order, so I guess we can go."

"Stoneworth," said the neighbor, "that was a nice little speech you give. But I ain't backin' down one inch. Not one."

His face jutted forward and his eyes narrowed.

"You d—" he glanced toward the dining room. "You dad-blamed carpetbaggers still think you can come down here and strip us to the bone. Well, I ain't havin' it. We'll see what Judge Harrington has to say."

He stalked out the door, but turned and called back, "I'm walkin' home, Deputy. Stay here and cozy up to these outsiders if'n you want to."

"Mr. Stoneworth," said Deputy Edwards, as the door slammed, "Snodgrass ain't the easiest feller to get along with. I had to write the restraining order, but I know you'll respect it."

"Of course I will," said Uncle Berk. "I know you're just doing your job. As I said, I'll be in town first thing Monday morning to see the judge."

He walked to the door and saw the officer out, shut the door behind him, then turned and walked into the dining room.

Seven very sad-faced people awaited him.

17

The Aftermath

Chairs scraped across the floor as the young people jumped to their feet. Aunt Nan met Uncle Berk at the dining room door. She put her arms around him and laid her head against his chest. All were silent, then Uncle Berk pulled away from his wife and waved the children back into their chairs.

"Y'all sit down now."

Nan walked back to her place and Uncle Berk slumped into his chair at the other end of the table.

"I don't know when I've ever been so angry," he said.

"You have good cause to be angry, Berkley," said Aunt Nan.

Uncle Berk leaned forward on his elbows and rubbed his hands over his face.

"Don't reckon I've ever come so close to throwing a person out of my house. I apologize to you, Erik, for that remark he made."

"It's not your apology to make, sir," said Erik. He slapped his

151

palm against the wooden table. "Why can't people understand? We probably hate the Nazis more than they do. We lost both my father's parents to the Nazis. They took our grandmother during *Kristallnacht*. She was arrested while visiting her sister in Dresden. We never saw her or her sister again."

Erik slid back down into his chair.

"Did you know that our Grandfather Gunther was a prominent scientist? he asked. "After Grandmother was taken, he saw the horror of what the Nazis were doing. With Grandfather's help we came to this country."

Erik swallowed hard.

Anna quietly took up the story. "As soon he could, Daddy contacted Dr. Oppenheimer at Los Alamos. They had corresponded for several years and had developed mutual respect and a strong friendship. Dr. Oppenheimer began the process that led to our father having security clearance. Dad became one of the scientists who worked in Oak Ridge to develop the atomic bomb."

"Wow! What happened to your grandfather?" asked Jackie.

Erik spoke again, "We tried repeatedly to contact him, but he had disappeared. Later we found out our grandmother had died at Dachau. We will probably never know what happened to Grandfather. We hate what the Nazis did and what they stood for. We are Americans. We are proud to be Americans."

"Absolutely!" said Anna.

"But because of my speech and my looks," said Erik said, his words ringing with frustration, "I am marked as a German, a *Nazi*, even!"

Dulcie watched him, sensing his pain. She bit her lip and shook her head.

"My tongue does not so easily forget its old language," Erik continued. "It does not form just right the words for the new language. For Anna, it is easy, but for me … I try, then I come face to face with such a … a *dumkopf* as this man!"

"You didn't make Mr. Snodgrass what he is Erik," Dulcie said quietly. "You're just a target for his rage."

She shook her head and struggled to find comforting words. "And, you had nothing to do with the property line matter. My mother says when you run into someone with that much bitterness, they are fighting deep, old personal battles. For whatever reason, Mr. Snodgrass sees us as the enemy."

"One thing for certain and sure, my pretty little niece," said Uncle Berk, "he's turning me into an enemy mighty quick!"

Aunt Nan reached over and covered Uncle Berk's hand with her own. "It's all right to hate the evil in the man, but wrong to hate the man himself."

Uncle Berk squeezed her hand in return. "You're a wise woman, Nan Stoneworth, and exactly right."

He leaned back in his chair. "I'm just having a mighty hard time separating the two."

"I *cannot* separate the two," said Erik, flexing and unflexing his fingers. "I … I *hate* the man *and* the way he acts."

Dulcie rose to clear the breakfast dishes.

"Look," she said, "we may have hit a brick wall, but we'll find a way around it." She paused, smiled, then continued. "Just think—what did we expect forty-eight hours ago? The adventure of exploring a cave? Maybe find a piece or two of an old military wagon? That's about it. Instead, what happened?"

She hesitated, trying to change the mood in the room. Her voice took on renewed excitement. "We've seen wonders so beautiful even *The National Geographic* couldn't do them justice! And some of them no other humans have ever, *ever* seen."

She smiled at Anna, thinking of "Anna's Diner," then she continued, "We've proved there *were* Rebel soldiers in the cave. We even know their names and their hometowns. And one of them was from Sandy Hook, Tennessee. How many people in all the world know that startling bit of information?"

She smiled, leaned forward, and looked around the table.

"And we have Civil War relics that could mean college for all six of us!"

153

"Dulcie," said Aunt Nan, "if I closed my eyes, I could easily believe I'm hearing your mother, both by what you say and the way you say it."

"That's true, Dulcie," Uncle Berk agreed. "You do sound like her—the same cheerful outlook. And what you say is all well and good, but we don't just have a collection of old guns. The cold truth is that we've also got a restraining order that won't let us do a cotton-picking thing with them. And Dwart Snodgrass has a deed showing that he owns the cave where we found them."

"He's awful, just awful!" exclaimed Dulcie. "And I detest what he's doing. But he's *not in control* of everything!" She bit her lip. "I … I think he's kind of … well … pitiful."

"I certainly do not pity him!" said Erik, his eyes blazing. "He deserves any agony he has been through, is going through, or ever will go through. I would not mind if he had a double-dose of misery with some salt rubbed in."

"One thing is certain," said Uncle Berk, "he's got the upper hand, and he's going to take every advantage if he can. Frankly, I don't know a thing we can do about it."

Aunt Nan stood up and began to help clearing the table. "Well, here it is noon," she told them, "and we're just now ready to leave the breakfast table. We got a later start for this day than we'd planned."

"Yes," said Uncle Berk, "and it's going to be a little longer before we leave this table. With everything else, I forgot one little matter."

He pinned Jackie with a look. "What's the deal, my young friend, about you baring your fangs at Rothal in the cave last night?"

For the next few minutes, the teens told the story of Jackie's encounter with Rothal Snodgrass and Tad Tesh. When Uncle Berk saw the multicolored bruise on Jackie's shoulder, he shook his head in dismay.

"And the biggest shame of all is that Rothal has a '*witness*' to verify his pack of lies as being *truth!*" Again, he shook his head.

154

"Well, at least *we* know what happened."

Uncle Berk looked around the table. "While the rest of you young folks weren't 'wounded in battle,' I imagine you have some bruises and a collection of sore muscles."

"That's for sure," said Aunt Nan, "and sitting here at this table for an hour and a half hasn't likely helped any."

Groans and moans from those at the table verified that she was right.

"Why did you have to bring that up, Mom?" asked Eugene. "Since that car pulled in the drive, I haven't even thought about my weary bones."

"Me, neither!" said Jackie. "But, man, oh man, now that my mind isn't on—" He stopped mid-sentence and clamped his hand over his mouth.

"A-ha!" exclaimed Poppy, snapping fingers on each hand and sporting a huge smile. "Did you hear what I heard? I think we just heard a confession interrupted midstream. C'mon, Jackie, 'fess up!"

Jackie looked at the floor and grinned. His freckles seemed to fade into the blush that rushed to his cheeks. "Well... I was merely going to concur with Aunt Nan that inactivity for such a long time had resulted in a certain stiffness—."

"Oh, no you don't, brother-mine," Dulcie interrupted. "You're as sore as the rest of us. Eugene came right out and admitted he's sore, and you might as well do the same. Only Erik's tongue has failed to betray him." She turned to the blond young man. "How about you, my friend?"

Erik flashed his winsome smile. "I am feeling the effects of our adventure. But it was well worth it. Soreness will wear off, but memories will linger."

"Well put!" said Dulcie. "Almost poetic. And far more gracious than the bungled mumbling of a certain someone. The same who made disparaging remarks about the female side of this team being soft."

"Okay, okay," interrupted Uncle Berk, laughing. "We're in

general agreement that the spelunkers are *all* stiff and sore. Let's do something about it. Let's take a hike down River Trail to the bridge over Blue Hole Creek. You can walk off some soreness and maybe we can figure out something about the property lines."

"That's a great idea, Uncle Berk," Dulcie agreed enthusiastically, "and we can talk about what to do with the rest of the afternoon."

"Give me half an hour to take care of some business on the phone," said Uncle Berk told them. "In the meantime, Jackie, will you write out the property line descriptions exactly as they were written on the Snodgrass deed?"

"Sure, Uncle Berk," Jackie replied.

Uncle Berk rose from the table. "When we head out, Eugene, bring your compass."

"Will do, Dad," said Eugene, then he turned to Dulcie. "You're the only one who hasn't seen our new foal. I've got a couple of things to do at the barn."

He winked at his cousin. "Come help me, and I'll show you one of the cutest little critters ever born."

"All right," said Dulcie. She looked at Poppy and Anna. "By the time you get the table cleared, and the dishes done, we'll be back, okay?"

Anna stood and began picking up the dishes. "That will be fine."

"Sure, no problem at all," Poppy agreed with a grin. "Go corral the foal, pet the puppies, cuddle the kitties, cluck at the chicks. We'll do all the hard work."

"Ignore her," said Eugene. "If that brother of yours keeps rubbing off on her she's going to forget that she must be respectful when dealing with her elder brother—namely, me!"

He laughed and opened the door for Dulcie. "You'll notice that I am showing proper respect for one older than myself—namely, you!"

"Oh, much older!" she said dryly. "Eleven whole days!"

They walked toward the barn. Now that the cold front had

156

passed, it was a delightful, sparkling clear, fall-in-Tennessee, kind of day.

"Dulcie," mumbled Eugene, kicking at the stones on the path. "Um, ... what does a guy ... uh ... how does a guy ..." his voice trailed off. "I need to talk to someone, ... you know, about, about, ... um ...." He finished in a rush, "Dulcie, how does a guy let a girl know he likes her?"

Dulcie didn't answer right away. She stopped at the barn door and turned to her cousin. "Everyone wants to be liked, Eugene, so start by being genuinely interested in her."

"Scares me spitless to be friendly. Especially if I sorta like a girl ... or think I might. When I try talkin' to her, I never know what to do with my hands, or how to stand, or what to say. And I stumble over my words, and .... What if she laughs at me? Or sticks her nose in the air and snubs me?"

Dulcie thought for a moment, then answered. "Maybe you're trying too hard. Don't focus on yourself. Instead of thinking, 'What's she thinking about me?' you might ask, 'How am I making her feel about herself?' Ask what she thinks about stuff."

"I don't even know how to start."

"Pay attention to her from a distance. What is she really excited about? Then you can ask her questions about things you know she's interested in. Every girl appreciates a guy who listens to her." She grinned. "Guys like that are rare."

He opened the barn door and they slipped into the semi-darkness. Inside, the smell of hay from the loft and stalls was sweet. As their eyes adjusted, the sunlight seeping in gave a golden glow.

"The little fellow's in the back stall," said Eugene, and guided Dulcie in that direction. He kicked at the hay at his feet. "The girl I'm talking about, she really doesn't talk much. She watches and listens. She participates, but doesn't say a lot."

Dulcie leaned over the stall railing. "Oh, what a sweet little one! Look at you, all cooped up in here. You're ready to run, aren't you, baby?"

"Yeah, he is. That's one reason I had to come out here, to let him and his mama out. Usually they are out by now, but we've had a couple of delays today."

He opened the doors and let the mare and her baby out. They raced out into the barnyard with the mother galloping along and the little one frolicking about.

"Just look at him! How does he keep his balance?" asked Dulcie. "He's so spindly. Why, he's all legs!"

She and Eugene walked to the fence and stood leaning on it while watching the animals.

"Yeah, he's not at all like your big blubbery cousin," said Eugene.

Dulcie glanced from the cavorting foal to Eugene. He wasn't smiling.

"You're thinking about Anna, aren't you?" Dulcie asked, picking up their previous conversation.

"Yes, I was talking about Anna," he mumbled. "I like her, but how could she possibly like me. I'm clumsy and awkward, and yeah, I might as well say it, I'm fat."

Dulcie laid her left hand on his forearm and looked him in the eyes—but he dropped his glance to his feet.

"*You* are not fat," she said firmly.

"How can you say that?" He looked up. "Just look at me! I'm sixteen years old, five feet and eleven inches tall, and I weigh 228 pounds. How can you say I'm not fat?"

"You are Eugene *Stoneworth*. You've always been stocky, Eugene, but you're a Stoneworth. All our men are well over six feet tall. You'll grow right through this heaviness and end up exactly the way you're supposed to be." Dulcie looked Eugene up and down. "You know, you aren't just a body, Eugene. You are a *person*. A kind, sensitive, and intelligent person. That's what will be important to any girl—not just Anna."

"Well, that's sure looking at things in a different way." Eugene didn't look like he believed Dulcie.

"It's the *right* way to look at it," Dulcie replied quickly.

158

"Anyone with a lick of sense looks past the outside, and sees the heart inside. I know Anna sees a lot in you that she likes."

"You do? Really? You *really* think so?" He grabbed her by both shoulders and looked her in the eyes. "Has she said anything?"

"That's for me to know and you to find out." She laughed. "But Eugene, there's *so* much about you that's likeable."

Dulcie, smiling, pushed him away. "Now let's get those chores done."

Eugene's steps seemed lighter as they walked back into the barn. "We just need to carry out some blocks of salt for the cattle. Let's go do it."

When they finished, they continued to talk as they walked back to the house.

On their way, Dulcie playfully punched Eugene's shoulder and said, "I'll bet you've lost a few pounds in just the last forty-eight hours! You'll make it through Misery Bellycrawl a lot easier next time."

"*That* would be a relief!" He laughed.

18

The Property Line

"Well, there it is," said Eugene. "From here we ought to be able to figure where the property line's located." He stood in the road near the bridge over Blue Hole Creek and pointed up the side of Cardwell Mountain. "You can see the very top of the cave mouth through the trees."

Uncle Berk, Aunt Nan and the six teens had walked down the lane from the house and followed River Trail toward the Snodgrass Farm. They were a short distance upstream from where the small creek ran into the river.

"See the two dark cedars just below the brow of the hill?" Eugene asked. "You can make out the cave just to the left."

"I see it," said Jackie.

Poppy shaded her eyes and squinted. "Me too, but how do we know where the property line is?"

Eugene responded, "Just as soon as Daddy gets the ten paces stepped off we'll be able to sight up the mountain with my compass and see where the line runs. It goes straight east from the corner here—that corner is what Dad's trying to find."

He fished a small compass from the bib pocket of his overalls.

Uncle Berk lined up at the point where the little stream emptied into the river, and began pacing it off.

"Seven, eight, nine, ten." Uncle Berk stopped, and with the heel of his right shoe marked an "X" on the shoulder of the gravel road. "There, that's bound to be close to ten paces upriver from the creek. That's what the deed calls for." He pulled a piece of paper from his pocket. "That's what Jackie wrote down from the Snodgrass deed, and that's what Snodgrass said this morning—ten paces."

He turned and pointed toward the river. "If you look right down yonder, that rock there must be the corner marker. It's ten paces upstream from the creek, so we're bound to be right in line with the northwest corner of our property. Now, Eugene, take your compass and aim straight east. See what it looks like sighting up the hill."

Eugene lined up the bumps on the ring of the compass face until they were pointing east. He lifted it to cheek level and sighted up the mountain. "It doesn't look good, Dad."

"Let me see, Son," said Uncle Berk. Eugene handed him the compass. He looked at the sights, lifted the instrument into position and peered up the hill. He brought it down, looked at the spot where he was standing, looked at the bridge over the creek, then sighted up the mountain again. Then, slowly, Uncle Berk let his hand drop to his side.

He shook his head and sighed. "It's no use. Even if we're off a little, the cave is well on his side of the property line."

Aunt Nan took a deep breath. "Now, what do we do, Berkley?"

Uncle Berk paced up and down the road. "I'll just have to go to the bank Monday and check our deed. They're holding it until the mortgage is paid off. I can't think why the boundary line would read any different on our copy than on the Snodgrass deed. The Andersons settled here about the same time as the Snodgrasses.

I'm sure they used the same survey and markers. Since the property was never out of their hands until I bought it from Mr. Anderson, the lines have never been resurveyed. It doesn't look good, kids." Uncle Berk lined up on the mark again. He checked the compass settings and sighted up the hill again. His shoulders slumped.

"Well, so much for that," he said. "Let's go back to the bridge over Blue Hole Creek."

As they walked along he said, "I'm having a hard time believing Anderson deliberately misled me. He has a fine reputation for being an honest man."

They stopped on the small bridge. Uncle Berk pointed about a hundred yards further down the road. "Mr. Anderson said the line began way down there next to that clump of trees. I know for certain that's where he said the northwest corner is."

He looked at the stream of water surging under the bridge, and then commented, "It's something how The Blue Hole pours out that steady stream of water all year long. At times, during rainy season, it's a real gusher. Notice how it's washed out this deep gully. I stopped clearing and cultivating along where the ground slopes down to it."

He paused abruptly—then said angrily, "Look what that sneaking Snodgrass has done! Look across at that nursery!"

"What about it, Mr. Stoneworth? It looks fine," said Erik.

"What's wrong with it, sir?" asked Anna.

"I got it!" said Jackie, snapping his fingers. "Snodgrass let you clear his land, plant your nursery stock on it, and when it gets big enough to sell, he'll—"

"Why, that no good—," said Uncle Berk, smashing his right fist into his left palm. "There's at least ten acres of his land over there that I've cleared and planted." His eyes flashed.

"I'll bet Snodgrass had himself a big ol' belly laugh every time he saw me out here sweating and straining, pulling up stumps, lugging rocks. I don't know how many times I've gone by and seen him loafing around in his yard."

Uncle Berk took of his cap and slapped it against his thigh.

"Sitting in that chair leaning back against a shade tree, whittling and spitting tobacco juice. He's probably been snickering the whole time because I've been up here slaving away, planting his land for him! Well, I've had it! I've a mind to go marching down there right now and tell him just exactly what I think of him."

"No, you will not!" said Aunt Nan, grabbing his arm and tugging to turn him around. "You're going back to the house, and calm yourself down. Monday you can go to the bank and check your deed, then go see the judge. Don't stir things up any further today."

"That low-down, lazy, ... well, I ought to …."

"Daddy," said Poppy, taking his hand, "I'm so glad you put off clearing and planting the rest of the property over there. You'd really be stuck if you'd done all that work."

Uncle Berk took two or three deep breaths and blew them out slowly. "You're right about that, Princess. I'm upset enough as it is. Guess it could have been a lot worse."

Aunt Nan looped her arm through Uncle Berk's. "Honey, let's head on back to the house."

They all turned and began walking back up the road.

"Young'uns, how're you going to spend your free afternoon?" asked Aunt Nan. "You can't go into the cave, and now with the trip to Murfreesboro shot down, you'll have to come up with something else. Berkley and I have plenty to do, but you youngsters may have to be creative. How 'bout something original—like cleaning the barn?"

"Mom, how unimaginative!" exclaimed Eugene. "And how insensitive, with relatives visiting from out of town." He winked. "And, today's Saturday. It'd almost certainly be against child-labor laws."

"Besides, " said Jackie, "my older colleague and I have discussed a plan that we want to experiment with."

Jackie flashed his engaging smile at Erik, who grinned back. "Now that a trip back to the cave has been eliminated, we have the perfect opportunity to put it into action. So, if you adults will permit us to do so, and provide a few useful items, Erik-the-Dauntless and I shall attempt to convince our other young associates to join us in a venture of a different sort."

Erik shook his head and laughed. The rest of the teens just listened.

"Well," said Uncle Berk, "if it's okay with your aunt, I guess we can turn you loose for the afternoon. But would you mind filling us in on a few details? In other words, what are you up to?"

Jackie shrugged his shoulders innocently, jumped over a stick lying in the road, and said, "I'm sure you're aware that all great scientists prefer not to disclose a hypothesis to the public until adequate research has been done to assure the likelihood of success. I know you'll understand."

"Okay," Uncle Berk said with a chuckle, "but would you like to divulge where on our property this outing is to take place, and what materials I'm to supply?"

"Said undertaking will involve the vicinity of The Blue Hole. We'll require a ball of string, a carpenter's square, a measuring tape, a level, a few old boards, a hammer and some long nails, and let's see… Did I forget anything, Erik?"

Erik nodded, and said, "A couple of poles seven or eight feet long. And Eugene, you should bring your compass."

"Beanpoles will work, Uncle Berk," Jackie told him.

"Wait just a minute, son," said Uncle Berk. "If you're thinking of trying to find out how deep Blue Hole is, I gotta nix that. It's been tried, and it's far too dangerous."

"Nope," said Jackie. "Wouldn't think of trying that. If we ever need to know the depth of that water-filled abyss, we'll just put the end of a string between Erik's teeth and have him dive in! No, this is nothing as dramatic as that. Let's simply call it, 'Project X.'"

"Sounds like something a twelve-year-old would come up with," said Dulcie, crossing her arms over her chest. "Jackie, why don't you just come out with it, and tell us what you're up to?"

"Just trust me, Sis. It could be as significant as our finding the guns!"

"Now I *know* you're exaggerating," Dulcie scoffed.

"The afternoon is shot, anyway," said Erik. "What have you got to lose?"

"I'm for it," said Poppy. "It's sorta like a blind date. We have no idea what we're getting into."

Anna shrugged. "Might as well find out, I guess."

Dulcie looked at Jackie. "All right. I'll go along, too. But I warn you, Little Brother, this had better not be another one of your pranks, or you're in big trouble."

"Okay, kids," said Uncle Berk, "go ahead, but I'm serious when I say there's to be absolutely no horseplay around The Blue Hole. No rafts on its surface and no submarines to plumb its depths. Okay? It really is too dangerous. I won't be here to bail you out if you get in trouble. Nan and I are going to run into town. Go ahead with your project. But be careful, and don't do anything foolish."

"Yea, for Uncle Berk," said Jackie, jumping up and down. "We need to round up the tools. And, since we had a late breakfast, we'll want an afternoon snack." He snapped his fingers, "Oh, Sis, bring your sketch pad and pencil, okay?"

With that the three boys dashed ahead to hunt the things they needed.

A few minutes later, Dulcie, Anna, and Poppy joined them behind the barn. Eugene hitched one of the horses to a ground sled. The boys loaded it with planks, some old tarpaper, and a variety of other items Jackie and Erik insisted they would need for "Project X."

"Giddyup, Beauty," Eugene called, snapping the reins. The sable-colored horse tightened the traces and began to pull. Eugene drove the horse out of the barn lot. Jackie ran alongside and the rest of the troop fell in line and made their way through the garden, across the orchard, and up the hill through the pasture toward The Blue Hole.

19

"Project X"

Late that afternoon a crew of grubby teenagers made their way back to the house.

"What do you think those kids are up to?" asked Uncle Berkley after the team clomped up the stairs to change out of their muddy clothes. "Reckon they found another cave to crawl into?"

Aunt Nan looked up the stairs after the kids. "I don't think so," she said. "Even though they were quite wet and mud-caked from the knees down, they were relatively clean, otherwise. There were a few leaves and twigs in their hair and on their clothes, but that's all outside stuff."

She shook her head. "Their shoes were an absolute mess! I made them take them off on the back steps and clean them before I even let them in the house."

"And just exactly why did they want that big sheet of butcher paper they wheedled out of you?" asked Uncle Berk.

"Honey, I don't know. They're evidently going to draw

167

something on it. They had Poppy's crayons and some of Dulcie's art supplies. When I questioned them about it, Jackie said, 'Military Secret!' winked at me, then took off up the stairs like greased lightning, laughing every step of the way. That boy ....''

Uncle Berk chuckled. "He is something."

"And Eugene!" said Aunt Nan. "Eugene baited me about it. He commented that he hopes we are ready to spend some money—for a good cause, he assured me."

"He knows we don't have any extra cash lying around. What could he be thinking?"

"We'll find out in due time," said Aunt Nan. "Poppy said we'd be given the opportunity to 'review the findings' tomorrow after church."

Uncle Berk's laughter rang through the kitchen as he slapped his knee, "That little girl is startin' to sound just like Jackie!" He sobered. "Just hope tomorrow's sermon is interesting enough to take our minds off the restraining order and the property line mess," he said. "If the sermon doesn't do the job, maybe the kids will."

Uncle Berk poured himself a cup of fresh coffee. "I guess you told the kids that the Saturday night bath arrangements are the same as last night?"

"Sure did; girls, back porch—boys, front porch. And never the twain shall meet. First, I apologized for the fact that our *outdoor shower system* is not working tonight," said Aunt Nan giggling.

"The Lord must have known how much we'd need that downpour last night. Since the kids are only semi-grubby tonight, perhaps we won't need a pre-bath shower. Maybe one tub of water will be enough for each trio."

Aunt Nan looped her arm through Uncle Berk's and leaned her head against his shoulder. "Isn't it fun to dream about having electricity and running water someday?"

She raised up and looked at him, her eyes shining. "I think, if I could only choose one, I'd go for the water! Our kerosene lamps do a pretty good job and we have the battery radio. But oh, to have running water!"

Uncle Berk leaned down and kissed his wife on the nose. "Honey, I'm afraid we'll have to sell a lot of plants 'fore we'll have either one."

Dulcie got up early Sunday. She was still quite sore, but not as stiff as the previous morning. She dressed before Poppy or Anna woke up and slipped downstairs. Aunt Nan was at the cookstove just beginning breakfast.

"Morning, Aunt Nan. May I help? Biscuits are my specialty."

"That would be great! If yours even come close to being as good as your mother's, they'll be delicious. I do believe Berkley would be ready at any time to make a meal of your mother's biscuits, with a bit of molasses or jam, and butter."

"Mama got me started making biscuits early," Dulcie replied, taking an apron from a hook behind the kitchen door and tying it around her waist. "In fact, I can't remember when I didn't know how to make them. She used to let me sit on the stool and help her when I was little."

"With thimble biscuits, right?"

"That's right," said Dulcie. "She'd let me help mix the ingredients and make the dough. Then we'd roll out the dough, and use the cutter made from the Pet Milk can to cut out the regular biscuits. With the scraps left over, I'd make my thimble biscuits. I'd roll the dough really thin, and Mom would hand me her special thimble. I'd cut out my biscuits with it. Little tiny ones. I was so proud of them! She'd put them in the oven right alongside hers. And they'd come out just right."

"The Stoneworths are such a loving bunch of people—with women like that raising up their children!"

"Yes," said Dulcie thoughtfully, "But, Mother says the Stoneworths have been mighty blessed by the choices they've made in marriage, too."

Nan smiled at the compliment from her niece, then looked toward the ceiling as thumping and loud laughter rumbled from Eugene's room.

"This is changing the subject a little," said Aunt Nan, "but will Jackie be able to sit still in church this morning? He has so much energy!"

Dulcie laughed. "He'll be just fine. He may be in a whirl on the inside, but on the outside he'll sit still. Except during the singing. Then he'll sing his heart out! Oh, and during the sermon, his mind will be racing a mile a minute."

"What do you mean?" asked Aunt Nan.

"You watch. When he comes down, he'll have his Bible and a notebook. From the time the preaching starts until it's over he'll write like a madman. He'll jot down every scripture quoted, and every point made. And, he'll list other scriptures that could have been used, add a poem by Coleridge, Keats, or even Lord Byron, if appropriate. And for good measure he may add a quote or two by Ralph Waldo Emerson or William Jennings Bryan, and who knows who else."

"Is that right?" Aunt Nan looked doubtful.

"I'm not kidding!" said Dulcie. "He glances at the minister once in a while and returns to his note-taking. He scribbles like—well, like an excited little kid coloring with crayons—one who doesn't mind getting out of the lines. Jackie doesn't miss a word the minister says. He'll have six or seven pages of notes by the time the sermon ends."

"Well, I can't wait to see that!" said Aunt Nan.

"And let me make a prediction."

"What's that?" asked Aunt Nan.

"He'll squeeze into the pew next to Uncle Berk."

"Why not sit with the other boys?"

"Because Jackie sings baritone. But, he's trying to learn the bass parts. He can't hit the low notes yet, but wait until his voice changes! He'll want to sit by Uncle Berk so he can listen to him sing the bass line."

Aunt Nan laughed. "It's going to be so nice to have all of you with us at church today. Anna and her mother come with Mr. Justice most of the time. And Erik comes once in a while. Gearheartd almost never attends. Mr. Justice will be thrilled to have almost his whole family with us today."

Dulcie carried two jars of jam into the dining room and set them on the table. "What's the church like, Aunt Nan?"

"Hebron Chapel is a wonderful church. It is an old church with a rich heritage. General James A. Garfield presented two or three sermons there during the Civil War. Later he became president, of course, and was assassinated. Some of the old timers, such as Mr. Justice, remember seeing him when they were tiny children."

"Is it the very same building?" asked Dulcie.

"Yes, though it's been remodeled and enlarged. Of late, the church has faced hard times. The Depression, then the war, took its toll on the congregation, with so many moving away. But it's still a fine group of people."

Aunt Nan glanced up at the clock on the wall. "Look at the time! I'd better get the other girls up."

"Wasn't it a wonderful church service, Erik?"

Dulcie and Erik walked together toward the car parked behind the church.

Erik nodded slowly. "Yes, I enjoyed it. I still sort of expect to hear the service read in German, since that's what I remember as a little boy. I haven't actually attended Hebron Chapel often enough to be comfortable yet," he admitted. "But everyone was nice. And I am amazed by the singing!"

"I know! I love to sing with so many other people! Many of these people have been singing all their lives, just like our family. By the way," she poked him on the arm, "I heard you humming along, and singing a few phrases."

He grinned and shrugged his shoulders. They leaned against

the car and waited for the rest of the family to catch up. Erik kicked at the grass between his feet. "I'm not sure I really believe there is a God, Dulcie. If there is, where was he at Dachau and Auschwitz when the Jews were being treated worse than animals?"

Dulcie clasped her hands in front of her. "He was there. He was with Uncle Berk in the P.O.W. camp."

She looked off across the field at the hills in the distance. "A lot of Hitler's men claimed to be good Christians, but they chose to ignore what the Bible plainly teaches—that we must respect every person's worth, and to love one another."

"You sure make that last one easy." Erik turned to Dulcie and reached out to brush one finger down her cheek. "In just the last few days—"

"Hey!" interrupted Jackie, racing around the side of the church building. "Did you hear what Aunt Nan and Mrs. Gunther cooked up?" He cartwheeled to a stop in front of them. "They talked on the phone early this morning, and because of 'Project X,' they've agreed we can keep our ol' team together a little longer."

"What do you mean, Jackie?" asked his sister.

"Dulcie, Uncle Berk is gonna take Erik and Anna to school tomorrow morning when he goes to town. So they get to go back home with us this afternoon and spend the night again. Mr. and Mrs. Gunther even brought school clothes for them to wear tomorrow."

He ran back toward the church shouting over his shoulder, "I'm gonna go catch Mr. Justice." He ran across the parking lot, did another cartwheel and came up with his shirttail hanging out.

"I'm so glad you and Anna can stay," said Dulcie. She and Erik settled back against the car again. "I thought you'd just spend the afternoon, and then go home. But now, we ... I mean the whole gang, will be together until tomorrow!" she finished in a rush.

Just then, Anna and Eugene walked up to them with the bundles of clothes the Gunthers had brought. "I got the keys from Dad," said Eugene. "We'll put these clothes in the trunk. Sure wish he'd let me drive home, but he won't, not with company along."

"Did you see 'The Wild Man from Borneo' come by here, by chance?" asked Poppy, as she joined the group. "I have his suit coat, his Bible, and his encyclopedia of sermon notes."

"Yes," said Erik. "He sped off to talk to Granddad Justice. Probably about Rebel Cave."

"Poppy, just put his stuff in the trunk," said Eugene, "and see if you can chase him down. Mom and Dad are about ready to go."

As soon as the Gunthers and Mr. Justice left following lunch, the group changed clothes and headed up the hill for the unveiling of Project X. "I'll say one thing," said Uncle Berk, as the group walked across the orchard. "This is certainly perfect for a Sunday afternoon outing. Just wish we didn't have the Snodgrass matter looming over us like a dark cloud."

"Didn't you hear what the preacher said about trusting the Lord, no matter what the circumstances?" asked Aunt Nan.

"Yes, and I heard what he said about forgiveness and loving your enemy, too. That part made me more than a little uncomfortable. I'm not sure I'm ready to—" Uncle Berk's head whipped down to look at his feet. "What in the world did I just step in? Mud!"

The young people exchanged knowing looks, but said nothing.

"Where did that come from? All the rain the other night must have caused a wet-weather spring." Uncle Berk pointed to a slight depression running from the pasture through the orchard. Jackie and Poppy bounced along beside him, and the rest followed behind. "I've never noticed a spring anywhere along here. Sure wouldn't expect one this time of year."

The path took them away from the low area and through a gate into the pasture. About halfway up the hill the path veered to the left and crossed the swag again. Here there was a wide band of moist earth with water running along the surface in its center.

"What on earth's going on?" exclaimed Uncle Berk, pushing

his cap back on his head and staring at the sight.

"Soon you'll see, Dad!" said Eugene.

"Man, oh man!" said Jackie. "It's working! Yippee, it's working!" He grabbed Poppy's hand, "C'mon, Poppy, let's go!" Up the hill they raced.

When the group reached the spring, Uncle Berk's mouth dropped open. "Look at the size of The Blue Hole! You've dammed it up! No wonder it's so huge! How did you do it?"

"It wasn't as hard as you might think, Dad," said Eugene, grinning. "The gully that drains the spring cuts through the limestone. It's about two feet wide there at the bottom except for a foot-deep trough that's about ten inches wide at the very bottom. We left that open with water running through it at first and worked from inside the trench to build the dam."

"Sir," said Erik, "we took a couple of two-by-sixes and made uprights and braced them in position on either side of the trench. Then we cut the old inch-thick planks to the right length and placed them horizontally against the uprights edge to edge, one on top the other. You can see how they're stacked."

"And Daddy," said Poppy, "each time we put a board in place we took a piece of tarpaper and lapped it over the top of the board and all the way down over at least the two previous boards. That was my idea."

"It was a good idea, too," commented Jackie. "As soon as we got a board in place with the tarpaper on, we nailed it to the upright."

"And when we had three boards in place," Eugene continued, "we took some rocks and wedged them into the trench at the bottom. And, with some mud and a flap of tarpaper over them, only a little water leaks through."

"This is amazing!" exclaimed Uncle Berk. He took his baseball cap off, stuck it in his hip pocket, and ran his fingers through his dark hair.

Erik continued the explanation. "So water built up behind the tarpaper and pressed it against the cracks to make the dam more

174

watertight. Some water is escaping, but the dam is secure enough that it held and the crater filled."

"The guys continued that process till it got high enough to run out through the ditch we girls dug around the hillside," said Dulcie. "The ditch filled up as far as we got it dug, then ran out and down the little low place—and made the mud you walked in."

"We were afraid the source of water might drain off somewhere underground and not fill the crater high enough for our plan to work," said Anna, "so we built this temporary dam to test it."

At this point Jackie assumed a dignified pose and got their attention.

"Sir and Ma'am, it is an honor that the 'Project X' committee has chosen me to make a brief statement."

Jackie cleared his throat. "Which statement is this: The Blue Hole, or rather, the constant flow of water therefrom, has three great potential benefits for the Stoneworth family and its enterprises. One, it can easily provide gravity-fed running water for the house and the barns and other buildings, including the greenhouse. Two, with additional work, it could irrigate the entire operation of Stoneworth Hills Nursery to such a degree as is deemed advantageous. Three, and this would be the biggest challenge, with installation of a turbine motor, it could generate electricity for the house, barn, and greenhouse, and perhaps additional outbuildings."

"There is more than an ample flow for running water to the house," added Erik.

Uncle Berk and Aunt Nan looked at each other with raised eyebrows, then Uncle Berk said, "Jackie, kids, this is great. And it would be a dream come true if such a system could be installed. Wouldn't it, Nan?"

"Oh, yes! Oh, my yes. Of course it would! But could it really work?" she asked.

"A permanent dam of reinforced concrete could be built to capture the full pressure of the retained water," Erik told them. "The flow would turn a turbine large enough to generate electricity for the house and barn. And maybe the greenhouses. I did a science project on hydroelectric power last year in school. I'm certain this would work."

"He won the science prize, Dad—ten dollars!" said Eugene. "That's how good his project was." He pulled the piece of butcher paper they had gotten from Aunt Nan out of the bib pocket of his overalls. "This shows a rough sketch of our plan, with an idea of where we could build a reservoir over there above the house."

He pointed across the hillside. "Dad, Erik knows what he's talking about. A reservoir over there would be high enough to provide adequate pressure for a bathroom upstairs."

"Oh that *would* be a dream come true!" exclaimed Aunt Nan.

"Yeah!" said Poppy, "No more, front-porch, back-porch baths!"

"You've sure given us something to think about!" said Uncle Berk.

"And, Mr. Stoneworth," added Erik, "we checked the creek all the way down to where it … uh … where it leaves your property. This is the only point where the waterway could be dammed and used as a water source without trenches dug through outcroppings of solid limestone. Here you will just be digging through soil."

"Uncle Berk," said Jackie, handing him a piece of paper, "here's a list of measurements we made and estimates on pipe, concrete and stuff. Of course it's a rough estimate. Prices probably have changed some since Erik did his project last year."

"I'm amazed at how thoroughly you've thought this through. What a team! Eugene, may I keep this sketch?" asked Uncle Berk.

"Sure, we made it for you."

"Been thinking, Uncle Berk—" said Jackie.

"I'm sure you have, Jackie," said Uncle Berk, laughing.

"Been thinking we oughta change the title of this little operation from 'Project X' to 'Project Water Flow.' Okay?"

Dulcie smiled proudly when her little brother got unanimous approval.

20

The Ride

"We've had a pretty full day already," said Aunt Nan. They walked across the lawn toward the house. "A big breakfast, and a bigger lunch. Why don't we just take it easy tonight? We could play some *Rook*. We have a new deck of cards to break in. I'm willing to make popcorn and hot cider. How does that sound?"

"Sound great to me!" said Anna. "I'm ready for a break. In fact, since we can't go to the cave, I wouldn't mind just resting this afternoon."

"Mr. Stoneworth," said Erik, "Dulcie and I would like to take the horses out. Would that would be all right, sir?"

"Dulcie, you've ridden quite a lot in Kentucky, haven't you?"

"Of course, Uncle Berk. Well, not a lot, I guess, but enough to be comfortable if the horse is gentle."

"Erik, you ride Beauty and let Dulcie ride Bonnie," said Uncle Berk. "Bonnie's not quite as spirited. You can handle Beauty. We've heard about the riding awards you've won."

"I'm so excited!" exclaimed Dulcie. "It's a perfect day for riding."

"Poppy and I are going for a walk," said Jackie. "We have some serious matters to discuss, right, Poppy?"

"Oh, yes!" she said with a grin. "A walk along River Trail away from prying ears will be perfect."

Eugene stuck out his lower lip. "Looks like we're not wanted, Anna. You think we can find some way to occupy ourselves?"

Anna flashed him a smile. "I have no doubt we can. Why don't we go sit on the porch swing and consider the possibilities."

They walked past Erik and Dulcie, who were changing their shoes for the ride. Eugene gently bumped Dulcie with his elbow, looked down, and winked.

Dulcie and Erik rode the horses down the lane that ran to the road in front of the house.

"Let's just take our time," said Dulcie. "That will let the horses warm up and let me get a feel for the saddle again. Maybe later we can canter down the road."

"Sounds good to me."

When they reached River Trail, Dulcie asked, "Erik, if we turn left, where does the road go?"

"It is a dead end. There must have been a homestead there at one time. The house and buildings are long since gone. Only part of a chimney still stands. There is a good view of the Collins River from that point. Do you want to ride down that way?"

"Sure, why not? Since I've never been here before, it'll be fun to see more of the area."

They chatted as they rode. Dulcie maneuvered Bonnie back and forth, stopping and starting several times so horse and rider could get a feel for each other. After a while, she eased up beside Erik, and they rode in comfortable silence until they came to an old fence blocking the road.

"Look at that view!" exclaimed Dulcie, her voice soft with

wonder.

In front of them the Collins River curved into a wide bend. The fields and woods rising from the opposite bank, bathed in the muted colors of fall, provided a picture-perfect landscape.

"Such a *dumkopf* I am! I didn't bring my camera when we have such beauty." He shot her a sideways glance. "In fact, more beauty than we usually have around here."

"Oh, Erik," she said, grinning at him, then glancing away. She pointed to the crumbled remains of an old house.

"Just look at that old chimney," she stammered. "You … you can tell by its size, and by the placement of the foundation stones, that it was a quite a house in its day."

"Hmmm … a showplace, no doubt. What stories it could tell." Erik's gaze seemed far away. "It is such a shame when family stories are lost. Memories fade if they are not renewed, not shared."

"That's true—and that's one reason why my mother keeps a journal—to pass on those stories. And now I have one, too."

Erik leaned down and patted Beauty's neck. "Have you ever looked at family pictures, and found old ones with no identification?"

"Sure" she said. "I love our old family pictures. My mother has most of them marked on the back with the names, but we have a few that no one remembers."

Dulcie smiled softly. "In the really old ones, you can tell what a proud day it was for the family. They were all dressed up. The sweet babies in their long gowns. And the parents are so dignified and sober in their Sunday clothes. And now no one even knows their names anymore." Dulcie's voice trailed off.

"Sad, is it not?" Erik turned in his saddle and looked at Dulcie. "Imagine the lives they touched. Maybe that little baby went on to be a mother, a teacher, or maybe a grandmother. Someone *must* remember!"

Tears gathered in Erik's eyes, and he quickly brushed them aside.

"You're thinking of your Grandmother Gunther, aren't you?"

He nodded, then answered, "They murdered her. They worked her, they used her, they starved her." He fought the tears. "She was Jewish. Because of her bloodline, they killed her. And she is no more."

"Oh, Erik! I'm *so* sorry," Dulcie said gently. "And your grandfather ... what do you think happened to him?"

The riders had dropped their reins over the pommels of their saddles, and the horses munched the browning grass by the side of the road.

"Grandfather's position in the scientific community protected him for a while. But shortly after he refused to join the Nazi Party, they began to focus on Grandmother. They learned she was Jewish and made her sew the yellow star on her clothes. After they took her, I think Grandfather knew he did not have much time left."

Erik pulled his sleeve across his eyes and took a deep breath.

"Grandfather rushed his plans to get us out. Since he was a full-blooded German, he was certain he was in less danger than his son—my father. Under Hitler, anyone was considered to be a Jew, no matter what their religious beliefs or practices, if they had one grandparent who by *race* was a Jew. Father, half-Jewish, married to an American, with quarter-Jewish children would certainly be a target for the Nazis. And Anna and I would be also. So Grandfather Gunther got us smuggled out of the country, first to England, then to America. I do not know how he did it. Things were difficult by then. He was supposed to contact us in London, but we never heard from him. Grandfather simply disappeared."

"And you still don't know what happened to him?"

"No. We only know about Grandmother because of her cousin who was with her in Dachau, and survived. Father says with all the refugees coming to America now that the war is over, maybe someone will find us who knows what happened to our grandfather. But so far, nothing."

Erik took another deep breath.

"Somewhere in Germany is Grandfather's old trunk. All of our family pictures are in that trunk. Strangers will find it and see the photographs. They will wonder who those people are, and with a shrug of the shoulders, cast them aside."

"But Erik, *you* are here and so are your parents and Anna. Through you, your grandparents continue to live. As long as you remember and pass on your memories, they will live on and on."

"I suppose," said Erik unhappily.

He lifted the reins, gave them a tug and started Beauty back down the road. Dulcie followed. The horses moved into a gentle trot and soon they approached the lane to the house. Arriving at the junction just ahead of them were Jackie and Poppy.

"Look Poppy," said Jackie in a voice loud enough to be heard. "Who woulda thought it?— Roy Rogers and Dale Evans!"

"Hey, you two!" called Dulcie. "Why, bless my hide, if it isn't Tom Sawyer and Huckleberry Finn."

"You're close," said Jackie. "Could well be Tom Sawyer and Becky Thatcher. But for sure, Huck Finn never was as cute," he bowed and swept his hands toward Poppy, "as my delightful companion."

Poppy giggled, flipped her auburn hair, and batted her eyelashes.

"Oh, for such a gift with words!" exclaimed Erik as they drew the horses to a halt and sat looking down at the full-of-life youngsters.

"And did your deep and private discussion," asked Dulcie, "solve any of the world's problems since we saw you last?"

Jackie shook his head. "Nope. We're focusing on something else."

"What is on your mind?" asked Erik, leaning forward and stroking Beauty's neck.

"While you four Tennesseans are in school tomorrow," said Jackie, "Uncle Berk's taking Dulcie and me when he goes to see the judge. So I'm picking Poppy's brain. Trying to figure every angle on the Snodgrass matter. Checking out ideas about anything we've seen or heard that might help us resolve Uncle Berk's problem."

"Any breakthroughs?" asked Dulcie.

"Not yet," said Jackie, "but I still need to talk to everyone else before we go to bed. Time's running out."

"All right, Sherlock," said Erik, smiling. "We will see you after our ride. Get up, Beauty."

The horse moved smoothly down the road with Bonnie and Dulcie alongside.

As they approached the Snodgrass property, Beauty, beginning to show his high-spirited nature, moved ahead of Bonnie.

Erik tightened the reins a little and called back, "Why not let them run a little? Let us cross the river at Shellsford and ride on up to the junction. We will trot back to the river, then walk the rest of the way back."

Dulcie said, "Okay, let's go."

At that moment, an object whizzed past her. Beauty whinnied loudly, reared up and whirled around, almost dislodging Erik. The horse plunged to the side, nearly falling, then regained his footing, and raced down the road with Erik fighting for control.

"Wait!" Erik yelled back. "We will run it off." Bonnie pranced nervously, but Dulcie held her firmly.

"Right!" Dulcie called.

"Yipeeee!" came a yelp of delight from the field behind her. She looked across the ditch beside the road and saw Tad Tesh slapping his leg and howling with glee. Rothal Snodgrass stood bent over, hands on his knees, laughing uncontrollably. In one hand was a slingshot.

"You idiots!" she shouted. "You could have killed him!"

Rothal stopped laughing long enough to yell, "One less Nazi!" then he continued to guffaw.

Absolute rage swept through Dulcie. She whirled the horse around, kicked both heels into Bonnie's sides, and angled her across the road. The horse soared over the ditch and charged the pair of startled boys. Tad Tesh turned and ran, but Rothal tripped over a root and fell. Dulcie jerked Bonnie to a stop just in time to keep the horse from trampling him. Instantly dropping the reins, she threw her leg over the side and slid to the ground in one fluid motion. Rothal was getting to his feet when she yanked the slingshot out of his hand and broke it over her knee. He threw up his arm and staggered back from her.

"You get to that house, you miserable excuse for a human being. That goes for you too, Tesh!" She shouted after the fleeing youth. "Get yourselves out of my sight, Rothal Snodgrass! I stopped this horse in time to keep from stomping you into the ground. When Erik gets back, it'll be a different story. I won't do a thing to stop him if he rips you apart!"

Rothal, glanced down the dirt road toward Shellsford and stumbled a few steps backward. "Well ...."

"You shut your mouth! Don't you ever pull a stupid stunt like that again! If you *ever* harm the Stoneworths or their guests, I'll... I'll... I'll call my daddy and he'll turn his people loose on you. Hatfields and McCoys from the Kentucky mountains will swarm this valley. They'll ferret out every single Snodgrass alive."

Rothal turned and bolted for the house.

"You tell your dad I said so." She choked back tears, then yelled, "Tell him I said, 'Put *that* in your pipe and smoke it!'"

Seeing Rothal's broad back disappear, Dulcie wrapped her arms around the warm, smooth neck of the horse, pressed her face against the animal and began to cry.

"Bravo, Sis, bravo!" yelled Jackie.

Out from behind a bush charged Jackie and Poppy. Each carried a large stick.

"Truth did bard Willie Shakespeare speak when he said, 'Courage mounteth with occasion.' Your courage took the day, Dulcie."

Jackie dropped his club, ran to her, and threw his arms around her. "You scared the liver out of me. I was afraid that gorilla would tear you to pieces before we could get here. But you had it under control the whole time!"

Poppy followed close behind Jackie and hugged them both. "You didn't need us at all. Dulcie, I'm so proud of you!"

"And, I'm so ashamed!" Dulcie sobbed. "I totally lost my temper. That coward ran, but I wasn't in control, even of myself. I *never* lose my temper like that —"

"Dulcie," said Jackie, "there's such a thing as righteous indignation. You were right; they were wrong!"

"But I wasn't righteous, I was … was infuriated! I was ready to fry them in lard!"

Dulcie knuckled the tears from her eyes and took a couple of deep breaths.

"Oh, my goodness, speaking of being out of control, Erik will be back any minute. If he realizes what happened, he's going to be *enraged*!"

She clucked at Bonnie and led her back toward the road, quickly mounted, then pointed toward home. "You two start toward the house, but stay within earshot. I'll head him off but I may need your help."

Dulcie leaned forward and heeled Bonnie into a gentle trot toward Shellsford. They hadn't gone far when the thunder of Beauty's hooves announced their return. Erik was flushed with delight, beaming from ear to ear as he charged up.

"Whoa, boy."

He reined the horse to a stop.

"What a ride! I do not know when I have had such a workout on a horse. You would think Beauty was a racehorse rather than a draft horse. He is something else. I do not know what got into him. Must have been stung by a bee or something. I will tell you one thing, had we been on a racetrack, we would have won a prize! Why did you not come to meet me?"

"Didn't you tell me to wait?" Dulcie stalled.

"Oh. Yes, I did." Erik laughed.

Dulcie thought fast, "Um, … Beauty is still prancing. Why don't we trot to the end of River Road? Then we'll walk them back to the barn to cool 'em off."

"Great idea!" he replied.

Erik didn't seem to notice Dulcie's flushed cheeks and

reddened eyes.

Later, while they were rubbing the horses down, Erik called, "Dulcie, did you notice this welt on Beauty's haunch before we went for our ride?"

"No, I didn't," said Dulcie.

"I did not either," said Erik. "I wonder if it has anything to do with his reaction today. It does not look like an insect sting. Maybe we should mention it to your Uncle Berk."

"And we'd better keep an eye on the time," said Dulcie, changing the subject. "Tonight's the night we're supposed to take it easy and play some games. Let's head for the house and wash up," she said.

As they walked toward the house, Erik took her hand. "I do not know when I have enjoyed myself more than these last few days. Being with you is so much fun and ... so peaceful."

Dulcie blushed a deep red. *If he only knew ...* she thought.

21

The Visitor

The laughter around the table was so loud that no one heard the soft knock on the back door. The two foursomes were playing cards in the dining room. They had finished the first round of Rook and were changing seats and opponents.

"Refreshments now, or refreshments later?" asked Aunt Nan.

"I'd just as soon wait until we finish this game," said Uncle Berk.

The gentle knock came again. Uncle Berk hurried through the kitchen, looked through the curtains, and opened the door.

"Why, hello, young lady. Come right on in here!" he said.

"Thank you, sir. I'm sorry to be a bother, but I wondered could I talk to y'all for a minute?"

Uncle Berk brought a lanky, longhaired girl into the dining room. She clasped and unclasped her hands. In spite of her effort, her hands shook visibly. It was obvious the red-eyed, hollow-cheeked girl had been crying.

Dulcie looked at the younger girl in her hand-me-down dress, and thought, *She's scared out of her wits!*

"This is Ruthie Snodgrass, kids," said Uncle Berk. "Ruthie, you know Eugene and Poppy. And I'm sure you've seen Anna and Erik Gunther at school. These two are Dulcie and Jackie Delaney. They're my niece and nephew from Kentucky."

When they spoke to her, she looked down at her hands "P... pleased to meet you," she said softly.

"Let's go into the living room where we can visit," said Aunt Nan.

Uncle Berk escorted the frightened girl to a chair by the fireplace. The others took seats on the couch or chairs nearby.

"I seen what happened this afternoon," said Ruthie, glancing at Dulcie and Erik. "Mighty sorry, Miss Delaney, Mr. Gunther, I'm so ashamed of what Rothal done—err—d... did. And Miss, I was plumb proud of you. Don't many people stand up to Rothal like you done."

Erik looked questioningly at Dulcie, who avoided his gaze. Her mind raced, *How much do I say—how much will she tell?* She simply said, "Thank you."

Ruthie looked around the room and turned to Uncle Berk. "I know it's out of place fer me to ask, Mr. Stoneworth, and I apologize, but would y'all mind pullin' the window shades down? If Pap or Rothal show up, they won't see me and I can slide out the kitchen door and sneak home the back way. Rothal's gone off with Tad Tesh, and Pap and Maw went to town. I don't reckon they'll be home right away, but it'd shore be bad if'n they catch me here. I left a bucket at our spring so I kin pretend I went to get water."

Uncle Berk and Eugene pulled the blinds so no one could see into the room.

"I don't know what y'all want with our cave," the girl continued, "or why that old hole in the ground is worth fussin' about. It's been nothin' but trouble, if'n you ask me. But my Pap's got his pride. He don't hold to no one taking advantage."

"Ruthie, we acted in good faith when we let the kids explore the cave. I was told it was part of my holdings. I'd never allow my children, or anyone else to trespass onto your property, if I could stop it," said Uncle Berk. "I told your father I'd accept the judgement of the law about the property lines. I'm a man of my word, and I'll do just that if the land belongs to your daddy."

He arose and leaned against the mantle above the fireplace.

"I'm mighty glad to hear it. I know we got papers sayin' it's ours. I seen 'em," Ruthie blurted out. "But I ... well, I been watchin' ya'll since you bought this place. Y'all are fine folks. I know that. I think my mama does, too. Maybe even Rothal, but he'd never admit it as long as daddy's got his back up about you."

Tears gathered in the girl's eyes. "It's just I don't want y'all thinkin' poorly of us. Or ... or that my Pap an' Rothal are bad," Ruthie stammered. "Oh, they act up sometimes. But, Pap's just so proud. He don't take disrespect off nobody.

"He come home yesterday mighty riled up. Mama an' me," she shifted her eyes to the floor, "well, we just try to stay out of his way when he's like that."

Unconsciously she rubbed a deep purple mark on her right cheek.

"Why, Ruthie, that's just terrible!" said Dulcie, noticing the bruise.

Ruthie dropped her hand as though scalded, her eyes huge. "Oh no, Miss. Nothin' happened."

Again she touched the mark on her cheek, "This? I'm real cl ... clumsy, always fallin' down. P... Pap says I got my mama's

189

two left feet. She … she's 'bout bad as I am."

Aunt Nan walked over to the child and tilted her face to the light. "Honey, that's a bad bruise. Are you sure that—"

"Oh yes, ma'am. I'm fine," she said quickly, then she turned toward Uncle Berk. "I was just wonderin' if maybe you could talk to my Pap again. If'n you could lay to rest your claim on the cave, I reckon he'd calm down some. Don't you?"

Uncle Berk didn't say a word.

"Mama says Pap's like he is 'cause he's got a bad hurt deep inside. Life's been awful hard on 'im. It's bore down on 'im somethin' fierce. Mama says his daddy's family was dirt poor, and so was his mama's family. None of 'em could he'p each other out much. It was hard on 'im growin' up that way."

"Lots of folks have had it hard, Ruthie," said Uncle Berk.

"Yessir," she said, but continued as if she hadn't heard him. "Mama says it was on account of the Civil War that Pap's kin was so poor. Pap's Grandpa Snodgrass was starved to death in Camp Morton Prison somewhere off up in Yankee country. That left his wife and young'uns to scrape by. Pap's Grandpa Murphy was killed by the Yanks at the Battle of Stones River, so his family might nigh didn't make it, neither.

"And them carpetbaggers that come down from up north after the war, why they was…they were just plain awful! From his childhood Pap's mama and daddy fed him the terriblest stories from them sad days. But Pap's daddy was only around till Pap was ten. He had a moonshine still at the cave. A Yankee revenuer killed 'im up there in a shootout."

"Oh my," Aunt Nan whispered, "your family *has* had its trouble."

"Yes, ma'am." Ruthie paused. "But that ain't the deepest hurt. 'Specially for Rothal. See, we used to have us a brother, an older brother …."

She broke down and began to cry.

Aunt Nan held the sobbing girl.

Uncle Berk pulled his handkerchief out of his hip pocket, and handed it to the crying child. "I wasn't aware there was an older son in the family."

"No, sir. I figured you didn't know. When y'all moved here he was off in the Civilian Conservation Corps, and he went right into the army when the war broke out. He never was around after y'all come. Then you went off to war yourself."

Ruthie swiped at her eyes with Uncle Berk's handkerchief and took a shaky breath.

"When my brother went to war, Ma planted a lilac in front of the window where the little banner's hangin' now. You know, the flag with the gold star that lets folks know we got one that ain't comin' home? The lilac's growed so tall you can't see the little gold star any more. So folks don't know. But Mama won't cut the lilac back none since it's for him."

Ruthie got up, walked to the window, lifted the edge of the window shade and peeked into the dark.

"I'm gonna have to go real soon," she said.

"Rothal adored that big brother of our'n. Hung on to every word he said. Thought the moon and stars rose on account of him. He saved all the letters from Arthel, first when he was in the CCCs, and then when he went off to war. More 'n that, Rothal wrote back. And kept talkin' about all the stuff they was gonna do together after the war. An' he worked hard at school to make our big brother proud."

Ruthie blinked hard to push away the tears.

"Time went by and we didn't get no more letters. Rothal would jump off that school bus an' run to look in the mailbox an' then

191

he'd look so sad. He got moody. Started havin' trouble at school an' about everywhere else. Ma got real quiet. And Pap got madder 'n madder at the Germans and the Japs, and 'specially at the Nazis." She glanced quickly at Erik and Anna, then looked at the floor.

"One day Rothal ran to the box and there *was* a letter. Only it warn't from our brother—it was about 'im. All it said was he died defendin' our country. 'Fore long, though, we found out he pined away in a German prison. He was all shot up an' they wouldn't get no doctor for him. An' then they starved 'im, just like the Yanks done his great-granddaddy Snodgrass. Rothal ain't been the same since. And Pap ain't. And Mama ain't." Ruthie took a deep breath. "An' I guess I ain't neither," she whispered.

"We ain't bad folks, really we ain't. But sometimes things just boil up inside, and Rothal just don't care no more! But I sure do apologize for what he done this afternoon, Mr. Gunther, Miss Delaney. And I'm glad you stood up to Rothal. I don't guess he's ever had a woman stand up to 'im. He needed that."

Ruthie seemed to struggle to find the right words. "He ... he may be hurtin' but that ain't no excuse not to be decent. And ... and for certain it ain't no excuse for doin' somethin' as dangerous as he done today. Now, I beg your pardon for takin' up so much of your time. But I just had to—"

Erik stepped toward her and said, "Miss Snodgrass, may I shake your hand?"

She extended a limp hand and he shook it. Then Anna shook her hand, followed by Eugene, Aunt Nan, and Uncle Berk.

But Dulcie said, "May I hug you?" and embraced her. So did Jackie and Poppy.

"Ruthie," asked Uncle Berk as they walked her to the back door. "What was your brother's name?"

"It was Arthell. Don't it have a ring to it? Arthell and Rothal. Would'a been good names for twins, I always thought."

"Did he have a middle name, Ruthie?" Uncle Berk asked.

"Oh yes! It was Bedford! My daddy was proud to name him Bedford—after General Nathan Bedford Forrest. Daddy says him and General George Patton were the greatest generals that ever lived."

"Arthell Bedford Snodgrass ... A. B. Snodgrass, then," said Berk, rubbing his chin and looking at the ceiling.

"Yes sir, only nobody ever called 'im that. Just Arthell." The mantle clock chimed the hour. "Oh, I just gotta go! I'll sneak out the back. Th ... Thank you for your hospitality," she said solemnly.

"See you on the school bus, Ruthie," said Eugene, and smiled at her.

She glanced shyly at him, smiled tentatively and nodded. With that she slipped through the kitchen door and into the darkness.

Eight numbed people slumped down on the couch and chairs.

"I sure don't feel like playing any more *Rook*!" said Jackie. The others agreed. They sat in silence for a while.

Then Dulcie spoke up. "Now we know why the Snodgrasses are *limping* through life."

For the next few minutes Dulcie, Jackie, and Poppy told the shocked family of the encounter with Rothal.

Finally, after the story had been told and questions answered, Uncle Berk said, "This is getting out of hand. We've got to do something about it. I'm going to make a phone call."

A little later he gathered the group together again. "I'm going to ask a favor of you. It's a bit late, but there's a neighbor we need to call on. Are you game?"

"Oh, man," said Jackie. "You gotta be talking about down river, the Snodgrass family."

"Right," agreed Uncle Berk. "From what Ruthie just told us, and based on the phone call I made, there may be a way to defuse the situation a little. I think we ought to try."

"I am willing to go," said Erik defiantly, "but one remark about my being a Nazi, and I will not be responsible for my actions."

"Erik," said Aunt Nan gently, tugging his arm so that he faced her. "We're always responsible for our actions. Think about what Mr. Snodgrass may say, and decide right now that you will not react *no matter what*. It is your *choice* what you do in the situation. He does not control you."

Aunt Nan squeezed his arm gently. "I know you'll do the right thing."

"I… I will try," said Erik.

"What about the rest of you?" asked Uncle Berk. "You willing to go?"

Some 'yes' votes were shaky, but moments later the group walked down River Trail in the bright moonlight to visit the nearest neighbors—without an invitation.

22

The Story

Dwart Snodgrass leaned forward in his chair on the ramshackle porch, and squinted into the gathering darkness at the visitors. "Well, if y'all got business here, I reckon you can c'mon up," he growled.

He pushed the chair back onto its rear legs and leaned against the wall of the dingy white clapboard house. "It's a mighty sorry time to be callin' on folks, if you ask me."

"Mr. Snodgrass, I know it's late, but I thought we should talk," said Uncle Berk.

"Said all I had to say yesterday mornin'. Don't like chewin' my tobacco twice."

He leaned over and yelled back into the house. "Ruthie! Light the lantern, an' bring it out here."

"Yessir, Pap," the girl replied.

Mr. Snodgrass waved toward the other end of the porch. "There's a chair over there for your Missus," he said, pointing at a chair near the edge of the porch. "Rest of y'all will have to stand or sit on the porch floor. I ain't gettin' up."

Nan nodded at the gruff man and took a seat. The older teens sat down on the porch near the wooden steps. Poppy and Jackie took similar positions on the other side. Uncle Berk stood on the ground with his left foot on the second step where he could look directly at the man in the straight-backed chair.

Ruthie came out the door carrying the lantern.

"Hang it on that post," her father directed. She hung it from a nail on one of the uprights that supported the sagging roof. Her eyes flew from her father to Uncle Berk and back again.

"Rothal!" Again, Mr. Snodgrass leaned over and yelled through the screen door. "Boy, be sociable. Why don't you finish cleanin' that shotgun out here by the lantern light?"

A flat voice answered from somewhere in the house. "I'm comin', Pap." There was the sound of movement, and the swarthy youth slunk through the screen door carrying a twelve-gauge, pump-action shotgun in one hand, and a rag and gun oil in the other. He wore a hunter's vest with a dozen shells on each side. He nodded at Aunt Nan and glared at the rest.

"Stoneworth," said Dwart Snodgrass, "you got somethin' to say or not? If you do, get it said."

"Mr. Snodgrass, I was talking on the phone to my banker—"

"Ain't sellin' the cave, Stoneworth. Leastwise, I ain't sellin' to you—"

"I'm not buying, either. I'm not here to talk to you about the cave, I—"

"Well, you ought to be!" said Snodgrass. He leaned the chair forward and glared at Uncle Berk. "You best be here askin' my pardon." He shook an angry finger at the teens. "I seen them younguns of yours sneaking down that old ditch on my property this afternoon. Seems they don't know what *private property* means. Well, I ain't a-gonna put up with it."

He leaned the chair back and folded his arms across his chest. "Next time I talk to the sheriff it'll be to get a restrainin' order to

196

keep you and your kind off *all* my property, not just out of my cave."

"I'm not here to discuss your property. It's about your son—"

Dulcie saw Rothal stiffen and look quickly at his father. Mr. Snodgrass sat forward abruptly and got to his feet.

"Now, don't be tryin' to blame Rothal—"

"I'm here to talk to you about your other son."

Mr. Snodgrass mouth snapped shut. He glared at Uncle Berk through slitted eyes. "You ain't got no call to speak of my boy." He cleared his throat. "You ain't even fit to speak his name."

Uncle Berk tried a different tack. "You know Silas Murphree at the bank?"

Snodgrass nodded.

"He's a member of Hebron Chapel Church. This evening I called him at home with some questions, and Arthell's name came up."

"Who do you think you are, stickin' your Yankee-carpetbaggin' nose into my family's business—my son's business?" Snodgrass shouted.

Uncle Berk held up both hands. "Look, Snodgrass, you and I don't have to be on the best of terms for me to know how much you cared about your son." He lowered his voice. "I thought you might want to hear how he died."

There was movement inside the house near the door. And the sound of a muffled gasp.

"Gerty, you and Ruthie, you stay in that house," Mr. Snodgrass shouted at the door. "An' I don't want to hear no carryin' on in there."

He turned back to Uncle Berk. "I ain't listenin' to no pack of lies. You're tryin' to take advantage of our poor boy's death. Ain't gonna work." He sat back down.

"Mr. Snodgrass, when I heard the name Arthell Snodgrass recently, I didn't recognize it. In the German prison we often went by initials only—kept as much from the Germans as we could. So your son was known as A. B. Snodgrass. Now, I didn't know him personally, even though we were in the same prison. He was in a different compound."

Mr. Snodgrass froze in place.

"There was an American colonel in there," Uncle Berk continued. "Just before he and I were captured, when we realized there was no way to escape the Germans, we did the unthinkable—we switched uniforms and dog tags. Because of special circumstances it was important that his identity be kept secret from the enemy. So he posed as a sergeant, which was my rank, and I pretended to be him. The Nazis thought I was the highest-ranking officer there. That's part of the reason for my scars. The Germans tried to get information from me. Since I wasn't really the colonel, I couldn't tell them what they wanted to know."

"Good thing you couldn't, you'd a prob'ly squealed," Snodgrass muttered.

Dulcie glanced up at Erik, saw his jaw muscle tighten—then relax. She smiled at him. *It's working*, she thought, *he's choosing not to react.*

"The prisoners thought I was the colonel, too. I kept records about our men, mostly by their initials and last names. One of the people who was able to get to me pretty regularly to report, was the colonel. When he did, I fed him information that I got from the others, and I let him know what the Nazis were trying to get out of me."

"What's that got to do with my son?"

Uncle Berk took one step up onto the porch. "The word is not good. But I'd want to know if it were my son."

He stopped. "Your son was captured on September 12th of last year, or thereabouts. Shortly before the Germans brought him to our prison, A. B. Snodgrass and the others were loaded into railroad boxcars—packed in like sardines, so close together they couldn't sit down. The Germans locked the boxcars and pushed them out onto railroad tracks in plain sight of allied planes. Our pilots flying over thought it was a supply train, so they bombed and strafed it. Many of our men were killed. When the cars were torn up enough that the men could break out, they lay down in the snow and formed "U-S-P-W"—United States Prisoners of War—with their bodies. The planes flew away. Some of our boys never got up out of the snow. Others made it as far as the prison. That's where I got to know the name A. B. Snodgrass. He was on my list as seriously wounded," Uncle Berk said. "And I remember the day his name was missing from the list. The day he died. That was February 2nd, Groundhog Day, of this year."

Dulcie blinked tears. She saw Eugene gently put his arm around Anna. She was crying openly. Poppy's hands covered her face. And sobbing could be heard coming through the screened door.

Snodgrass leapt to his feet. "Y'all hush, in there!" he snapped, his voice thick. "This man's lyin' through his teeth. He's just tryin' to cozy up to us. Tryin' to git our land!"

"No he ain't, Pap! He's tellin' the truth and you know it!" It was a voice they hadn't heard before, the voice of Mrs. Gerty Snodgrass.

Snodgrass slumped down heavily in the cane-bottomed chair, then leaned back against the wall. Rothal made a show of loading the shotgun and sighting down the gun barrel.

Uncle Berk waited in silence.

"Stoneworth," said Dwart Snodgrass. He lit his pipe with shaking hands. "I already knowed all about that boxcar business."

Uncle Berk's eyebrows shot up. "Really? I'm surprised your son was able to write. And that the mail got through. My family went for months, almost a year, without knowing where I was, or if I was even alive."

Uncle Berk cleared his throat, then added. "I'm glad he wrote."

"No," Dwart paused. "No, he didn't write. Well, he did write us one little bitty note."

He rubbed his stubbled beard and blinked his eyes. "Said he'd write more when he was strong enough. It was dated January 31, 1945. He give it to a soldier boy that come by here, and brung it to us when he got back."

"What was the soldier boy's name?" asked Uncle Berk.

Snodgrass snorted, "Huh! You ain't gittin' that outta me. You'd just turn around an' say, 'Oh, yes, I knowed 'im well.' I'll just let you in on this much—that soldier boy was tall and skinny. Now, what are you gonna make of that?"

"The skinny part doesn't help. We were all skinny." Uncle Berk rubbed his jaw, and gazed up at the porch ceiling. "Tall ... If he was real tall, it would have been Tony, Antonio Giancarlo, from Milwaukee. Or ... or Tex Hargrove of Beaumont, Texas.

"If you have the address of the soldier, write him a postcard and ask if he knew Col. Stony Blackstone in Germany. Ask him to write and describe the colonel for you."

Uncle Berk turned away from Snodgrass, and then back again. "Oh, if it was Tex Hargrove, he has a two-inch scar on his right cheek. And straight in line with that scar, part of his lower right ear lobe is missing."

Once more, there were muffled sobs in the darkened house.

Dwart Snodgrass again banged his chair forward and stood up. "Might as well tell you. You've 'bout wore out yer welcome. I still figure you cooked up this little visit to soften me up to git my cave. I ain't—"

Uncle Berk marched up the stairs and across the porch. He reached his hand out to Aunt Nan.

"Mr. Snodgrass," he said, "I've never seen the likes of you! I told you this visit has nothing to do with the cave. It has to do with the fact that every father and every mother who loses his son in defense of our freedom deserves to know how that boy died."

Uncle Berk stomped across to the steps, one hand in the small of Aunt Nan's back, guiding her. He turned to the bitter man.

"I *could* have lied to you. Told you I knew Arthell, that I held his hand at the end. But I didn't. This visit has to do with the fact that we are neighbors, and likely will be for a long time to come. I thought making this call was the decent thing to do."

"We don't need *your* kind of decency," said Mr. Snodgrass. "We got along just fine before you Yankees moved in here. I reckon we'll go on just fine without snugglin' up with you outsiders."

"Look," said Uncle Berk. "We try to do the right thing. If we ever fail at it, it'll be an act of thoughtlessness, and not intentional. Now, about the cave—"

"Yeah, here it comes. I figured you'd get to it sooner or later. It's *my* cave!" he snarled. "An' it's gonna stay mine!"

"Like I told you yesterday, I am perfectly willing," said Uncle Berk, "to let the law decide about the land. What the law determines, I will abide by. And whatever the outcome, as I said before, I'll try to be a decent neighbor. My wife and children will do the same. I hope you will, too. I think the A. B. Snodgrass, the Arthell Bedford Snodgrass who died for our country in that German prison camp, would want you to do the same. Honor your son's memory, Mr. Snodgrass."

Uncle Berk reached his hand to Aunt Nan and helped her down the steps. The children followed in silence.

23

The Swing

Erik placed one hand on Dulcie's arm as they walked into the house. "Will you sit on the swing with me for a little while?" he asked.

Dulcie blushed under the gaze of the rest of the family. "I suppose so. It's a little cool," she said, smiling at him. "Let me find my sweater."

"Not for too long, you two," said Berk. "It's getting late."

The moon was dipping low across the Collins River when they sat down on the swing. They rocked back and forth in silence for a few minutes, and then Erik spoke.

"So you jumped Bonnie over that ditch and almost rode her right over Rothal, huh?"

Dulcie described her encounter with Rothal and Tad Tesh.

"Oh, Erik, I could have killed him or crippled Rothal for life. Now that it's over, it scares me half to death."

"He would have deserved it after the idiotic stunt he pulled," said Erik. "You must have struck some kind of terror into him, from what Jackie, Poppy, and Ruthie said. But why did you keep it from me? I would rather have heard it from you."

Dulcie ducked her head.

"I'm not altogether sure why I didn't tell you."

She plucked at a pulled thread on her sweater. "Partly, because I didn't want you to go chasing after Rothal and maybe make the situation worse. But mostly because I was so thoroughly disgusted with myself."

She glanced up at him. "I guess I just didn't want you to ... to misjudge me ... I mean, I totally came unhinged! I jumped that ditch on Bonnie without even thinking that I could have killed Rothal."

"But you did not. You stopped in time."

"Only because Bonnie is so responsive! I don't even remember when it hit me that what I was doing was so stupid, but Bonnie stopped on a dime the minute I pulled up on the reins. Otherwise, Rothal would've been trampled under her feet."

Dulcie looked across at the silver light shining on the river. "And the Snodgrasses would have had one more reason to hate us. "

Erik reached over and took her hand. "Nothing makes a man prouder than to have the woman he ... um ... he admires, stand up for him."

With his free hand Erik tipped her chin towards him and continued.

"Especially when she has beautiful curly black hair, pretty dimples, her eyes well up with tears in the soft moonlight—"

"Oh, hush!" she said, pulling away, and scooting to the far end of the swing. "Why, it had nothing to do with *you*."

Dulcie bit her lip to keep from laughing.

"You egotistical thing." She tossed her head and looked away. "I was ... I was upset about what he did to that poor horse!"

"Fib! You fib! You not only lose your temper, now you fib, too!" Erik laughed.

"Well, maybe I was a little concerned about you—" Dulcie turned back to him.

"Erik, you should have seen our little kids arrive on the scene. They came carrying clubs longer than they are tall. They stopped when they saw Rothal hightail it to the house, but if they'd been needed …." Dulcie giggled. "You would have doubled up laughing if it hadn't been so serious. There they came, ready to take on the enemy, swinging their weapons of war! What a wonderful, *ridiculous*, moment."

Dulcie hopped off the swing and struck a pose. "I'm standing there, all 5 feet and 2 inches of me, shaking my fist at Rothal Snodgrass as he scrambles for the house. And I'm yelling at the top of my lungs, threatening to have the Hatfields and McCoys swarm over the area to ferret out every Snodgrass around! I must have been a sight!"

Erik reached out and grabbed her raised fist and pulled her back down on the swing beside him. "What are … who are … the Hatfields and McCoys?" asked Erik.

"They are two feuding families of the Appalachian Mountains. They're my Daddy's relatives—on both sides."

"*That* threat must have made Rothal weak with fear," kidded Erik.

"He probably didn't even hear me, or if he did, he's probably never heard of the Hatfields and McCoys." Dulcie giggled again. "But I had to say *something*. That was the only thing I could think of. It's hard to come up with something creative when you don't cuss."

"You still have not answered my question. Why did you not tell me *at the time* what happened."

"I did explain! I told you how I lost my temper … I was ashamed, and—" Dulcie sobered. "Look, Erik, I've seen hints of your anger lying just under the surface. If you had realized what spooked Beauty you would have gone after Rothal and there would have been a horrible brawl."

"Not necessarily," Erik responded quietly.

Dulcie disagreed. "As much as I'd like to think Rothal was running from me, I know better. He ran home to arm himself to face *you*. Rothal is a coward, but he's a bully, too. My daddy says no one's more dangerous than a bully who's scared. Eugene told me that in Rothal's lunch bucket he carries brass knucks to school. Tonight, with your own eyes you saw him fingering that pump shotgun. What I did was to try to prevent a confrontation between the two of you."

"And you did, but ...." Erik sighed. "I would still like a chance to get back at Rothal."

"Erik, didn't pitiful little Ruthie's visit—or our trip to their house—help you understand the Snodgrass family at all?"

"I suppose, a little. That young lady has—what do you call it? Spunk. Yes, she has spunk, and she explained some of their pain. But why does Rothal make me the enemy?"

"Because, to him, you sound like the enemy, look like the enemy, carry yourself like the enemy. You are tall, blond, with pale blue eyes. You look like Hitler's ideal Aryan. And there's enough of the German touch in your speech that when Rothal sees you, his knee-jerk reaction is 'Nazi.' He can't go to Europe and fight the war over again. But with all the anger bottled up in him about his brother, he can try to make you pay for what happened to Arthell."

"But that is not fair!"

"No, of course it's not," she said. "It's terrible—and sad."

"That brings up another matter, Dulcie."

"What's that?"

"The Snodgrasses are not the only ones who feel that way about us. There are others, too."

"I know," said Dulcie, shaking her head, then shivering violently. "We'd better go in. It's getting late and I'm getting cold."

"I could warm you up!" he said, scooting closer.

"Oh no, you couldn't!" she said, slipping off the swing and onto her feet, but smiling back at him. He got up and put his arm around her as they looked across the moonlit lawn and the nursery

206

toward the Collins River.

"Erik, haven't the last four days been wonderful? What adventures we've had!"

Dulcie looked down at her hands, "Do … do you suppose we'll ever see each other again?"

"I promise to peek across the table at you tomorrow at breakfast," he teased.

"You dunce! I mean after Tuesday. I know Jackie and I can't come back next Thanksgiving. We're having the family reunion at our house then. And next summer I'll have to get a job so I can go to college, or to help support the family if Daddy's health keeps getting worse."

"All four of us plan to attend college in Nashville. We'll see each other then. At least I hope so."

"Me, too!" said Dulcie. "But that's almost two years away. That seems like forever! Will you write to me, if I promise to write back?"

"Sure I will!"

"You write first. It wouldn't be proper for me to be the first to write."

"All right."

Dulcie shivered again. "I do hope the Civil War guns are ours. They'd sure help pay for college."

"Certainly would. But Dulcie, I do not see how they can be ours. We saw where the property line runs. What are the odds we can prove the lines have been changed? If the cave belongs to Snodgrass, then the guns belong to Snodgrass, too. We lose all around."

Erik shoved against one of the porch uprights. "Man! It angers me to say that."

"Maybe he'll give us a finder's fee," said Dulcie.

"Why, yes, that is it!" said Erik, grinning. "Dwart Snodgrass will likely say, 'Y'all jist he'p yoreselves to them guns. Ah been tryin' to come up with some way to show my 'preciation fer y'all.' Pardon my sarcasm, Dulcie, but I think the chance of that—"

"Hey, out there!" called Uncle Berk, as he stuck his head out front door. "You two better get in here. You're about to run out of *moonshine*—I mean moon*light*. It's time for us to get to bed. You already missed 'Lum and Abner' on the radio. Come on in now."

The couple walked hand in hand across the porch toward the door. Dulcie looked up at her tall friend and said, "That was a pretty good Dwart Snodgrass imitation, Erik." She giggled. "With a little work, we might get you a job on the Grand Ole Opry with Minnie Pearl."

"That Snodgrass!" Poppy sniffed, standing in the bedroom with her hands on her hips. "Did you hear the way he talked to his wife and children?"

The girls were in their nightgowns, getting ready for bed.

"Of course I did," said Dulcie. "Can you imagine your dad talking to your mother that way?"

Poppy's eyes grew huge. "I think she'd clobber 'im."

Dulcie laughed at the thought of sweet Aunt Nan taking a swing at Uncle Berk.

Anna didn't laugh. "It's hard to understand, Poppy. I just don't know how people become what they become and do what they do. I don't understand why the people of my birth country let the things happen there in Germany that they allowed...."

"Well," said Dulcie, "do you remember what I told you about my grandmother?"

The other girls nodded.

"Maybe part of the answer is there. Grandmother Crowe told me stories about bad boys and girls being eaten up by mice and rats. In my imagination I saw horrible pictures that made me so afraid that I still have a hard time thinking about rodents."

"That was so awful!" said Poppy.

"When she locked me in the cellar and made scratching sounds on the door, it drove the bad thoughts and pictures deep, deep

208

inside. Now my feelings tend to react to anything that triggers those old memories." Dulcie lifted her curls and loosened the tangles with her comb.

"Oh, Dulcie, do you think you'll ever get over it?" asked Poppy.

"Sure, Poppy. I *am* getting over it."

"Are you really?" asked Anna. "How?"

"I'm not sure if I can explain it," said Dulcie, "but I'll try. Well, to start with, we think in pictures, right?"

The other girls nodded.

"Grandma 'showed' me horrible pictures. My feelings came from the pictures I saw. The more vivid the pictures, the more afraid I was. I reacted automatically. How can I change all that?"

"That's exactly what I want to know," said Anna. "How *do* we stop what you call 'knee-jerk' reactions to things."

"Like what kinds of things, Anna?" asked Dulcie.

"Well, I've heard people say 'that's just the way I am.'" Anna bit her lip. "For example, if I go into a rage at Erik about something, I might say, 'Oh, well, all of us Gunthers have short tempers. That's just the way we are.' See what I mean?"

"But that's just an excuse!" said Dulcie. "It's like what Aunt Nan told Erik before we went to see the Snodgrasses. We have a choice about how we react. For example, I have to change the pictures I see when I think of mice. If I change the pictures, I'll change how I feel. If I change how I feel, I'll change how I act."

"So how do you do that?" asked Poppy.

"First, I take a deep breath and get quiet, then I try to imagine mice playing, and see the mamas gently taking care of their little ones. If ugly pictures try to come back, I remind myself that those aren't true pictures. They're all messed up like the reflections you see in a carnival mirror. So I reject the ugly images. I imagine myself being unafraid—and I *feel* unafraid. I look at the little mouse in my mind, and I pick it up and pet it. It's soft and cute and playful. I change what I see and feel, and that helps me change my actions."

"Dulcie," said Anna, sliding under the covers, "I've seen you looking at the pictures you sketched of the three bats in the cave. Is that a part of changing the pictures in your mind?"

"Uh huh." She grinned. "I didn't realize you noticed."

"You touched the pictures with your finger," Anna told her.

"Yes, I did. Every time I see that picture, I imagine myself stroking the bats and feeling what warm, soft, little guys they are. I just keep making myself have good feelings about them."

"Do you think it's working?" asked Poppy.

"I know it's working—though it's not easy. I'm not having the nightmares any more. And I'm not nearly as afraid as I used to be. I could never have even looked at the bats if I were."

"We started out talking about that awful Dwart Snodgrass," said Anna," and about how people become what they become and do what they do. And here we are talking about bats! Mr. Snodgrass is certainly not a bat!"

Dulcie sat on the edge of the bed. "No, but the same idea works," she said. "Creating ugly pictures in people's minds will create strong feelings against other nations, or religions, or races—or whatever."

"Makes sense," said Poppy, raising up on her elbow and looking past Dulcie at Anna. "If you can get one group to see another group as ugly and evil and threatening, people will dislike—or even hate—them. And be afraid of them."

"And those feelings," agreed Anna, "can lead to such terrible things as what the Germans did to the Jews."

"Closer to home, that must be why Mr. Snodgrass is so hateful," Dulcie said sadly. "He sees awful pictures when he thinks about us, about other people, about life."

"Hey, that's right," said Poppy. "Remember what Ruthie said about her dad's parents, about how—"

"Yes! That's it!" interrupted Anna. "She said they told him horrible stories about how the Yankees treated them during the war."

"And then," said Dulcie, "the Northerners, the ones they called 'carpetbaggers,' came after the war and took advantage of the horrible state the Southerners were in."

"And there are the awful things that happened to the Snodgrasses' son last winter," Poppy went on.

"So what kind of pictures does Mr. Snodgrass see when he hears a German accent, or a northern accent? Ugly, ugly, ugly, ones!" continued Poppy, answering her own question. "No wonder he has ugly feelings!"

"But he's responsible, too," said Dulcie. "It's up to him to *choose* to turn off the old pictures. Quit adding Technicolor."

"And stop pumping up his hate juices," said Poppy.

"Right," agreed Dulcie. "He needs to replace *ugly* pictures with *nice* ones. That would change the way he feels."

"I guess," said Anna, stifling a yawn, "that to change, Dwart and Rothal Snodgrass have to stop seeing us as wicked, threatening mice—or worse, as Nazis.

"An' we've gotta help by trying our best not to act like rats," said Poppy, grinning.

24

To the Courthouse

"One more stop, and then to the courthouse to see the judge," said Uncle Berk to Dulcie, Jackie, and Poppy. He pulled the car away from the curb in front of the high school, where Anna, Erik and Eugene were trudging slowly up the walk to the building. "Think those three will have trouble paying attention today?"

"Not if the teacher mentions the Civil War in Tennessee," said Dulcie.

"Or caves," said Poppy.

"Or hidden treasure!" said Jackie.

A little later, pointing to a building just ahead, Poppy said, "There's my school."

"It breaks my heart that I can't go to class with you today, Poppy," said Jackie, grinning.

"Yeah, I'll bet! I'm surprised you aren't crying."

"Now, I'll be fair to you," Jackie responded. "If the judge says we can go in the cave, I promise not to discover anything *really* exciting until you get there."

"You will *not* go cave exploring *at all* until I get home! Even if the judge wants to go along, or … or … or the speleomonster will eat you alive!"

"Now, Poppy," said Uncle Berk, pulling in front of the school, "don't you worry. After Jackie gets all the wood cut and stacked in the woodshed, he'll be too tired to go cave exploring. I only agreed to feed 'em until Sunday. Today he has to *earn* his food. Dulcie gets off easy because she sent us those pear cuttings."

"Sounds fair to me," said Dulcie.

"Ah, poor me," said Jackie, hand to forehead. "He's gonna work me to death. If Willie S. were here he'd say, 'O! What a rogue and peasant slave am I … I shall despair. There is no creature loves me; And if I die, no soul will pity me.'"

"Let me out of this car before I throw up," said Poppy, laughing. "See you after school."

Uncle Berk and Dulcie both chuckled, but then he grew somber. "I sure hope the judge will tell us the restraining order was all a big mistake, and just to forget it."

"You don't sound very confident, Uncle Berk," said Jackie.

"I'm not. I don't see any way we could be misreading the Snodgrass deed."

Uncle Berk took a deep breath and blew it out. "I don't want to take something from the Snodgrass family that is rightfully theirs."

"Well, I do!" said Jackie. "They ought to get some kind of justice for being so nasty!"

"Justice is not up to us, Jackie," said Uncle Berk. "It's up to the law."

Uncle Berk pulled the steering wheel to the right. "Here's the courthouse," he said, pulling into a parking place. "At least we'll have an answer one way or the other."

He pointed to a large building just down the street. "I'll run over to the bank and get my deed, just in case the judge is able to see us right away. Want to go along?"

"No," said Dulcie, "we'll be in the office where they have

214

records of all the deed and property sales. Back home, I studied the land grants of the early settlers in Muhlenberg County as a history project. I had to track what's happened to their land since, so I learned how to search deed books and plat maps. I want to show Jackie how it's done. I can use your property as an example and find out who's owned it down through the years."

Berk scratched his head. "All right, but I think I already know that," he said, shrugging his shoulders. "You go on. I'll see you in a little bit."

At 9:50 Uncle Berk, deed in hand, walked into the room where Dulcie and Jackie were poring over musty old books. "C'mon, kids, we're to meet Deputy Edwards at the judge's office in a few minutes, so you'd better wrap it up. Can't be late. You learning anything, Jackie?"

"Yes sir, I'm getting the hang of it. Pretty interesting." He pocketed notes he'd made and put the huge title book back on the shelf.

He continued, "Bunch of this land was given as grants to men who fought in the Revolutionary War, just like in Kentucky."

Dust from the old book clung to Jackie's jacket. He brushed it away. "I'm ready to go. Are you, Dulcie?"

"Sure am." She picked up her sketchpad and tucked her pencil into her pocket.

Deputy Edwards was waiting outside the judge's chambers when the trio arrived.

"Hi there, Mr. Stoneworth, children. 'Fraid I have bad news. Judge Harrington's docket is full today. I took the liberty to set an appointment for tomorrow morning at 11:45. That was the earliest time available."

Uncle Berk's shoulders slumped. "That's a disappointment!" he said. "I sure had hoped to get this thing behind us today. And the kids wanted to make at least one more trip into the cave, but I reckon that's out, too."

"Yes sir, it is. The restraining order remains in effect until the judge or the sheriff lifts it. I'm awful sorry." He fingered the badge on his jacket as he spoke.

"The sheriff says Mr. Snodgrass has been troublesome enough that he'd prefer to have the judge handle it. Snodgrass said that's what he wants. Told the sheriff he figured you'd have a harder time buyin' off the judge. Can you imagine the gall!"

"It won't come to that, Deputy Edwards. That's not the way I do business. I'll honor whatever the judge's decision is." Uncle Berk sighed. "I went over my deed with one of the bank officials this morning. It sure looks like Mr. Anderson started way north of where he should have when he showed me the boundaries. It's hard to figure how he could'a made that kind of mistake by accident."

"Sure is," said Deputy Edwards. "The Andersons were considered honest, law-abiding citizens. Maybe his dad showed him the property lines after the old-timer went senile."

"Could be that's what happened," agreed Uncle Berk, rubbing the back of his neck. "Sure leaves me in a bind."

"Frankly, most of that land's not worth more than a dollar or two an acre," said the deputy. "Hardly seems worth making a fuss over."

"It is to me," said Uncle Berk, grimly. "I've already planted nursery stock on part of it. Anyway, maybe we can get it settled tomorrow."

"See you then, Mr. Stoneworth." The deputy nodded at the children and went on his way.

"Good grief, Uncle Berk," said Jackie. "It looks like the judge could have seen us for a few minutes. It wouldn't take long just to look at your deed. Now, with us leaving tomorrow, we won't get to go back in the cave at all. What a raw deal!"

Uncle Berk pushed open the heavy door to the outside and held it for the teenagers. "Jackie, I don't think your cave-exploring ambitions are a high priority to the judge. Anyway, if he reads the deed the way everyone else does, you won't be going back into the cave, period. Snodgrass won't let you."

He sighed and ran his fingers through his hair. "Well, I need to get to the bank to return the deed. On second thought, I think I'll see if the bank will let me take it home. Tonight, we'll go back over it with a fine-toothed comb."

"Uncle Berk, may we wait for you in the office of deeds?" asked Dulcie, turning back to the courthouse.

Uncle Berk looked puzzled. "I guess that'll be fine. I do have a little more business to take care of while I'm in the bank. And I need to see the vet to get some salve for that welt on Beauty's haunch. The skin's broken. I want to take care of it before it festers."

"That should give us plenty of time," said Dulcie, "to … to finish up the—"

Jackie jumped in, rolling his eyes. "Yeah, to finish up the assignment she gave me. So much for having two days off from school!"

"Tell you what," Uncle Berk reached into his pocket and withdrew a fistful of coins. He counted out a few and handed them to Dulcie. "Here's fifty cents. If you get tired of messing around in those dusty ol' books, you walk over to the City Drug and Fountain and get yourselves a chocolate malt."

"Wow!" said Jackie. "Thanks!"

An hour and fifteen minutes later Uncle Berk found the kids still poring over the old records.

"Uncle Berk, this is fascinating stuff," said Jackie. "In 1827, not far from Shellsford, a Mr. Josiah Greer traded a hundred and twenty-five acres of land in return for a mule named 'Black Jack' and an iron wash kettle. Can you imagine that?"

"Yep," said Uncle Berk as they left the courthouse. "Mr. Greer may have inherited a big chunk of one of those grants and needed a kettle and a mule a lot more than he needed land he couldn't clear and cultivate."

As they went by City Drug, Uncle Berk said, "You missed your opportunity to get that malt. But I tell you what we'll do.

Tomorrow, when we take you to the train, we'll come early and stop here. If Eugene and Poppy skip their last class they can join us. Say! If Julia and Gearhardt are willing, Anna and Erik can come along and we'll have a little going-away party for you with chocolate malts for everybody."

"That would be swell, Uncle Berk!" said Dulcie.

"Man, oh man! I guess so!" said Jackie.

"Okay," said Uncle Berk, "but give me my half dollar back. I'll spend it on you tomorrow."

Dulcie and Jackie looked at each other. Jackie shrugged, and Dulcie said, "I only have forty-five cents. I … I spent a nickel."

"At the courthouse? What could you spend a nickel for in the courthouse?"

"Shhhh," said Jackie, looking around as if to see if anyone was listening. "It's a military secret. Tell you later."

Uncle Berk flung his arms out, palms up, shrugged his shoulders, and gazed heavenward. "What's this world coming to?"

He grinned and stuck his cupped hand out to Dulcie. "Gimme my forty-five cents. Let's go."

The afternoon sped by. At home, Uncle Berk put on his work clothes and went to the barn to dress Beauty's wound and handle other chores that had begun to stack up.

Meanwhile, something curious was going on at the house.

"Jackie," said Aunt Nan, "watch for your uncle to start back to the house. If you see him coming this way, head him off. You'll have to delay him some way. We have about twenty minutes before the school bus comes. Anna and Erik are going to ride out on the bus with our kids. Mr. & Mrs. Gunther should be here about the same time. They're bringing the finishing touches."

Dulcie started unfolding bunting and watched Jackie ponder a plan to distract Uncle Berk. *When he gets that thoughtful look and moves his jaw slowly from one side to the other, he takes on another 'Smith Delaney look.' His wheels are turning, for sure.*

"I got it!" said Jackie. "I'll run out and tell him to come back to the barn because I want to show him something and discuss something important. I'll take him back to the foal's stall, and try to talk him into letting me name him. I'll tell him I like 'Blaze,' and we'll discuss why that's a good name or why it's not. And then I'll—"

"You'll handle it just fine," said Aunt Nan. "Right now, get me the step ladder. When I'm up on it, you can pass me the end of that banner, then give me the hammer. I've got some tacks in my apron pocket."

Soon they had streamers running across the dining room. A banner hung across one end of the room with the word "CONGRATULATIONS!" in big letters. They were so busy, no one noticed Uncle Berk until they heard him stomping his feet on the mat just outside the door.

Jackie shot through the kitchen.

"Don't take off your shoes, Uncle Berk! I've gotta show you something. And I need to talk to you real bad."

"Well, there they go," said Aunt Nan, leaning over to peek out the dining room window. "Jackie is talking a mile a minute, and Berkley—seems to be a little reluctant to go back to the barn lot."

She lifted the lace curtain and peered around the edge. "No, Jackie hooked him. He's going into the barn now."

"We're just about ready. And there comes the school bus," said Dulcie, clapping her hands.

The bus turned around at the end of the long drive and Eugene, Poppy, Anna, and Erik got off and started to the house.

"And here come the Gunthers," said Aunt Nan.

The long car turned up the lane and stopped long enough to pick up the four walkers, one on each fender and one on each running board. When they pulled in at the house, the teens jumped off and the Gunthers got out. Mr. Gunther opened the back door and lifted out a flat box.

"Great," said Dulcie, "they got the cake. Do you think they had time to have it decorated?"

"Probably so," said Aunt Nan. "Julia certainly knows how to

get things done."

A little later everyone was in place and Aunt Nan went to the back door and waved to her husband and nephew to hurry to the house. When they got to the door, Aunt Nan called excitedly, "Just kick your shoes off and come in your sock feet, Berkley. There's something on the dining room ceiling, and it's running down the wall. Hurry!"

Uncle Berk hurried, but Jackie beat him. Grinning from ear to ear, he rushed in and joined the others in the dining room. The minute Uncle Berk stepped through the door they began to sing,

"For he's a jolly good fellow,

For he's a jolly good fellow,

For Berk's a jolly good fellllllooow,

And he owns Rebel Cave!

And he owns Rebel Cave!

And he owns Rebel Cave!

For Berk's a jolly good fellllllooow,

And he owns Rebel Cave!

Uncle Berk's face was comical. Confusion danced across his features. He glanced around at the banner stretching most of the way across the dining room with its bold message of CONGRATULATIONS!

"All right, what's the joke? Did y'all fall off a turnip wagon and damage your brains? Or find a keg of Rebel Cave moonshine? Just look at that cake!"

In the middle of the dining room table was a large one-layer chocolate cake. The top was decorated with a picture of a cave entrance and there was a message:

For Berkley,

Owner of Rebel Cave!

"Okay, what gives? Did you see the judge?" he asked. "What *is* going on here?"

"No," said Dulcie, "we didn't see him, but you *are* the owner of the cave."

"Your visit with Judge Harrington tomorrow is just a

technicality, Uncle Berk," said Jackie, "a trifling technicality."

"That means the guns are ours, too, Daddy," said Poppy. "Isn't that great!"

Uncle Berk held up his hands. "Hey, hey! Back up a little and explain it to me one step at a time. What are you talking about?"

"C'mon, everybody," said Eugene. "Grab your coats, and Dad, put your shoes back on, and let's all take a little hike. We'll tell you the story. Cake can come later."

They quickly donned jackets and shoes and walked across the property toward the north boundary. When they reached the brow of a small ridge that sloped down to Blue Hole Creek, they stopped.

Erik pointed to the stream flowing down a ravine to the right, and said, "When we were trying to decide where to dam the creek to set up the hydropower turbine, we first checked out The Blue Hole. But before we worked on the temporary dam, we decided to explore the stream to see if there might be a better spot."

Eugene picked up the story. "As we made our way down the streambed we saw that the rocky ridge between here and the buildings would present problems, but we came on down until Jackie saw what we thought might be a good location."

"Not for the primary dam, you understand," chimed in Jackie, "but for a secondary one that would—Dulcie, you should take it from here."

"Okay!" said Dulcie. "It's as clear as if it were yesterday—"

"But it was really day-before-yesterday," Jackie interrupted.

"Hush—you'll get a turn later," Dulcie admonished, reaching over to place her hand on his shoulder.

"Let me take all of you back to Saturday and tell you how it happened. When we're through, Uncle Berk, you'll be as excited as we are. And we'll go eat that cake and celebrate.

"Saturday, we were standing right here ...." Her voice took on a new excitement as she relived that day and the surprising discovery they had made.

25

The Flashback

The Discovery on Saturday

"At this point," Erik said on Saturday, "a dam placed this low wouldn't be much good for irrigating." He pointed over the ridge to the house in the distance. "And, we're too far down the hill for a dam to provide water for the house."

"True," said Eugene, "but a small irrigation dam here could supply water for this lower quarter of the property and we wouldn't need to dig such long ditches."

"That would save money on pipes, too," Anna commented.

"I think I see just the spot for a small secondary dam," said Jackie, pointing to a spot below them. "There, right after the stream levels out and starts across the field toward the river, it gets broader for a short distance."

He then indicated a spot a little further down the creek. "See where it gets narrow again? A small dam at that point would stop the flow and create a sizeable pool."

"Sure," agreed Eugene, "that should work." Then he squinted and shook his head. "No, wait. See that flat area and the sunken hollow over there? That kills the plan."

"Why?" asked Anna.

"A lot of the water would run out that way," he said, pointing across the creek to a low area going around the base of the hill to the right. "In fact, if you dam up the creek, most of the water would drain off down that—"

"Eugene!" Dulcie grabbed Eugene's arm. "That's it!"

She pushed up on to her tiptoes and surveyed the field. "At least, it might be. We'll have to check it out!"

"What are you talking about, Dulcie?" asked Erik, looking confused.

"Look! It appears that at one time the creek made a sharp turn to the right at the point where it levels off. I'll bet that overgrown, filled-in gully is where the stream originally ran. The creek followed along where we can see the heavy brush, and then swung down toward the river way over there."

She pointed to the clump of trees by the river. "I bet it goes through Eugene's Culvert!"

"Dulcie is right," Erik agreed excitedly. "That does definitely look like an old watercourse." He continued, speaking slowly and carefully as if he were thinking it through as he spoke. "At some point during a period of unusually heavy rain, the torrent surging down the hill was too great to make the sharp turn. It must have rushed straight ahead over the bank and gouged a new channel more directly toward the river. When the flooding stopped, the new channel continued to carry the water."

"And through the years the old channel gradually filled in," Eugene added.

"You know what this might mean?" asked Dulcie excitedly.

"Yep, I think I got it!" said Jackie. "If the Snodgrass deed was written *before* the new channel was cut, back then the creek didn't run into the river where it does now."

"So the bridge over Blue Hole Creek isn't by the property corner shown on the old deed, as Mr. Snodgrass thinks it is," exclaimed Dulcie. "Instead, the corner is by Eugene's Culvert."

"Then the property line would be exactly where Mr. Anderson told Mr. Stoneworth it was!" said Erik.

"That means the cave *is* on our property!" said Eugene.

"Yahoo!" yelled Jackie.

"But wait!" said Dulcie, her face set in determined lines. "Don't get too excited. We have to prove it. First, we must find out where the old streambed hits the Collins River," said Dulcie. "We need to follow it to see if it actually goes through Eugene's Culvert."

"And then?" said Erik.

"We'll have to find proof the creek changed to the present location *after* the Snodgrass deed was drawn up," said Dulcie, shading her eyes as she gazed at the old watercourse.

"That's right!" said Erik. "If the stream changed *before* the deed was drawn up, Mr. Snodgrass is right about where the property line starts."

"Well," said Eugene, "it shouldn't take long to follow the old channel. Let's go do it."

As the group worked its way through the underbrush, Poppy spoke up for the first time in several minutes.

"Would it help if I told you when the new channel was probably cut?" she asked.

"Yeah, that would be most considerate, Miss Smarty-pants," called Eugene from the back of the line. "That would be extremely helpful. Why not give just the year and dates. Don't bother with the hours and minutes."

"Oh, shoot," said Poppy. "I don't know the exact time here, but near Murfreesboro, a few miles from here, on the 24th of June, 1863, the rain started before four a.m. It rained solid for the next couple of weeks, except for a little break on the first of July."

"Poppy, don't carry on such foolishness," said Eugene.

"You kidding, Poppy?" asked Dulcie. She stopped to untangle a persimmon branch from her hair, "or are you telling us straight?"

"Telling you straight. You remember about the Battle of Stones River, where Grandpa Carver and Grandpa Stoneworth fought?"

"Sure," said Dulcie.

Poppy continued, "I wrote three papers and gave two reports in my history class on that battle and what happened afterward. The battle ended on the third of January 1863. For the next six months both sides dug in and there wasn't much fighting. But on June 24, 1863, Col. John Wilder, from Indiana, and his mounted infantry, armed with Spencer repeating rifles, started out through a driving rain for his attack on Hoover's Gap."

"They actually used guns like our seven-shooters?" asked Erik.

"Yep! Our boxes have 'Wider' printed on them," said Poppy. "They should have said 'Wilder', of course. Wilder's 'Lightning Brigade,' using Spencers, took Hoover's Gap in a day. The rest of the army followed. For two solid weeks the Union Army slogged through mud and pouring rain. That rain just never stopped until well into July. There's not been a rainstorm to equal it since. Some say there's been nothing like it for a thousand years."

"Then that really *could* be when this stream changed channels," said Anna.

By this time the teens had followed the old streambed and stood where it ran under the road and into the Collins River.

"Here we are at Eugene's Culvert," said Erik. "And right out there," he continued, pointing just up river, "is the rock that is probably the real property corner."

Eugene stepped off ten paces upstream from the culvert, and sighted up the hill with his compass. He handed it to Anna and she passed it on. Soon all had seen where the property line would run up the mountainside. Rebel Cave was well inside the Stoneworth property—if this was truly the location of the corner.

"This certainly gives us something to work with tomorrow at the courthouse," said Dulcie.

"If we can drop just one more piece into the puzzle, it'll settle it," said Jackie. "What I mean is, we must *prove* that the Snodgrass deed is talking about *this spot* as the property corner, not the place upstream from the bridge. If this *is* the corner, then Uncle Berk owns the cave, the guns, and everything in the cave. Somehow, we just *gotta* find the proof."

26

The Missing Piece

"So, folks," said Dulcie, bringing back to the present the group standing above the small stream that Monday afternoon, "in a nutshell, that is the story of what happened on Saturday. We figured out the creek changed courses right down there." She pointed across the stream to the beginning of the old, overgrown, now-filled-in gully.

"Well, I'll be!" said Uncle Berk, shaking his head. "You really can see the old watercourse."

"Oh Berkley!" said Aunt Nan. "It's almost too good to be true."

"It really is astonishing," said Mr. Gunther. "Children, I am very proud of all you have done!"

"And wait 'til you see what we found at the courthouse to nail it down!" crowed Jackie, grabbing Aunt Nan around the waist.

"We *smack-dab* nailed it down! But I think we could explain it much better with some refreshments. Don't you?"

"Berkley," said Aunt Nan, handing him the knife, "you do the honors of cutting the cake. Then I'll serve it and the drinks. Oh yes, and the ice cream the Gunthers brought. We've gone all out for this celebration!"

Aunt Nan carried the plates and silverware into the dining room. "Now, while we eat, Jackie and Dulcie can tell us about their visit to the courthouse."

"Uncle Berk left us at the courthouse," Dulcie told them, "while he went to the bank to get his deed. There we did a search on this property, the Snodgrass place, and the abandoned homestead next door. Did you know that Pervis Greer, a Revolutionary War soldier, was the original owner of the land on both sides of the river? He built his home where the old chimney still stands. In 1823 he sold this property to Harmon Anderson. And Mr. Anderson sold the property north of us to Buford Snodgrass in 1825. That's where Buford's great-grandson, Dwart Snodgrass, lives now. You take it from here, Jackie."

Jackie touched the corners of his mouth with his napkin and said, "When Mr. Greer died in 1842, his estate went to his children. A son inherited the house and land on this side of the river, and the land on the other side went to a daughter. That's as much as we had time to research before Uncle Berk interrupted our search."

"But you said you hadn't found anything much," said Uncle Berk. "Sounds to me like you'd found quite a bit."

"Well, yes," agreed Jackie, "but nothing that made any difference regarding your situation. No other sales were made till you bought this place from the Andersons. Land had passed from one family member to another without being divided up."

"So naturally," said Uncle Berk, "no one challenged the boundaries or had them resurveyed."

"Right. So Dulcie and I were at a dead end when we left to

meet Deputy Edwards. But he said the judge didn't have time for us, so while you went back to the bank, we kept looking. Then Dulcie had a brainstorm that gave us the breakthrough. Your turn, Sis. My ice cream is melting."

"Okay," Dulcie said, laying down her fork. "Wait'll you hear this! Jackie and I could hardly keep it under our hats!

"We hit the dead end with your property, then it dawned on me that the land across the river might hold the key. Obviously, where they came together with the property over here, they'd share the same boundary marker. The west boundary for the property on this side of the river would be the east boundary for the land on the other side. So we searched for records of sales, and the plat books for *that* property."

"And we found what we needed!" exclaimed Jackie.

Dulcie continued. "In 1867 the Greers sold the land west of the river. An Armond Tankersly bought the land across from the Snodgrass property on the other side of the river. Let me show you on our sketch."

She placed her sketchbook on the table in front of Uncle Berk and Aunt Nan. Dulcie pointed to a large diagram showing the properties.

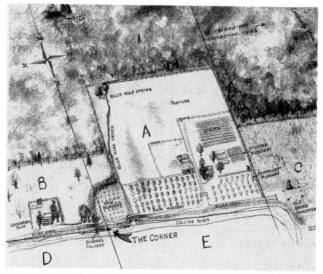

"Your place, Uncle Berk, is marked 'A', the Snodgrass property is 'B', the old Greer homestead is 'C.' Greer property across the river is in two parts. The part Harmon Tankersey bought in 1867 is shown as 'D.' The last piece, shown as 'E,' is across the river from here and was sold in—" She paused to look at her notes.

"October 13, 1869 to a Carl Calvin," said Jackie, laying his fork on his cake plate and rubbing his hands together, "and here comes the exciting part, just wait till you hear. Just you wait!"

"We won't have to wait as long," Aunt Nan chuckled, "if you'll be quiet."

"Both deeds, for 'D' and 'E' – the two properties on the other side of the river," said Dulcie, "have this phrase '… *beginning at a rock on the east side of Collins River ten paces upstream from where Blue Hole Creek enters the river—'*"

"Dulcie," interrupted Uncle Berk, slapping his thigh in exasperation, "that doesn't help at all! We already have that wording on our deed and we know what it means—you've marked the property lines at the wrong place!"

"But wait, Uncle Berk," said Dulcie. "We're not through. Both of these deeds, written long *after* the Snodgrass deed and after the original deed for your property, have a very significant phrase added."

She held up a piece of butcher paper on which she had written:
"by the old channel, (not the new channel cut by the flood of 1863)."

Uncle Berk sat in stunned silence as this soaked in. Then he jumped to his feet yelling, "That's it! That's it! The creek changed channels *after* the old deeds were written. The boundary is not by the new channel—Snodgrass has the corner marker too far up stream. He has it on our property! The cave really is ours! And the new nursery is on our land!"

"Thank the Lord!" said Aunt Nan. "This is too good to be true!"

Erik ran his forefinger along the sketch of the Collins River until he came to the old channel. He tapped that point with his finger. "In the late 1860s, evidently some water ran in each channel. The surveyors who prepared the deeds for the land across the river wanted to be sure no one made a mistake in locating the property corner. So they made it clear that the corner was by the old channel—at what we call 'Eugene's Culvert.'"

"But," said Eugene, "since our land was never sold until we bought it, no one has questioned the boundaries. Not until now."

"By looking at our sketch," said Poppy, "it's easy to see where the water course changed and moved Blue Hole Creek. Mr. Snodgrass is so sure his land includes our acreage because he's going by the statement on his deed that his property line is ten paces beyond where the 'creek enters the river'."

"Only, he doesn't realize the channel doesn't enter where it used to. It changed during the flood of 1863," said Eugene.

"But Dulcie noticed there *was* an old channel," said Erik, "and that tipped us off to what had happened."

Anna chimed in. "Then she and Jackie found the wording on the deeds for the property across the river. That gave us the proof we needed!"

They all crowded around the map. They traced the dark green line showing where the old channel had run, and poked fingers at the point where it entered the river.

They barraged Jackie and Dulcie with hugs and slaps on the back.

"Without a doubt, that is the corner! What an accomplishment, young people—what an amazing accomplishment!" said Uncle Berk.

"It was a team effort," said Dulcie. "Jackie and I got to do the detective work at the courthouse and find the needed proof, but we all played a role."

"Hey, Eugene," said Erik, "your little sister was right about when the channel was cut!"

"That's right," agreed Jackie. "Poppy was on target when she said the flood of June 1863 cut the new channel."

"She sure was," said Eugene, beaming proudly. "Now let's

look at our guns—Wow! It sure feels good to say that—OUR guns!" he repeated.

Soon all, including the adults, were chanting it:

"Our guns, our guns, our guns!"

"Wait, just a minute," said Uncle Berk. "Jackie, I see why you said the meeting with the judge was just a 'trifling technicality.' You kids already knew about the old channel this morning. You just hadn't told *me*."

"That's right, Uncle Berk," said Dulcie. "We had a terrible time keeping it to ourselves until we were certain. We knew about the old channel, but we couldn't prove when the creek changed beds or that the boundary marker in the deeds wasn't located where Mr. Snodgrass said it was."

"Now we have the evidence that settles it once and for all," said Jackie.

"We really do!" said Uncle Berk, grinning from ear to ear. He clapped Eugene on the back. "Now we can look at the guns—I mean, *our* guns!"

"I want to examine the seven-shot bullet tubes Erik and Anna have told us about," said Mr. Gunther.

"The restraining order isn't lifted yet," said Aunt Nan, "but nothing says we can't look at our guns."

"Oh, hold on a minute. I need everyone's attention," interrupted Uncle Berk. "There's still one small mystery to solve." He turned to his niece. "Dulcie, I want to know what you spent my nickel on at the courthouse. You can't bribe a judge with that amount."

"No," said Dulcie, giggling. "But you can make a phone call and set a celebration in motion! That's what I did." She tossed her hair and stuck her nose in the air. "I'm not sure you'll *ever* get your ol' nickel back." She grinned.

Uncle Berk scooped Dulcie into a bear hug and swung her in a circle. "I consider it well spent. Now, go get the guns."

A short time later the Gunthers left Anna and Erik to spend one last night with the team.

While the other two girls got ready for bed, Dulcie sat on the edge of her bed and wrote an account of the day in her journal.

Anna said, "Dulcie, I wish I had a copy of your journal. So many things have happened—and I want to remember them all."

Dulcie flipped the cover of the notebook closed and tucked it into her suitcase.

"I'll copy some of my notes for you, Anna," she said. "I'm glad I've got the journal to help me recall these jam-packed days. One thing is certain—I'm taking home a treasure store of memories of you two—and of our whole gang. I'm going to miss you terribly!"

"Did you ever dream we'd have such an adventure?" asked Anna. "I don't want it to end."

"Me, either!" said Poppy.

"Anna, I'll get to see Poppy and Eugene at our family reunions, but I'll have to wait 'til we get to college to see you again—Oh, I can't stand it." Dulcie flopped back on the bed. "It's going to be almost two years!"

"At least we'll get to have breakfast together tomorrow," said Anna, "and the going-away party. My parents said we can even go with you to the train." Anna yawned. "Now, let's get some sleep." She playfully stuck out her lower lip. "*Some* of us have to go to school tomorrow."

27

The Judge

At 11:40 Tuesday morning, Dulcie, Jackie, and Uncle Berk walked into the Warren County Courthouse and made their way to Judge Wallace Harrington's chambers. The young people were dressed in their good clothes for the train trip home to Kentucky, and their uncle was decked out in his Sunday best. The secretary showed them into the rich oak-paneled room where Deputy Sheriff Edwards stood, pistol strapped to his side, waiting to make the introductions.

"Your Honor," said Deputy Edwards. "This is Berkley Stoneworth, and his out-of-town guests, Miss Dulcie Delaney and Mr. Jackie Delaney—Judge Harrington, folks."

Following a round of greetings and handshakes, the judge dismissed the officer and invited the others to be seated in the large leather chairs that faced the judge's desk.

"Mr. Stoneworth," he said, "I regret I've not had a chance to meet you before this, to thank you for your service to our country during the war. Welcome home."

"Thank you, sir. It's wonderful to be home."

"Deputy Edwards tells me you haven't exactly had peace on your side of the Collins River for the last few days."

"That's right. It's about the boundary between our property and the parcel of land owned by Dwart Snodgrass."

"I apologize, Mr. Stoneworth," said Judge Harrington, with a smile, "for the somewhat irregular way the deputy handled the matter. He was in a bind. I think he took the action he did largely to appease Mr. Snodgrass. That's really all he could do until a proper disposition of the matter could be arranged."

Uncle Berk held up one hand as though to dismiss the judge's comment. "I find no fault with what Deputy Edwards did. I just want to get the matter settled once and for all."

The judge looked at Dulcie and Jackie and said, "And just exactly what role do these two play in your situation. Are they here for a civics lesson?"

Uncle Berk's pride shone from his face. "My niece and nephew have done some valuable research here at the courthouse about the history of the property. Based on what they've found, I think we've determined where the exact location of the northwest corner of my property is. It, of course, is also the southwest corner of the Snodgrass property."

"Sounds interesting," said the judge. He turned to Dulcie and Jackie. "What did you find?"

For the next several minutes, using the map Dulcie had drawn, they pointed out the location of the corner as claimed by Snodgrass. They showed the two channels of Blue Hole Creek. They showed the references to the old and the new channels in the deeds, and the copied notes from the plat books.

Judge Harrington slapped the top of his mahogany desk. "What superb detective work! I must say I am impressed. Your evidence seems to settle the matter."

He beamed at the teenagers, then turned back to Uncle Berk.

236

"However, to make your claim to the property, including the cave, firm and undeniable, we need to take one additional step."

"What's that?" asked Uncle Berk.

"I'm lifting the restraining order," Judge Harrington said, picking up the order and glancing over it, "with the understanding that you'll have a certified surveyor locate and mark all corners of your property."

"But that could cost me as much as $35!" exclaimed Uncle Berk. "That's more than a week's wages!"

"I'm aware of that, and I wish I could force Snodgrass to pay half the cost. But I can't. He's not interested in proving anything. It's already settled in his mind. So it is up to you to do the proving."

"I won't say I'm happy about this, Your Honor," said Uncle Berk, "but I'll do it."

"Fair enough," the judge responded. He took the restraining order and wrote across it in large letters, "VOID."

"Mrs. Callahan," he called.

When the secretary came to the door, he handed her the paper and told her to record his action. After she left, he looked at the trio sitting across from him, glanced at his watch and said, "I have a few minutes before my next case. I'd like to tell you a few things off the record."

"Certainly," said Uncle Berk. "Dulcie, Jackie—'off the record' means nothing said here is to be repeated outside this room. Agreed?"

"Yes, sir," said Dulcie.

"Got my word on it," agreed Jackie.

"First, never underestimate Dwart Snodgrass," the judge warned. "Never underestimate his cunning or his bulldog stubbornness. And know this, he is ruthless. He has no concern for the feelings of others."

"Sir," said Dulcie, "we've seen that."

"I'm sure. He runs roughshod over one person after another. Needless to say, there's always tension between him and his neighbors."

Uncle Berk nodded his head. "He sure has a way of putting an ugly twist on things."

"Yes, and just when a wound between him and a neighbor begins to heal, he curls his lip and snarls a remark that yanks off the scab and leaves the other person bleeding again."

"Sure not the way to get along with folks," Uncle Berk retorted.

"There is another 'off the record' matter I'd like you to hear," the judge said, leaning back and putting his hands behind his head. "By itself it would not be adequate to prove you own the cave. However, if it ever came to court, I could provide interesting testimony on your behalf."

Jackie sat up straighter and leaned forward. "Really, sir? You could?"

"I sure could." He checked his watch again.

"Let me tell you a story. The use of Raccoon Hollow Cave, now known as Rebel Cave, for making moonshine whiskey has been going on since before the Civil War. I'm sorry to say so, but my grandfather and great grandfather used the cave as a location for a still—or distillery. They were in cahoots with the Snodgrass men."

"Our daddy has mentioned moonshine, but I don't exactly know what it is," said Jackie.

"Moonshine whiskey is liquor made without government license. And without paying the required taxes. It's illegal to do it that way, so it was made in secret hideaways."

"The cave must have been perfect for that," said Dulcie.

"And it was successful for a long time," said the judge. "A still requires water. The cave has water. It requires secrecy. The cave is certainly isolated. Especially in the summer when the trees are full. Also, smoke from the still's fire goes back into the cave part of the time instead of coming out."

"It sure does that," agreed Jackie.

"You young people have visited the cave, so you know about the pool and the waterfall?"

"Yes, sir," said Dulcie with feeling. "They're impressive."

"You ought to see them in a really rainy season. That pool becomes a swirling torrent. Grandpa Harrington used to talk about finding everything ruined, with the copper boiler floating two-thirds of the way to the ceiling."

"Wow!" said Jackie.

"Flooding was one problem. Revenuers—government representatives responsible for shutting down the stills—were another. The story told in my family is that in 1869, revenuers made a raid, tore everything to pieces, and took my granddad off to jail. Mr. Snodgrass got away. An interesting aside to that story is that it's thought one of the revenuers was Shelah Waters, a spelunker who spent a lot of time exploring Higgenbotham Cave. Waters, who was a former Yankee officer, was later shot from ambush near Spencer, not far from here."

"When your granddad went to jail, did that put an end to the cave being used as a distillery?" asked Uncle Berk.

"No. The final straw was around the turn of the century when Dwart Snodgrass's daddy died in a shoot-out up there."

Dulcie winced. *That's what Ruthie Snodgrass told us about,* she thought.

"But, sir," said Jackie, "what's the evidence that the cave belongs to Uncle Berk?"

Judge Harrington burst out laughing. "Oh, I got off track there for a moment."

The judge leaned toward Uncle Berk. "Mr. Stoneworth, you bought your place from the Anderson heirs, right?"

"That's right."

"When my granddad told tales about the still, he'd laugh about how he and Grandpa Snodgrass would bring old Mr. Anderson a jug of "white lightning"—or moonshine. It was their way of showing appreciation for his looking the other way while they used *his cave* for their operation."

The Judge grinned. "He'd always chuckle about how Mr. Anderson would act reluctant to take the whiskey, being an upstanding citizen and all, but he'd take it, saying it was 'fer medicinal purposes, ye understand.' That old man kept enough of that 'medicine' for his whole family and all his animals.

"My Granddad had a punch line at this point in the story. He'd slap his leg and say, 'Mr. Anderson—he must have had the wellest, or else the drunkest critters around!'"

Uncle Berk chuckled, then asked, "So it *was* common knowledge among the older generation that the property belonged to Mr. Anderson?"

"Without a doubt. But as I've ordered, you need to have it surveyed to nail the matter down tight."

Judge Harrington picked up a gold pen and wrote quickly on a small piece of paper, then leaned across the desk and handed the slip to Uncle Berk.

"I've written down the names of a couple of reliable surveyors. Tell them I said to be reasonable about what they charge, or else!"

He stood up and walked around to the front of his desk. "Well, I'm already five minutes late for my next appointment."

"We thank you, sir," said Uncle Berk.

"Good to meet you, Your Honor," Jackie commented.

"Thank you for telling us about the cave, and about your granddad," said Dulcie.

"I'm glad I got to spend some time with you," said the judge to the children. "If you're ever back down this way to stay a while, contact me. I just might have some detective work for a crack team like the two of you." He smiled.

Uncle Berk, Dulcie and Jackie all shook hands with the judge, and walked out of the courthouse into the bright sunlight.

"What a relief!" said Uncle Berk. "I'm so glad it's over and that it worked out like it did!

"That's for sure!" said Jackie.

"I do need to run back to the bank for a few minutes," said Uncle Berk. "Want to go along, or just walk around town?"

"I'd like to walk around a little," said Dulcie, "and then stop at Magness Library. Would you like to do that, Jackie?"

"Sure," Jackie agreed. "But first, let's go by Puckett Ford and

Mullican-Henegar Chevrolet. Eugene says they have pictures of some really swell cars that'll be out before long. They may have even gotten in a new model or two."

"You two have fun," said Uncle Berk. "I'll see you later."

When the trio got to City Drug at 2:30, Aunt Nan and the other four young people were anxiously waiting. Uncle Berk, Jackie, and Dulcie filled the group in on their meeting with the judge.

"So the judge already knew we owned the property?" asked Eugene.

"Yes, but he couldn't absolutely prove it. It needs to be settled permanently with a survey," said Uncle Berk.

"But it isn't fair," argued Poppy, "for us to have to pay for the whole thing."

"Maybe not," said Dulcie, "but there's no way Mr. Snodgrass is just going to take your dad's word for it. The survey will prove beyond the shadow of a doubt where the boundaries are. Once it's settled, no one will be able to argue with the outcome."

"That's true," said Eugene. "So we can say the guns are really ours."

"Yep!" said Jackie. "Really ours."

"Now," said Dulcie, "the question is, what do we do with 'em?"

"You young people are going to be busy with school," said Uncle Berk, "so I volunteer for Aunt Nan, Mr. & Mrs. Gunther, and me to serve as the 'Gun Committee.' We'll find out their worth and the best way to dispose of them. We'll make recommendations and you can each make your own choices."

"That sounds fair," said Dulcie, nodding.

"Exactly how are we going to divide them up?" asked Eugene.

"Well," said Poppy. "There are twenty-one guns. There are six of us, and there are three families. That means seven guns per family. Each family could keep one and each teen would have three to keep or sell—whatever they want."

241

"Hey, that would work," said Jackie. "We could hang one over the fireplace to help us remember this week and all the great stuff we've done."

"Erik, you haven't said much today," Aunt Nan noted. "What do you think of this idea?"

"It is fine," said Erik quietly. "I have not really been thinking about the cave or the guns. I have been thinking about how much I will miss Dulcie … oh … and Jackie. I … I mean, I might not see them again. Certainly not till we get to college. And then …"

"Why, Erik," said Uncle Berk, "why wouldn't you see her, with her right next to you. You need spectacles, son?"

Aunt Nan shook her finger at Uncle Berk. "Now Berkley, don't tease the boy."

"I do not mean *now*, sir," said Erik.

He turned toward Dulcie. She knew he could see tears welling up in her eyes. "I mean when she gets on that train and goes off to Kentucky—"

"Oh, now I get it!" said Uncle Berk, clapping his hand to his forehead. "I do declare, it completely slipped my mind to mention something to you."

He paused and grinned. "You kids aren't the only ones who can keep a secret. The business I've been doing at the bank the last two days was to arrange a loan to put in the dam at The Blue Hole. That means water and electricity for the house. We can irrigate the nursery and farm! And I'm hiring you six to do the bulk of the work next summer—if you want the job, that is.

The young people sat in stunned silence and looked at each other in unbelief.

Uncle Berk continued, "It'll be hard digging the ditches to lay the pipeline, but there's a few fringe benefits involved. Like time off for a little cave exploring."

Pandemonium broke out with shouts and squeals, hugs and handshakes. They bombarded Uncle Berk with questions.

Then Dulcie said, "We have a presentation to make. The plans for next summer make this even more important. Jackie—"

Jackie got up and struck one of his poses: "Speaking on behalf of both the Kentucky branch and the Tennessee branch of the Stoneworth family, I wish to recognize two of those present for their contributions to the experiences and achievements we've enjoyed during the past few days. Anna and Erik, would you please rise?"

The two young people looked at each other. Erik shrugged, and the twins slipped out of the drugstore booth and stood by Jackie. Dulcie handed Jackie two scrolls tied with blue ribbons. Jackie gave one to each of the young people.

He said, "As you unroll your scroll, you will find it designates you by name and says to each of you the following:

> *Over these past few days you have exhibited a free and adventurous spirit, admirable dedication to your comrades, ardent commitment to tasks at hand, and especially, support and encouragement to your associates. In these ways and many more you have demonstrated that you are each worthy of being, and hereby are proclaimed to be, an Honorary Stoneworth Teen.*

"You'll notice," said Poppy, "that they're signed by all representatives of the Stoneworth family who are present—from both the Kentucky and the Tennessee branches. That makes it official."

Both Erik and Anna smiled widely, but looked somewhat embarrassed. Then Erik spoke. "I hardly have words for such an occasion as this. But we gladly accept the honor."

"Yes," said Anna, "it *is* an honor. And I can't imagine what it'll be like to be with you other Stoneworth teens all next summer, if it brings as much excitement and fun as we've had this past week."

"And I don't know how I'll be able to wait for summer to come!" said Dulcie.

"Between now and then," said Eugene, "I'm going to learn everything I can about caves. That'll make the time pass faster and when cave-exploring time comes, I'll be ready!"

"I'm going to keep boning up on the Civil War," said Poppy.

"Me, too!" Jackie nodded.

"I suppose I should really concentrate on learning all about hydroelectricity," said Erik.

"Well, we're going to need to know a lot about irrigation," said Anna, "so I guess I'll take that on. It doesn't sound exactly feminine, but who cares about that?—I'll go for it!"

"Let's see," said Dulcie, with a grin. "What does that leave for me? —Oh, I know! I'll study up on how to boss—"

A chorus of friendly "boos" interrupted her mid-sentence.

"You already have that down pat!" teased Jackie. "You should try for some other area of expertise."

"All right! All right!" Dulcie grinned. "Let me think about it."

A little later the exuberant group left the drugstore and made their way to the train station. Julia and Gearhardt Gunther joined them there for the send-off. Mr. Gunther took pictures of the six adventurers with Erik's Leica camera, and then, after another round of handshakes, hugs, and good-byes, Dulcie and Jackie got ready to board the train.

"Oh, I forgot something," said Uncle Berk, looking at his watch. "I'll run to the car and be right back." He hurried away.

"Aunt Nan," said Dulcie, "thank you so much for letting us come. We'll never, ever forget it."

"That's for sure," said Jackie, "and we sure can't wait 'til next summer!"

"Amen!" said Eugene, echoed by a round of 'amens' from the rest of the Tennessee gang.

"I can't wait till next summer either," Aunt Nan told them with a smile. "I'll be so glad to have you two back." She put one arm around Jackie and the other around Dulcie and gave them a squeeze. "And how exciting it will be to get started on that project to get water and electricity in the house."

Uncle Berk ran puffing back into the train station. In his arms he carried a long, narrow, well-wrapped package. "You mustn't forget," he said, pausing to catch his breath, "to take your new fishing rod."

"Fishing rod?" Jackie and Dulcie said in a baritone/soprano duet. "Fishing rod?"

"Why, of course! You don't want to forget your 1863 Colonel Wilder Seven-shooter Fishing Rod." He winked.

"Yeah!" said Jackie. "I won't let it out of my *sight.*"

"Thanks, Uncle Berk!" said Dulcie.

Uncle Berk chucked Dulcie under the chin. "You think you're the only Stoneworth who knows how to spend a nickel on a phone call? As soon as I got to the bank after our meeting with the judge I called your Aunt Nan and asked her to wrap this and bring it along. You've earned it."

The conductor sang out his, "All aboard!"

The Kentucky-bound pair climbed the steps, waved once more, and made their way inside. Soon the train was on its way down from the Cumberland Plateau. It was dark by the time they changed trains at Tullahoma for Nashville and Kentucky. During the homeward trip, Dulcie and Jackie hashed and rehashed their recent experiences and talked of plans for the next summer. Then they discussed how excited their daddy would be to see their "Wilder fishing rod," and what they might do with their seven guns. Jackie sat beside the window, and as their conversation began to die down, he said,

"Dulcie, Christmas is just a little more than three weeks away. You know what I want for Christmas?"

She said, "Uh-uh, but if you'll let me stretch out on this seat and put my head in your lap, I promise to stay awake long enough for you to tell me."

He scooted closer to the window to make room and began to explain. "Poppy and I are going to be writers. Between now and next year, she's not just going to study the Civil War, she's going to learn all she can about Colonel Wilder, and I'm going to learn all about General Nathan Bedford Forrest. We're going to write reports, and someday maybe even write books about them—" He looked down at Dulcie's closed eyes. "Are you listening?"

"Just barely," she answered in a sleepy voice. "Listen to the rails as the train wheels go over them. They're saying, 'clickity-clack, clickity-clack, taking you back, taking you back.' They're taking us back home now, but in a few months, they'll be taking us back to Tennessee."

"Yep, and you know, Dulcie, I have an idea that big old Rebel Cave has lots more secrets for us to discover."

"Wouldn't be surprised."

"We might even meet the Ghost of Rebel Cave."

She stifled a yawn. "You would bring that up, just when I'm getting sleepy! Let's not talk about that. You started to tell me about what you'd like for Christmas. What *do* you want?"

"Well, if I'm going to do all that writing, I'll need a typewriter. That's what I want." Jackie yawned and leaned his head against the window.

"How 'bout you? What do you want, Dulcie?"

"Let me think a minute." She closed her eyes. Jackie slowly and gently ran his fingers through her curls. The rails kept singing, "taking you back, taking you back, taking you back."

Just before she drifted off to sleep, Dulcie said, "Jackie, I just decided what I want for Christmas."

"What's that, Sis?"

"A pet."

"What kind of pet?"

"A white mouse."

RESOURCES YOU'LL ENJOY

We hope this book and those that follow in the "Stoneworth Teen Adventure" series will be a springboard to exploration, actually or through reading and study, of caves, nature, history, and even of how we can live life more fully.

Would you like to know more:

- About exploring caves?

- About how you can get started spelunking?

- About how you can explore caves safely?

- About commercial caves you can visit?

- About how Henshaw Cave and Higgenbotham Cave became *Cumberland Caverns?*

- About where to find more books about caves?

- About the Civil War and battle of Hoover's Gap?

- About Dulcie and Jackie and their background?

- About other "Stoneworth Teen Adventures?"

- About getting other books by the authors?

  *Check out the exciting pages ahead in this
  RESOURCE SECTION*

A note from author Philip Dale Smith...
I'll let you in on something!

As you know, just around the mountain from Rebel Cave are Henshaw Cave and Higgenbotham Cave. But there's something the Stoneworth Teens didn't know, and Private Jason Littlejohn and his companions didn't know during the Civil War. At the back of Henshaw Cave, past where workers dug saltpeter to make gunpowder, past the formation called "Moby Dick," past the waterfall, at what seemed to be the end of the cave, there was a narrow crevice. At times air surged out of that crack. Sometimes it poured in.

Years ago, Tank Gorin and Tom Barr, two of my spelunker friends and I went exploring in Henshaw Cave. We found that crevice. It looked too narrow to crawl into, and it didn't seem to go anywhere. But air gushed out. I decided to try it. I had to turn on my side to squeeze into the crack—at places it was less than ten inches wide. I wriggled and squirmed along for some time, then discovered I could turn upward. I soon came up through the floor of a room big enough to walk in! A little later I found myself in a huge room with a well-beaten path across the floor. On ceiling and wall were dates as early as the 1800s. I was in Higgenbotham Cave! The caves connected!

Tank Gorin and Roy Davis soon leased the mountainside and opened the cave to the public. Today thousands of people each year visit it as

Cumberland Caverns

One of America's largest caves, it's huge and magnificent.
You can see it, too! Check out its web site at
cumberlandcaverns.com
931-668-4396
1437 Cumberland Caverns Rd.
McMinnville, TN 37110
Wouldn't the Stoneworth Teens be surprised? And wouldn't Pvt. J. Littlejohn? Underground, you never know what awaits.

Visit a cave near you!

Has reading about the Stoneworth Teens and their cave adventures whetted your appetite about caves? Best not dash out and crawl into the first hole you come to! A good way to get a feel for caves and find out if you really enjoy "the world beneath" is to visit a commercial cave. These caves are lighted and have guides to help you enjoy and understand your experience of visiting a cave. Many of them have gift shops where you can buy books about caves, as well as souvenirs. About 100 caves are a part of the

National Cave Association

A visit to any member cave or cavern should be an enriching experience. Check out their web site at:

www.cavern.com

Their mailing address is:

P.O. Box 280
Park City, KY 42160

They'll be happy to send you a directory of commercial caves and perhaps brochures from caves near you.

When you're serious about exploring wild caves...contact the
National Speleological Society
Headquartered in Huntsville, Alabama, it is the world's largest organization of cave explorers and enthusiasts. They can steer you to the nearest of some 200 local chapters, called grottoes, of cave explorers. The NSS web page is

www.caves.org

The mailing address is:

2813 Cave Avenue
Huntsville, AL 35810

This organization touches virtually every aspect of caves and cave exploring. There are sections that focus on special areas of interest such as climbing techniques, plant and animal life in caves, and use of caves by ancient man. When you contact the NSS, be sure to ask for their free booklet,

A GUIDE TO RESPONSIBLE CAVING

Books about Caves . . .*

A Guide to Responsible Caving by Adrian (Ed) Sira -
Free booklet from the National Speleological Society

Caving Basics by Tom Rea

Adventure of Caving by David McClurg

The Complete Guide to Caving by Andy Sparrow

On Rope   (Vertical Rope Techniques)
by Alan Padgett & Bruce Smith

Caving Practice & Equipment by David Judson

Cumberland Caverns by Larry Matthews

Exploring Caves - Journeys into the Earth by
Nancy Holler Aulenbach & Hazel A. Barton

America's Neighborhood Bats by Merlin Tuttle

Bats, Strange and Wonderful by Laurence Pringle

Batman, Exploring the World of Bats by Laurence
Pringle (Wouldn't Dulcie love the last three? ☺ They're super!)

www.kidscience.com   *Caves*

www.homeschooling.about.com   *Exploring Caves*

www.cavern.com   *National Cave Association web site*

www.caves.org   *The National Speleological Society web site*

Note to teachers, parents, and presenters: The NSS has
excellent resources for teachers, including slides and videos
that can be rented.

*Check with your local bookstore, online source, or at
www.Cavebooks.com or www.Speleobooks.com.

Books about the Civil War...

These fascinating books, including novels filled with adventure, will take you back to the world of Private Littlejohn and his companions. You'll get to know what their lives were like and why the artifacts discovered by the Stoneworth Teens are so valuable. And you'll enjoy even more the *next* Stoneworth Teen Adventure. As Jackie Delaney would say, "You just wait!" But while you wait, read:

Pink and Say by Patricia Polacco This is a picture book that is not just for little kids! It is a fascinating and touching story for all.

Cold Mountain by Charles Frazier A Confederate soldier slips away from a hospital just before the war ends and tries to make his way home.

Corporal Si Klegg and his Pard by Wilbur Hinman Written by an officer, it gives an in depth look at the real life of a soldier in the war. Delightful, but dialect of long ago is a challenge.

Boys War: Confederate and Union Soldiers Talk About the Civil War by Jim Murphy   *(Real diaries and letters of boys 10-15)*

Red Badge of Courage by Stephen Crane

Charley Skedaddle by Patricia Beatty & Angela Jones

Life of Johnny Reb and *Life of Billy Yank* by Bell Wiley

Tullahoma by Michael R. Bradley (Includes Hoover's Gap)

Check these books out at your library or get them at your favorite bookstore. You can also find them at online bookstores such as amazon.com and barnesandnoble.com.

There are many excellent websites related to the Civil War. The few listed here will provide you with many links to others.

www.civil-war.net/index.html

www.educationworld.com *Civil War Stories*

www.myschoolonline.com *The Civil War Reference Desk*

Would you like to know more about Dulcie and Jackie and the extended Stoneworth and Delaney families?

Turn Back Time
winner of the
2001 Benjamin Franklin
Award for Popular Fiction

It's an upbeat Depression-Era novel with mystery, adventure, and romance. Dulcie and Jackie are small children, but they play an important part, especially Dulcie. This novel is written for adults and young people who like an exciting and challenging book.

Would you enjoy this novel? The judges for the Benjamin Franklin Awards are chosen from among top editors, writers, agents, and other leaders in the field of publishing. **About *Turn Back Time*, the Benjamin Franklin Award judges said:**

"One of the best books I have ever read."
"Excellent description"   *"Effective dialogue"*
'Well put together"   *"Great for all ages"*
'Well written"   *"A keeper!*
"Grabbed me ... from start to finish"

This book is the first in a series that tells the early story of Dulcie and Jackie and their family. Don't miss it!

Check for this book at your favorite bookstore or copy the order form on the last page of this book.

Heirloom-quality children's picture books that make a difference!

ISBN 1-886864-00-4
$14.95

OVER is not UP! By **Dale Smith** Just about every family has a child like Bitsie. When this little sleepy-head was called, she didn't get up, she just turned over—and OVER is not UP! The sun was up, the birds were up, and the flowers, even her pets—but not Bitsie. This book was a Benjamin Franklin Award national finalist. Its simple story line make it an ideal gift for children from two years to kindergarten. Illustrated by award-winning artist Donna Brooks. It is printed on acid-free paper, as are all our picture books, so the child you get this book for will be able to pass it on to his or her children.

ISBN 1-886864-10-1
$14.95

Nighttime at the Zoo By **Dale Smith** is based on and includes, a lullaby that his mother sang to him when he was a child. It depicts children visiting a zoo at dusk as many animals get ready for the night. The music for the song appears on each appropriate page and on the back end papers. North Carolina "miracle artist" Gwen Clifford used colored pencils to draw the bright, detailed pictures. Many boys and girls around the nation are going to sleep listening to this delightful song sung—or read—to them. It can become your family tradition, too.

Check for this book at your favorite bookstore or copy and send the order form on the last page of this book.

More life-enriching children's picture books.

ISBN 1-886864-08-X $15.95

The Rabbit and the Promise Sign **by Pat Day-Bivins and Philip Dale Smith** was named "Best Book of the Year" for children by the North American Book-dealer's Exchange. This charming Easter fable features magnificent illustrations by Donna Brooks. It is a story of assurance, hope, and love. The who receives this beautiful book will eagerly await the opportunity to see the "rabbit in the moon," and will remember the message of Grandfather Rabbit in the story. This highly reviewed and praised work is our best-selling children's book.

ISBN 1-886864-16-0 $15.95

Little Tom Meets Mr. Jonah, **by Philip Dale Smith and Pat Day-Bivins.** Little Tom, a mischievous kitten who thinks he's big and tough, has an important lesson for every child. He disobeys his father, gets trapped in a box of fish, and ends up on board ship with Jonah, the character from the Bible. During the kitten's escapade he learns that thoughts lead to actions, actions have consequences, and that we're responsible for the results of our actions. He also learns how wonderful second chances can be! You will love the beautiful illustrations by Donna Brooks.

Check for this book at your favorite bookstore or copy and send the order form on the last page of this book.

Order Form (copy this form)

You may order our books from your favorite book-store or online source, or may order directly from Golden Anchor Press.

Fax to: 253-537-5323   Phone: 253-847-9441

Mail to: Golden Anchor Press
PO Box 45208
Tacoma, WA 98445

Website: http://www.goldenanchor.com

Please send the following books: I understand that I may return any product for a full refund–for any reason, no questions asked.

Number   Title   Cost

_____ _____ _____

_____ _____ _____

_____ _____ _____

Shipping: 1st book $3.00, Each additional book $2.00

Name: _____

Address: _____

City/State/Zip_____

Sales tax: Please add 8.4% for products shipped to Washington addresses

Payment:: Check ____   Credit Card: Visa ____   Mastercard ____

Card number: _____

Name on card: _____Exp. Date ___/___

Order Form (copy this form)

You may order our books from your favorite book-store or online source, or may order directly from Golden Anchor Press.

Fax to: 253-537-5323   Phone: 253-847-9441

Mail to: Golden Anchor Press
PO Box 45208
Tacoma, WA 98445

Website: http://www.goldenanchor.com

Please send the following books: I understand that I may return any product for a full refund–for any reason, no questions asked.

Number   Title   Cost

_____   _____   _____

_____   _____   _____

_____   _____   _____

Shipping: 1st book $3.00, Each additional book $2.00

Name: _____

Address: _____

City/State/Zip_____

Sales tax: Please add 8.4% for products shipped to Washington addresses

Payment:: Check ___   Credit Card: Visa ___   Mastercard ___

Card number: _____

Name on card: _____Exp. Date ___/___